THE RIVALS

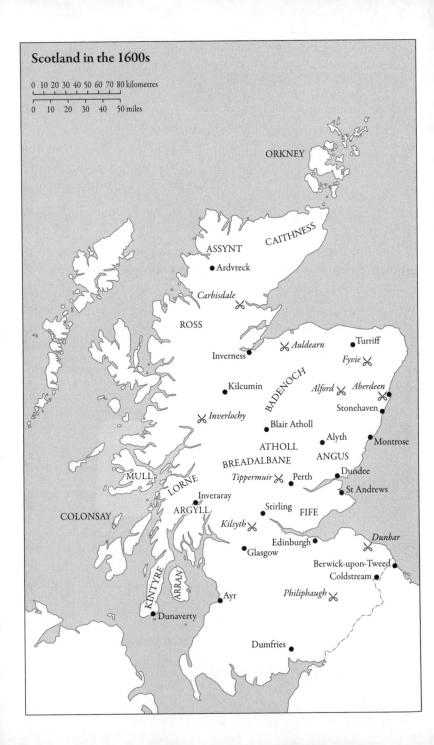

THE
RIVALS

MONTROSE *and* ARGYLL
and the Struggle for Scotland

MURDO FRASER

BIRLINN

First published in 2015 by Birlinn Ltd
West Newington House
10 Newington Road
Edinburgh
EH9 1QS

www.birlinn.co.uk

ISBN: 978-1-78027-306-8

British Library Cataloguing in Publication Data
A catalogue record for this book is available from the British
Library

Typeset in Adobe Garamond Pro at Birlinn

Printed and bound by Grafica Veneta
www.graficaveneta.com

Contents

Illustrations

Acknowledgements

This book would not have been possible without the generous assistance of the following people, to whom I am very grateful. The inspiration came in a series of well-lubricated debates with Hamish Mair on the respective merits of Montrose and Argyll. I am hugely obliged to Kate Wane, who spent many invaluable hours cheerfully researching and copying original sources. Harry Reid, David Torrance, Magnus Linklater, Alastair Stewart and Graeme Rose were all kind enough to read all or part of the text, and provided helpful comments. Lynne Mitchell typed the original manuscript, without complaining (much) about my handwriting. Hugh Andrew and the team at Birlinn provided encouragement, guidance and good counsel throughout the whole process. Finally, I have to thank my family for their support and patience during my frequent absences in the seventeenth century.

INTRODUCTION

Caesar and Pompey

St Giles High Kirk, or Cathedral as it is sometimes (incorrectly) known, stands on the Royal Mile at the heart of Edinburgh's Old Town. For centuries this magnificent church has been at the heart of Scottish public life, and has provided the setting for innumerable public events. Within its walls lie memorials to great figures from Scottish history, among them James Graham, 5th Earl and 1st Marquis of Montrose.

There could therefore have been no more appropriate venue for the memorial service to mark 400 years since James Graham's birth, held on Monday 21 May 2012. It was on the 21st of May that he was hanged at the Mercat Cross of Edinburgh, just outside the east wall of St Giles, 362 years before. Organised by the 1st Marquis of Montrose Society, which exists to keep alive the memory of this great Scottish hero, the service was attended by a Scottish Government minister, members of the Scottish Parliament, representatives of many of Scotland's ancient noble families, historians, writers and academics. At the close of proceedings the Marquis of Graham, eldest son of the current Duke of Montrose, laid a wreath at the elaborate Victorian tomb of his illustrious ancestor.

On the opposite side of St Giles, a little away along, stands another ornate memorial to a Scottish hero of the seventeenth century. Archibald Campbell, 8th Earl and Marquis of Argyll, lies in effigy in the church, although his physical remains rest many miles to the west in the Campbell family mausoleum at Kilmun in Argyllshire. Many of those attending the memorial service took a moment to pay their respects to the man who was Montrose's great rival. For a decade these two noblemen fought for the soul of Scotland. This is the story of the rivalry between them, and how it shaped a nation.

Both Montrose and Argyll had been, in their own way, loyal to the Stewart Kings Charles I and II. Both had been honoured by the older Charles; both were betrayed to their deaths by the younger. Both would declare themselves supporters of the Presbyterian Church of Scotland, both champions of the Covenanting cause. Both were heroes, inspiring leaders of men. Both were vilified and condemned as traitors, both died brave deaths and were celebrated as martyrs.

In their day both Montrose and Argyll could lay claim to the title of being the most powerful man in the realm. Today Montrose is undoubtedly the better known of the two, mainly for his genius on the battlefield – his great campaign of 1644-45 is still studied by military historians. Less is now known of his adversary. Until very recently the only biography of Argyll was John Willcock's *The Great Marquess* from 1903, now long out of print, although this omission was righted by Professor Allan Macinnes with the publication of his meticulously researched *The British Confederate* in 2011, which focusses on Argyll's role as a British statesman. In contrast there are numerous biographies of Montrose, perhaps the most famous being that of the great Scottish writer John Buchan from 1913.

The Civil War historian Edward Hyde (1st Earl of Clarendon and Charles II's Lord Chancellor) compared Montrose and Argyll to Caesar and Pompey, in that one could not endure a superior while the other would not have an equal. Buchan extended the comparison to Pym and Strafford, Fox and Pitt, 'secular types of conflicting temperaments and irreconcilable views'. Buchan claimed that in every national crisis there is some personal antagonism where the warring creeds seem to be

James Graham, Marquis of Montrose

summed up in the persons of the two protagonists. Certainly there are stark contrasts between Montrose and Argyll, in terms of their political and religious views, in terms of character, and in terms of temperament. And history is brought to life when seen through the lives of the personalities involved, rather than in a dull narration of dates and deeds.

The parallels between the rivals are striking. Both came from ancient and powerful Scottish families. They were not far apart in age, Argyll being five years older than Montrose. They both studied at St Andrews University and both demonstrated prowess in archery. Both would have considered themselves loyal subjects of Charles I, although ironically it was Argyll, as the young Lord Lorne, who was the royal favourite. And in the conflict which developed between Charles and the Presbyterian people of Scotland, both sided initially with the Covenanters against the King.

The struggles of the Scottish civil war of 1644-45 could easily be personified as a contest between those in Argyll's camp and those in Montrose's, although it was only at Fyvie in Aberdeenshire that the two sides actually met in combat (it ended in a draw). In time both would declare themselves loyal to Charles II, who in turn would betray each of them. Both were executed in Edinburgh, some eleven years apart, and while Montrose suffered the ignominy of a commoner's death by hanging, Argyll at least had the nobleman's privilege of beheading by the Maiden. Both had their severed heads displayed on the same spike on the Tolbooth. It would not be until Victorian times that suitable memorials to both would be erected in St Giles.

The rivals were very different in terms of their personalities. Montrose was the gambler, bold and brave, but rash; Argyll was more cautious and considered, but ultimately more influential and successful. Allan Macinnes, who states that Argyll can be deemed second only to Cromwell as a British statesman of the

Archibald Campbell, Marquis of Argyll

mid-seventeenth century, draws an amusing comparison with another Scottish obsession (other than religion and fighting) – football. Montrose is the stylish team playing with elegance and flair, a joy to watch, but in the end falling at the last hurdle. Argyll is the team playing 'ugly' football, grinding out results, and finishing on top. (If this makes Montrose Celtic, and Argyll Rangers, then some might say that there is an even more striking parallel based on levels of debt and unpaid bills!).

Modern day references to the two Marquises tend to favour Montrose over his rival. For those with little understanding of the complex politics of seventeenth-century Scotland, it is easy to concentrate only on the military records of the leaders of the time. And judged in these terms any contemporary of 'The Great Montrose' is bound to come out poorly in comparison. Montrose's abilities as a soldier and a leader of men were second to none. His brilliant military skills are remembered and commemorated today. Three times on the battlefield he defeated armies which included Argyll, who on each occasion – at Inverlochy, Alford and Kilsyth – had to flee ignominiously from the scene to save his skin.

Montrose is celebrated in song, while Argyll appears in ballads (such as *The Bonnie Hoose o' Airlie* or *The Execution of Montrose*) only as a scoundrel. While the romantic Cavalier Montrose was writing poetry, the faithful Covenanter Argyll wrote sermons. At least if the Church of Scotland were ever to create saints of Presbyterian martyrs, Argyll would be a prime candidate for canonisation (the thought of which would have him turning in his grave). But it is unlikely to make him a popular hero for a secular Scotland in the twenty-first century.

Where the chivalrous Montrose is an obvious heroic figure, Argyll, with his more obvious ambition and opaque motivations, is harder to admire. Even Presbyterian writers have found him difficult to fathom, one saying: 'His nature is complex, involved, and difficult at times to read'.[1] In fiction he has often been portrayed negatively. Walter Scott, who as a Tory was always inclined to the Royalists, wrote of Argyll: 'Something there was cold in his address and sinister in his look . . . all dreaded the height to which he was elevated'. There is a more sympathetic portrayal in Neil Munro's novel *John Splendid,* where the tensions between Argyll's conflicting roles as Highland chief and British politician are highlighted. The Marquis' chaplain, Alexander Gordon, says of him: 'It is the humour of God Almighty sometimes to put two men into one skin', while the eponymous warrior, a loyal clansman, in the aftermath of the Battle of Inverlochy, vents his frustration at his chief: 'You're for the cloister and not the field . . . I'll find no swithering captains among the cavaliers in France'.

One recent historian, while praising Montrose as 'a much adored and courageous leader, a poet and a patriot' damns Argyll as 'a most unpleasant man, cowardly, cruel, dishonourable in his dealings and entirely without compassion', leaving little room for doubt as to the writer's leanings.[2] A recent BBC/ Open University resource described Argyll as 'a cynical opportunist whose overt political ambition created divisions in the Covenanter ranks and caused former colleagues to take up arms for the King'.[3] Even amongst those who would concede that Argyll was on the right side of history with his political views, there are many who would appear to apply the descriptions borrowed from *1066 and All That* – Montrose would be 'wrong but wromantic' and Argyll 'right but repulsive'.

It is convenient to see history in black and white terms, with every story having a hero and a villain. In a Hollywood treatment of their lives (*Boldheart?*), Montrose, principled, dashing and brave, would be played by the star, with the scheming, cowardly, devout Argyll making a fine part for a character actor used to portraying the black-hearted villain. But this is all far too simplistic. Whatever Argyll lacked as a soldier, he more than made up for as a politician. He skilfully led the Covenanting faction in their disputes with Charles I, uniting the nobility, clergy and the people in a great national crusade. It was Argyll who was the defender of the populist cause, who was the people's champion, not Montrose. In mid-seventeenth-century Scotland it was Argyll who was regarded by the populace as the real hero. And it is Argyll's political ideas, and his championing of the power of Parliament against the unfettered rule of the King, that have better stood the test of time.

In reality both were heroes; both, at times, villains. Both were capable of courage and generosity, and equally capable of great cruelty. Both were military commanders and statesmen, although Montrose excelled as the former and Argyll as the latter. Both have left remarkable legacies and played a major role in shaping Scotland's history. Any history of the period needs to tell both their stories, and of the extraordinary rivalry between them.

Why does any of this matter to us today? This is not just a tale of two aristocrats from long ago. The rivalry between Montrose and Argyll, reflecting the greater national conflict between Royalists and Covenanters, was a struggle for the soul of the nation. Would it be the King's rule which determined how his subjects would live their lives, how they would worship their God, how their civil affairs would be conducted, as the Stewart monarchs desired? Or would the King rule only with the people's – or at least the upper and middle classes' – consent? It was this essential question which tore apart the nations of the British Isles in a bloody civil war.

Argyll and his allies might not have considered themselves as the progenitors of Parliamentary democracy, and Montrose certainly would not have been comfortable at being seen as the defender of autocracy, but the history of Britain would have been very different if the outcome of their rivalry had been other than it was. A victory for the Royalists would have meant no Presbyterian church in Scotland, and a monarchy out of step with the ambitions of the people. It is unlikely that their demands could have been suppressed indefinitely, and the outcome might well have been a much bloodier revolution – as happened in France – than the one which eventually transpired.

Our current constitutional settlement, with a sovereign Parliament and our monarchy having no more than a ceremonial role, owes its birth directly to the conflicts of the seventeenth century. It may not have been until 1688 that the principle that Parliament could choose its King would be established, but the arguments were made and fought over in the time of Montrose and Argyll. And the conflicts between the two ensured that it would be the people who decided how to organise the Church, not the monarch.

We neglect the study of our history at our peril. In Scottish schools today, the history of our nation that is taught (such as it is) tends to focus on a few key periods – the Wars of Independence, the Jacobites, the Highland Clearances. These are all significant in our nation's story, but it is quite wrong to ignore the struggles between King and Covenanters, between Montrose and Argyll. Arguably these conflicts were of far greater significance in our country's development than the adventures of the Old and Young Pretenders, but it is Bonnie Prince Charlie who still gets all the attention.

And just as we should not neglect our history, we should not forget our heroes. Both Montrose and Argyll were flawed personalities, as we all are, but no one could argue that they were other than great men who played a huge part in writing our nation's story. It is depressing how little is known about them today. As our country continues to debate its future, it is more important than ever that we understand where we have come from, and that we remember – and celebrate – those who were such an important part of that journey. If all this short volume achieves is to help stimulate interest in a neglected period in our history and its two principal characters, then it will have contributed to that objective.

PROLOGUE

Inverlochy

1–2 February 1645

'This disaster did extreamlie amaze us.'
Robert Baillie, *Letters*

In all his years of campaigning, he had known few nights as cold as this one. Wrapping his great plaid ever tighter around him in an effort to keep out the winter chill, Sir Duncan Campbell of Auchinbreck picked his way in the darkness through the groups of men encamped beneath the grey walls of Inverlochy Castle. Some were still awake, and as he passed he caught snatches of conversation – here a word or two in English, there a soft prayer or lines from a psalm recited in Gaelic, for the army of the Covenant held both Lowlander and Highlander, and all were devout Presbyterians. Most men slept, some in tents, hardier ones in the open air with only their kilts or cloaks pulled around them, but keeping close to the still-burning camp fires.

The young scout who had summoned Auchinbreck from his quarters within the castle walls led him carefully to the edge of the camp, where the view to the east was no longer obscured by the light from the fires. It was a clear, cloudless night, and the moon was up. The scout had reported movement on the hillside barely a mile distant, on the lower slopes of mighty Ben Nevis. It did not take the veteran soldier long to see that the youngster was right: dark shapes cast shadows as they shifted about. No friendly force would have come so close and then stopped to make camp, Auchinbreck knew. Whoever these men were, they were intent on doing him and his army harm.

Even with the bright moon, in the darkness of the night the strength of the hostile force could not be made out. The Covenanter army was 1,900 strong, made up of 500 experienced warriors from the Marquis of Argyll's regiment which Auchinbreck had recently commanded in Ireland, 1,000 additional Campbell clansmen freshly levied, and 400 Lowland soldiers. Auchinbreck could be confident in his numbers; the only force in the land capable of posing a threat to his camp was that of the rebel James Graham, Marquis of Montrose, and it was more than a day's march to the north, at Kilcumin at the south end of Loch Ness. The roads between there and here were well guarded, and no reports had been received of Montrose moving towards the Covenanters. But the presence of this unknown company so close at hand, and so obviously intent on attack, was a matter of the gravest concern.

His head full of questions, Auchinbreck made his way back to the castle to report to the man who was in one his military general, his clan chief, and his political leader: Archibald Campbell, 8th Earl and Marquis of Argyll. At the age of 37, the red-haired, squinting Argyll headed not just the mightiest clan in the Highlands, but also the Covenanter cause which had taken control of Scotland's government and gone to war against the country's king, Charles I. The outstanding political operator of his age, he had manoeuvred himself into the position of the most powerful man in the land, and was now in personal command of an army assembled for revenge. That winter the Campbell lands of Argyllshire had been devastated by Montrose's marauding army of Irish and Highlanders, spoiling and burning as they went, and leaving not a man alive who was capable of bearing weapons. Now Argyll was taking his troops north through the Great Glen in pursuit of his enemy, and this new development was an unwelcome distraction from the urgent task in hand.

A hasty council of war was convened when Auchinbreck returned with his news. The likelihood was that the strangers constituted only a small force under MacDonald of Keppoch, or another chieftain who was a hereditary foe of the Campbells. Nevertheless the threat was one which had to be taken seriously. Argyll was himself an experienced soldier, but disabled following a fall from a horse a few weeks before, and 'unable to use either sword or pistol'. He was not just *MacCailein Mor*, Chief of Clan Campbell, but the effective leader of the nation, and the risk of him being killed or captured was one deemed too great to take. The Marquis was 'compelled by his friends to go aboard his barge'[1] – his galley, the *Dubhlinnseach* (the Black-sailed) – which lay at anchor nearby in Loch Linnhe. With him went his entourage of Sir John Wauchope of Niddrie, Sir James Rollock of Dincrub, Archibald Syderff, Bailliff of Edinburgh, and the Reverend Mungo Law, whom Argyll had invited along 'to bear witness to the Wonders he purposed to perform in that Expedition'.[2]

It was only with the greatest reluctance that the proud Argyll consented to this withdrawal. Just weeks before he had suffered the humiliation of being forced to abandon his seat at Inveraray in Argyllshire when surprised by Montrose, escaping by boat down Loch Fyne and leaving the town to be sacked and burned by the invaders, and here he was again taking to the water to avoid potential capture, or worse. It did little for the morale of his clansmen, facing an unknown enemy, to see their chief put himself out of harm's way and leave them to defend his honour. In place of *MacCailein Mor*, command was given to Auchinbreck, 'a stout soldier, but a very vitious man',[3] who was more than up to the task.

Throughout the remainder of the night there were inconclusive skirmishes between the Covenanter scouts and the strangers facing them, but it was only at daybreak, on Sunday 2 February

1645, Candlemas Day, that all became clear to Auchinbreck. This was no mere raiding party which faced him. On the slopes of Meall an t-Suidhe, below the great Ben, a considerable army of 1,500 men was gathered. To his dismay he saw the Royal standard raised, and heard the pipers playing a tune which denoted the presence of the Marquis of Montrose as the King's General, followed by Clan Cameron's distinctive pibroch: 'Sons of dogs come and I will give you flesh'. Here was the very man whom the Covenanters had been pursuing – and now he had turned the tables on them. It was simply unimaginable that he could be here with his entire force, when they should have been many miles away to the north.

Three days before, James Graham, 5th Earl and 1st Marquis of Montrose, had been camped at Kilcumin (now Fort Augustus). Since raising the King's standard in Scotland in opposition to the rule of the Covenanters (and more particularly their alliance with the English Parliamentarians in their war with King Charles) the previous September, he and his Irish and Highland troops had seen spectacular success, destroying two Covenanter armies. Handsome, athletic, and charming, the 32-year-old nobleman was every inch the dashing Cavalier, and already fulfilling every expectation that his Royal master had for him. But now he was at risk of being caught in a trap. Ahead of him at Inverness was one force of Covenanters under the MacKenzie Earl of Seaforth; somewhere behind was another led by his former ally, but now bitter rival, the Marquis of Argyll. Seaforth seemed to present the easier challenge, so the plan was to head north by Loch Ness-side to meet him.

Never good at gathering intelligence on the enemy, Montrose was unaware of just how close Argyll was to him, until Iain Lom MacDonald, the celebrated Gaelic bard of Keppoch, arrived at his camp to give warning that Argyll's army was less than 30 miles away at Inverlochy. Montrose was astonished at the news and the outbreak of boldness in his adversary, whose dealings until now had been characterised by caution. 'Argyll dare not pursue me through Lochaber,' he had asserted.[4] Suddenly dealing with Seaforth was no longer the priority; Argyll presented the much greater danger, and opportunity. Montrose had the clan chiefs loyal to him sign a bond at Kilcumin, swearing to fight to the death for the King against the 'present perverse and infamous faction of desperate rebels now in fury against him'. Having thus reminded his men of the cause for which they fought, he set out to tackle his rival head on.

Montrose had a smaller force than Argyll, and the Campbell clansmen, thirsting for revenge for the harrying of their lands by the Irish, would be a far tougher nut to crack than the Lowland levies whom his Royalists had faced in their previous victories at Tippermuir and Aberdeen. Marching back down the Great Glen for a frontal attack on Argyll's army was therefore out of the question. Instead Montrose determined on a surprise attack from the rear, which meant outflanking the Covenanters. And so he took his men through the hills on a remarkable journey which has gone down in history as one of the great feats of Scottish military leadership.

This route march took Montrose's army from the morning of Friday 31 January to the evening of the following day. It was the middle of a particularly bitter winter in a time when the whole country was suffering severe temperatures, and the ground which the marchers were crossing, up to a height of 2,000 feet, was blanketed in snow. With hardly any supplies it was a gruelling experience even for the hardened warriors at Montrose's disposal. Most had 'not taisted a bitte of bread these two days, maircheing high mountaines in knee deepe snow, and widdeing brookes and rivers up to there girdle'.[5] A few, very few, had horses or ponies, the rest made it on ill-shod foot, with nothing to see but white hills all around, a sudden flash of powder snow erupting as a disturbed mountain hare took flight, a solitary wolf watching suspiciously from afar, and relentlessly and endlessly the back and legs of the man in front toiling his way forward in the footsteps of the men ahead of him. They drove one another on through the vicious cold, the stronger helping the weaker, pushing forward in a superhuman effort out of loyalty and love for their gallant commander, who walked with them every step of the way. Up beside the River Tarff they went, on to Glen Turrett and Glen Roy, then across the River Spean, always trying to keep away from any roads which might be watched by the enemy, and on to Ben Nevis. At last the starving, exhausted men arrived at their destination overlooking the enemy camp, and tried to snatch a few hours' sleep before the battle that awaited them.

Even before a shot was fired that morning the Covenanters had suffered the double blow of seeing their leader depart the field and of being taken by surprise by their great enemy, whom they had imagined was on the run. But Auchinbreck still had the advantage of numbers, and the ability to choose his position. As soon as day broke he drew up his men on dry ground a little to the east of Inverlochy Castle, facing the enemy. In the centre he put 'a strong battaillon of highlanderes with gunes, bowes and axes'[6] – probably Argyll's own regiment, seasoned fighters all. Behind were the Campbell levies, and on each wing the Lowlanders, one under Lieutenant-Colonel Lachlan Roughe of the Earl of Tullibardine's Regiment, and the other under Lieutenant-Colonel John Cockburn of the Earl of Moray's Regiment. 50 musketeers were positioned in the castle itself.

Montrose's men had spent a cold and uncomfortable night, and with nothing but raw oatmeal to eat and cold water to drink, they prepared for battle on empty stomachs. Catholic priests blessed those facing death with the sign of the cross, the very sight of which both dismayed and enraged their Presbyterian opponents. Then Montrose set out his forces for the fray, dividing them into three. He personally led the centre, comprising Highlanders from Atholl, Appin, Lochaber, Glen Garry and Glencoe, and put the Irish on the flanks, commanded by his Major-General Alasdair MacDonald on the right, and Colonel Magnus O'Cahan on the left. Montrose's few cavalry were commanded by Sir Thomas Ogilvie.

The battle began with Montrose ordering the advance. He had great confidence in the tactic of the Highland charge, sending his wild Highlanders and Irish towards the enemy at a run, an approach which had been devastatingly effective in his two previous encounters with Covenanter armies. The Irish on both of the Royalist wings rushed forward. They had been commanded 'not to giue fyre till he gaue it in there breastes', and held off from discharging their muskets until at very close range, where 'they fyred there beardes, both winges make a cruell hauoke of the enemies; leaping in amongst them with swords and targates, they quickly put them to disorder, and disperses them all over the fields'.[7] The Lowland troops, despite the battlefield experience many had gained with the Covenanter army in England, were simply no match for the furious onslaught of the Irish, and Auchinbreck's wings disintegrated.

The same pattern was repeated in the centre, where Argyll's regiment buckled under the 'strenth and furie' of the main Royalist charge. A wave of bright swords and sharp Lochaber axes broke upon the Campbells, the ferocity of the attack driving them back; everywhere men falling with blood gushing from gaping wounds, and all around the dreadful cries of the wounded and dying. The front lines were forced to retreat towards the reserves behind, but rather than make a stand of any sort, these, having witnessed too closely the fate of their more experienced comrades, 'queit there standing, brakes their ordour, and flies confusedly towards the castell'[8] seeking the illusory protection of the fortress's stout walls; men running in panic, pushing their comrades out of their way in their desperation to save their own skins. Montrose sent forward Sir Thomas Ogilvie with his small company of horse to set about the fleeing Covenanters, forcing them away from the castle and down to the shore of Loch Linnhe.

The battle proper was over in a matter of minutes, and then the bloody rout began, with the remnants of the defeated army pursued by the Royalists in all directions. Many fled into Glen Nevis where they were overtaken and cut down; others headed south towards what is now Fort William; some in desperation threw themselves into the Loch, whose cold waters quickly claimed even the strongest swimmers. The pursuit continued for seven or eight miles from Inverlochy, and 'if they [Montrose's men] had not beene wyried with a long mairch, standing all the night after in battell, and fanteing for want of food, there had been few or non eschaped'.[9] In total 1,500 of Auchinbreck's army lost their lives. While quarter was granted by the victorious Royalists to the Lowland troops who surrendered, for their ancient enemies the Campbells there would be no mercy from the Highland and Irish clansmen, and not a man escaped the sword. Only in the centre did the Campbell chieftains make a stand, 'stout and gallant men'; but surrounded and outnumbered they had no chance, and one by one they fell and their standards tumbled to the ground. Auchinbreck himself came face to face with the mighty Alasdair MacDonald, who gave him the choice of dying by means of hanging or beheading. The veteran Campbell soldier had faced death on many occasions, and replied coolly, *'dha dhiu gun aon roghainn'* (two evil alternatives that give no room for choice). MacDonald decided for him, with one swing of his great sword removing the top part of his head. It was less trouble than building a gallows.

From his position on board his galley Archibald Campbell had a limited view of the battlefield, but as the fleeing, terror-stricken Covenanters reached the loch shore it became quickly apparent what had happened – 'the Day lost, and most Part of his Friends cut off'.[10] There was no prospect of rescuing even a few of the survivors, for as the pursuing Royalists came within range they started to open fire on the *Dubhlinnseach*. The risk to the life of the Marquis of Argyll was such that the order had to be given to withdraw. The sturdy rowers strained at their oars, the galley turned and, slowly gathering speed, slipped out towards the safety of the open sea and away from the horror unfolding on the land behind.

On his side, the Marquis of Montrose lost perhaps as few as four men killed, although amongst them was his captain of cavalry, Sir Thomas Ogilvie, who suffered a wound in the leg and died a few days after. In his summary of the victory Montrose praised the bravery of his opponents: 'A little after the sun was up both armies met, and the rebels fought for some time with great bravery, the prime of the Campbells giving the first onset, as men that deserved to fight in a better cause. Our men, having a nobler cause, did wonders, and came immediately to push of pike and dint of sword, after this first firing.'[11] His respect for the Campbells had not led him to ensure that mercy was shown to them in the aftermath, but to be fair the ancient hatreds between the clans were such that neither side would have expected quarter, and the Campbells were themselves just as capable of atrocious behaviour.

The MacDonalds and other clans celebrated the rout of their old enemies, the eyewitness Iain Lom MacDonald writing a famous poem to mark the occasion:

Through the braes of Lochaber a desert be made,
And Glen Roy may be lost to the plough and the spade,

Though the bones of my kindrid, unhonour'd unurn'd –
Mark the desolate path where the Campbells have burn'd –
Be it so! From that foray they never return'd!
Fallen race of Diarmid! Disloyal, untrue,
No harp in the Highlands will sorrow for you:
But the birds of Loch Eil are wheeling on high,
And the Badenoch wolves hear the Camerons' cry –
'Come feast ye! Come feast, where the false-hearted lie!'

The mood could not have been more different aboard *Mac-Cailein Mor's* black-sailed galley as it cut its way through the dark, still waters of Loch Linnhe, past the snow-clad hills of Ardgour; no noise aboard to disturb the funereal hush but the grunts of the oarsmen, the creak of the rowlocks, and the repetitive splash of wood hitting water. Standing white-knuckled at the rail, alone in his thoughts, Archibald Campbell, Marquis of Argyll, Scotland's most powerful man, who had just witnessed not merely the destruction of his army but a devastating, desperate reverse for mighty Clan Campbell the like of which it had never before experienced, the loss of friends and kinsmen, with his personal reputation in tatters, accusations of cowardice from his enemies for fleeing the scene of battle set to haunt him, and his political career now in serious jeopardy, was turning over and over in his mind one burning question:

How had it come to this?

I

Chosen People

1607–37

In the spring of 1633, Captain David Alexander of Anstruther in Fife, of the ship *Unitie,* was contracted to lead an expedition in search of a new land. Seafarers had reported the sighting of a previously unknown island lying in the Atlantic Ocean to the west of the Outer Hebrides, and there was great excitement as to the opportunities that this might present. The Captain was to be paid £800 Scots in advance and £400 Scots on his return for his expenses, which included the cost of providing his ship fully equipped, and a crew of a skipper, mate, and ten sailors. By the 20 April of the following year he had to travel from Anstruther to the Hebrides, and from there 'searche, seek, and use all utter and exact diligence'[1] to locate the island, make full note of its size, assets and population, and report back by 1 August.

In addition to his costs Captain Alexander was to be rewarded with an undisclosed sum, for his 'aine paynes', should he be successful. His employer in this venture, putting up the reward, was the young Archibald Campbell, Lord Lorne, the eldest son and heir of the 7th Earl of Argyll. On 13 May 1633 King Charles I granted a disposition to Lord Lorne and his heirs male of this soon to be discovered land, but leaving the name and location blank for subsequent completion: 'that isle lying without the whole known and inhabited isles of the Kingdom of Scotland, called Hebrides Insulae, and now lately known by the name of _____, and lying _____, or of whatsoever other name or designation the same be of, with the castles, towers, fortalices, manor-places, houses, buildings, burghs of regality, burghs of barony, towns, seaports, avons, harbours, mills, woods, and the fishings of salmons and other fishes, with the lochs, cunnings [rabbits], cunningares [rabbit warrens], coals, coal heughs, parts, pendicles, and personance of the said isle whatsoever, with the mines and minerals of gold and silver, tin, lead, brass, copper, etc.'[2] This Atlantis, with its unsuspecting population inhabiting their towns and castles, was to be annexed to the Sheriffdom of Tarbet and form part of Lord Lorne's heritable office of Sheriff, and he would have power to appoint weekly markets, yearly free fairs, erect parish kirks, and create burgesses and other officers as required.

Sad to say, Captain Alexander was to be disappointed. There was of course no mystery land to be discovered, and not even a solitary rabbit could be found to repay the skipper's employer for his investments. But the ambition demonstrated by this expedition, and the confidence being placed in him by his King, is illustrative of the 26-year-old Lord Lorne's growing stature in Scottish society.

Archibald Campbell had been born into a powerful Scottish family holding an ancient earldom. The Campbells – Clan Diarmid as they were sometimes known – were originally from the Lowlands but had moved north and west into the Western Highlands. By the early seventeenth century they had become the most powerful clan in the Highlands, based in Argyllshire while maintaining extensive estates in the Lowlands, including in Dumbarton, Stirling, Clackmannan, Perth, Angus, Fife and Midlothian. The Chief of Clan Campbell was traditionally addressed using the Gaelic title of *MacCailein Mor,* 'son of the great Colin', in a reference to the thirteenth-century founder of the House of Argyll. The Campbells found favour with the Scottish monarchy over many centuries, and the heads of the family were ennobled first as Lords in 1445, and then as Earls in 1457. Through a combination of military might and shrewd political manoeuvring, Clan Diarmid greatly expanded their landholdings in the Highlands, swallowing up the territory of smaller clans. Their great rivalry was with the once mighty Clan Macdonald, which by the early seventeenth century had fractured into smaller factions, individually too weak to challenge the Campbell might.

The Stewart Kings of Scotland had taken great strides in bringing the once lawless Highlands under their rule. Royal authority was exercised by local clan chiefs, answerable, at least in theory, to the monarch, but with substantial local autonomy. Someone holding the dual offices of a powerful and wealthy earldom such as Argyll and the leadership of a large clan like the Campbells was in effect a 'mini-king', able to pursue his own expansionist policies at the expense of weaker neighbours. Clan society was still highly patriarchal, and with every able-bodied man expected to be a warrior, the chief of Clan Campbell had a ready-made standing army at his disposal, waiting to do its master's bidding. Much more so than a Lowland nobleman, the Highland chief had a force of men always at his back, hungry for a fight for clan pride, personal glory and, perhaps most important of all, plunder.

The 7th Earl of Argyll, father of Lorne, was a remarkable character with a turbulent life. He was known as *Gillespie Grumach*, 'Archibald the Grim', for his supposedly sullen nature (the nickname is sometimes also applied to his son). This appears to have been no handicap in public life, and the 7th Earl was honoured by the Scottish monarchy, carrying the crown, sceptre and sword of state at the openings of the Scots Parliament by King James VI.

Archibald Campbell, the future 8th Earl and Marquis of Argyll, was born, it is believed, in 1607, although there can be no certainty about the date. On his birth, as heir to the earldom, he was granted the courtesy title Lord Lorne. Lorne's mother died the year he was born and his maternal cousin, William Douglas, Earl of Morton, became his guardian. Lorne, as was usual for many members of the Scottish nobility, went to St Andrews University to study at the age of 14. He left after studying for less than three years and without gaining a degree, but this was not unusual, as only those who were studying to become professionals, such as lawyers, would seek to graduate formally. For many young nobles university life was not just about formal education but also afforded the opportunity to participate in a wide range of recreations. Even then St Andrews was noted as a venue for golf, and the young Lord Lorne became an enthusiastic player of the game (which he described as: 'That excellent recreation of Golf-ball, than which truly I do not know a better.')[3] He was also clearly an accomplished archer, winning the annual student 'Silver Arrow' competition in 1623.

This same medal was won some five years later by the man who would become Lorne's great rival, James Graham, 5th Earl of Montrose, also a student at St Andrews (in the intervening years it had also been won on separate occasions by David Leslie and Lord Elcho, both of whom Graham would later meet in battle). Montrose had been born in 1612, the only son of John, the 4th Earl. Some unfortunate omens surrounded the birth of the young Lord. His mother was reputed to have consulted witches about her son's birth, and his father was said to have commented to a neighbour that his son would trouble all of Scotland. We are also told, rather improbably, that the infant Montrose swallowed a toad.

In contrast to the Campbells who straddled both Highlands and Lowlands, the Grahams who held the Earldom of Montrose had land interests mainly in Perthshire and Stirlingshire, around the Forth and Earn valleys. Their ancestor Sir John Graham had been a follower of William Wallace and had died in battle against the English at Falkirk. The Grahams gained their peerage in 1451, and thereafter Lord Graham was made the Earl of Montrose. Unlike the still occasionally turbulent Highlands with its warlike clans, by the beginning of the seventeenth century Lowland Scotland was mostly peaceful, well settled, and relatively prosperous, although the twin threats of famine and plague were never far distant. Here English (or more accurately Scots) was the dominant language, although many Lowlanders would be familiar enough with the Gaelic which held sway in the Highlands. The backbone of the economy was agriculture with tenant farmers holding land from the nobility such as the Grahams. In the growing cities and towns there was an emerging middle-class – the burgesses – whose expanding economic power was leading to greater demands for political influence. It would be a shrewd politician who would enhance his own power by being seen to champion these ambitions.

Montrose's mother died when he was just five, and when the 4th Earl died in 1626 the young heir inherited the title at the age of 14, having lost both parents but with older sisters at home to care for him. At twelve he was entrusted to William Farrat and studied at college in Glasgow, but on the death of his father returned to the family seat at Kincardine in Strathearn. He then went to study at St Salvator's College in St Andrews in 1627. Like Lord Lorne, Montrose was a keen sportsman, and enjoyed not just archery but also golf and hawking. He had a particular fondness for gambling, regularly attending the Cupar races, and donating his winnings to the Church. More often than not he would lose out, on occasions squandering substantial sums at cards; it would become clear in later life that he enjoyed the risk and excitement of playing for high stakes. He was also noted for his generosity towards servants and the poor.

History does not tell us a great deal about the early life of Montrose. We do know that at the age of 17 he married Magdalen, the youngest daughter of Lord Carnegie (later Earl of Southesk), whose castle at Kinnaird was close to the Graham family seat at Old Montrose. The young Montrose had his fair share of female admirers, but the marriage was most likely one arranged for him by his family and guardians as a suitable coupling for the head of one of Scotland's great families. In due course there were to be five children, four boys and one girl. Marriage, and the birth of heirs, were encouraged for young noblemen at an early age to ensure the continuation of the family line, and as Montrose was an only son it was particularly important that this vital matter was attended to before he set off into the wider world.

It was expected of the sons of earls at the time that they would earn their spurs in military adventure, and both Montrose and Lorne naturally fell into line. Having done his duty in producing two male heirs, Montrose left his native shores to travel through Europe, from France (where he was Captain of the Scottish Guard at the Royal Court) to Italy. He had time to progress in his studies, taking a particular interest in reading about great heroes of history. Already, it seems, he had a vision for himself as a romantic hero. Gilbert Burnet, the Royalist bishop, wrote that he was: 'a young man, well learned, who had travelled, but had taken upon him the part of a hero too much, and lived as in a romance, for his whole manner was stately to affectation'.[4]

On his return to home shores Montrose arrived in London to be presented to King Charles I. Young noblemen were expected to be formally introduced to the monarch, and this rite of passage would have been eagerly anticipated. Dressed in his finest clothes, James Graham arrived at the glittering Court of St James looking forward to his reception, and the compliments of his peers which would inevitably follow. But it was all to go horribly wrong. The Marquis of Hamilton, the King's chief counsellor in Scotland, was suspicious of Montrose and warned Charles that the young man's ambition might present a threat to Royal authority. So when the Earl came before the King he received a chilly reception, Charles simply giving him the Royal hand to kiss, and then turning aside. It was a devastating blow for an eager Montrose. Humiliated in front of the assembled Court, who would all have observed the deliberate slight, he must have left and returned to Scotland fuming. He had from this point no reason to show loyalty to, or love for, his King.

In contrast to Montrose we know a lot more about the activities of the young Lord Lorne. In 1625 the Privy Council of Scotland issued a warrant authorising the Archbishop of Glasgow and Sir William Livingston of Kilsyth to go to Ayr to fit out a ship for a mission to subdue the rebellious Clan MacIain. Lorne was instructed to join the expedition with his forces. It was clearly successful, for shortly thereafter Lorne travelled to London where he met the then newly-installed King Charles, and, unlike the reception which awaited Montrose, he was warmly received. Charles even tried to arrange a marriage between his relative Elizabeth Stewart, sister of the Duke of Lennox, to Lorne, not realising that she had already formed a romantic attachment with the eldest son of the Earl of Arundel. Such was the King's anger that the lovers were thrown into the Tower of London for three months. Any disappointment which Lorne felt was clearly short-lived, for within four months he was married to Margaret Douglas, daughter of his guardian the Earl of Morton. He was 19 and she was 16. The couple were to have two sons and four daughters.

By this time the relationship between Lorne and his father, who was remarried with a new second family, had become strained. There was dispute over the peninsula of Kintyre which had come into Campbell hands recently and therefore did not form part of the entailed estate which was Lorne's rightful inheritance. Money worries were very much at the forefront of the young nobleman's concerns, and indeed this continued to be the case throughout his life. Large estates required careful hands-on management, and the cost of maintaining military forces and upholding justice and the rule of law throughout large parts of the Highlands was high. In this respect Lorne was no different from any other nobles of his generation, but the sheer scale of the Campbell family interests made his position all the more precarious.

Relations between the 7th Earl of Argyll and his heir deteriorated further when the father renounced the Reformed faith and became a Roman Catholic, and left the country to enter the service of the Spanish king. It may simply be a later invention, but the attitude of the 7th Earl to his son and heir might be summed up in what he allegedly told Charles I about Lorne: 'Sir, I must know this young man better than you can do: you have brought me low that you may raise him; which I doubt you will live to repent; for he is a man of craft, subtlety and falsehood, and can love no man; and if ever he finds it in his power to do you mischief, he will be sure to do it'.[5] Even at an early age the young nobleman was developing a reputation as a skilled political operator. He developed an unusual habit, which served him well in later life, of abruptly leaving the room and shutting the door behind him when a conversation took a turn he did not care for.

The contemporary historian Patrick Gordon observed that Lorne was 'of a homely carriage, gentle, mild, and effable, gratious and courteous to speak too' and had 'suche plaine and homely aspect, as he seemed rather inclined to simplicitie then any ways tented with a loftie and unsatiable ambition, though he proved the deepest statesman, the most craftie, subtill and over-reacheing politician that this age could produce.'[6] Edward

Hyde, Earl of Clarendon, wrote of him: 'His wit is pregnant, and his humour gay and pleasant, except when he liked not the company or the argument.'[7] Burnet, hardly a political sympathiser, added that he was 'a solemn sort of man, grave and sober, free of all scandalous vices, of an invincible calmness, and a pretender to high degrees of piety: but he was a deep dissembler, and a great oppressor in all his private dealings, and he was noted for a defect in his courage on all occasions when danger met him.'[8] This accusation of personal cowardice was one which would gain currency with Lorne's political opponents.

Lorne's progress in public life continued despite his father's hostile attitude towards him. In 1628 he was appointed a Privy Councillor, and thus at the very heart of national decision-making. His military exploits continued with the capture and subsequent execution of the famous outlaw Gilderoy, more accurately called Patrick McGregor, who with his band of outlaws had terrorised parts of the Highlands.

Portraits of Lorne as a young man show him attired as a courtier, with lace cuffs, tunic with slashed sleeves, cloak and knee breeches. He had long red hair, small blue eyes, and a long nose. He had a pronounced squint in one eye, which does not seem to have affected his prowess in archery. He wore a full moustache and a goatee beard in the fashion of the day. The most famous portrait of Lorne, or the Marquis of Argyll as he had then become, is David Scougall's perhaps deliberately unflattering portrayal from 1652, showing the subject as an older man, in clerical garb with a skull-cap, and looking rather dour and severe.

Montrose is described as being of middle stature and gracefully built, with chestnut hair, keen grey eyes and a high-bridged nose. Portraits show him with long, flowing hair, and the popular moustache and small beard of the time. Unlike Lorne he is often depicted in military gear. Contemporaries describe him as strong in body and limbs and highly skilled in riding a horse and in use of arms. Montrose's chaplain George Wishart wrote that, 'He was a man of a very princely carriage and excellent address, which made him be used by princes, for the most part, with the greatest familiarity. He was of a most resolute and undaunted spirit, which began to appear in him, to the wonder and expectation of all men, even in his childhood.'[9]

Like Lorne, and indeed like most young noblemen, Montrose was ambitious. As we have seen, he was noted for his personal courage – Clarendon wrote 'Montrose was in his nature fearless of danger' – but also a somewhat superior attitude: 'He was naturally jealous, and suspected those who did not concur with him in the way not to mean so well as he. He was not without vanity, but his virtues were much superior . . .'[10] He would be a good leader, but not a man fitted to be second-in-command, or even a good team player. Fitting the image of the romantic warrior, Montrose also wrote poetry (of variable quality, it has to be said, although one unsympathetic historian probably went too far in describing it as 'no less execrable than his actions as a member of society'!).[11]

By the fourth decade of the seventeenth century both Montrose and Lorne had followed a pattern in their lives that might be expected of prominent Scottish noblemen of their day. They had each benefitted from a rounded education, they had both married young and started families, they were both involved in the administration of estates, and they had both begun to make a mark in the public life of the country, a country which was about to enter a turbulent period in its history.

*

Scotland had already seen remarkable change in the previous 100 years. This proudly independent nation, which had for so long defined itself in contrast to its much larger and richer southern neighbour, had taken a huge step towards integration with England with the Union of the Crowns in 1603. When Queen Elizabeth of England died leaving no issue, her heir was James VI of Scotland, who had long coveted the much wealthier, and more secure, English crown. On his accession he became sovereign of three kingdoms – England, Scotland and Ireland – and celebrated the formation of 'Great Britain'.

The Scottish throne had always been a precarious perch for a Stewart monarch. James was well aware of several of his ancestors being murdered or deposed by jealous nobles. The ancient Earls of Scotland had always exercised substantial power, and even strong and popular monarchs had both struggled to contain their ambitions, and envied their wealth. In contrast, the Tudors in England had enriched the Royal family, centralised power, and dealt ruthlessly with nobles who opposed them. The crown of England was a prize worth waiting for, and when James inherited it it was as if all his Christmases had come at once.

James I and VI, as he became, believed in the Divine Right of Kings. He was God's anointed on Earth, and as such he was beholden to no man. His theory was set out in two tracts he authored, *The Trew Law of Free Monarchies* in 1598 and *Basilikon Doron* in 1603: 'The state of monarchy is the supremest thing upon earth, for kings are not only God's lieutenants upon earth and sit upon God's throne, but even by God himself they are called gods.' Such a philosophy did not go down well in the comparatively poor kingdom of Scotland with its history of strong earls and a weak monarchy, but in England it was what many expected from the heir to Henry VIII. For all that, James was a shrewd politician and knew the limits of even his own substantial power. He would not push the nobles or people of England too far.

The political changes that Scotland had witnessed were matched, if not exceeded, in scale by the religious developments.

The Reformation had come to Scotland comparatively late, in 1560, but if anything it was more comprehensive (although less bloody) than in any other European country. The leading Reformer John Knox was a disciple of the Geneva-based French theologian John Calvin, and had returned to Scotland with detailed plans not just for a Protestant church but for a whole Reformed society. The country responded with enthusiasm. The Church became the centre of life for the people, providing not just religious focus but also the beginnings of both universal education and a welfare system. Only in the remote Highlands and Islands and parts of the North-east did Catholicism continue to hold sway, protected by the patronage of powerful Catholic families like the Gordons, Earls of Huntly.

Scots Protestants took much of their inspiration from the Old Testament story of the Israelites as God's chosen people. A nation which feared God, and followed His laws, was a nation which would be blessed. There would be earthly rewards in the form of peace and prosperity for the country as a whole if it were true to the Reformed faith. The ancient Israelites were in a covenant relationship with Jehovah, and Scotland would enjoy divine blessing by following their lead. The Calvinist view of God's elect – that those who would be saved and enter heaven were pre-ordained from the beginning of time – encouraged the belief in the Scottish people as enjoying particular divine favour. Religion was not simply a private matter, although a personal relationship with Jesus Christ was essential, but an issue of national interest if the country were to prosper. Any attempt to dilute the true faith would bring God's condemnation on the land.

The Scots Kirk rejected the Episcopalian structure of church government favoured in England with its hierarchy of bishops and archbishops all deriving authority from the monarch as head of the Church. Instead the Kirk was ordered on Presbyterian lines with a system of church courts made up of clerics and laymen (elders), all of whom were equal in terms of authority. Every year the Kirk met in General Assembly and this gathering elected a Moderator to lead its affairs. But the head of the Church, unlike in England, was no mortal man but Jesus Christ himself. This is what led the great churchman Andrew Melville to tell King James, no doubt much to his annoyance: 'Sirrah, ye are God's silly vassal; there are two kings and two kingdoms in Scotland: there is King James, the head of the commonwealth; and there is Christ Jesus, the King of the Church, whose subject James the Sixth is, and of whose kingdom he is not a king, not a lord, not a head, but a member.'

The Reformation marked another significant change in Scottish policy. Historically Scotland had allied itself with France as a counterbalance to the threat from England – the 'Auld Alliance'. But now France was Catholic, while it was Protestant England which had nourished the Reformers like Knox, and it was to England that the Scottish nobility increasingly looked for support. When James VI was named as Elizabeth of England's heir, the transformation was completed. England was no longer the enemy but now the friend and neighbour, a change that was to be permanent.

Despite the Union of the Crowns, Scotland retained its own Parliament, but it met in future without the presence of the King. Away in the bright lights of London, James had little continuing interest in Scotland. He was taken up with the power and majesty of the English throne and the attentions of attractive young men. He interfered in Scottish affairs when he had to, but he knew where to draw the line, unlike the son and heir who was to follow him.

James had no love for the Presbyterian Church in Scotland; it was far too democratic and egalitarian for his liking. He preferred the hierarchical structure of the Church of England, of which he was the figurehead. But trying to bring the Scottish Kirk entirely into line with the English was simply not worth the effort. James appointed bishops, and these were rather reluctantly accepted by the Scots, but he did not go so far as to seek to impose the Anglican liturgy on Scotland.

James died in 1625 and was succeeded by his son Charles, who had been born in Dunfermline in 1600. Like his father, Charles Stewart believed passionately in the Divine Right. Charles was brave, principled and devout, but unlike his father he lacked wisdom and guile. He did not know when to back down, and this stubbornness was to prove his undoing.

Almost from the start the new King had difficulties dealing with his Parliament in London. While the Crown held extensive executive powers, all legislation had to be passed through Parliament, and only the House of Commons could approve the raising of taxes. Parliaments could only meet at the King's summons and would only be called when the monarch needed support for a particular measure, such as the levying of a new tax. Charles expected the Members of Parliament to do his bidding, and quickly became exasperated when they demonstrated that they were of independent mind. It was a relationship which was destined to end tragically.

The King's strong religious faith was heavily influenced by his Queen, Henrietta Maria. She was a French Roman Catholic and it was widely suspected that privately Charles' own sympathies lay with her religion. In a Scotland where there was deep antagonism towards 'Popery', this simply increased the tension between the King and his subjects, particularly when Charles turned his attentions to the Kirk. He could not understand why in a part of his Kingdoms the structure of the Church did not allow him, as God's anointed on Earth, his rightful place at the top of the tree, when this was happily accepted throughout England. It was time to force the pace of change, and in so doing

Charles put himself on a collision course with virtually the entire Scottish nation.

In 1634 Charles asked the Scots bishops to suggest alterations to the English Prayer Book prior to its introduction in Scotland. This did not go down well with the Scots Presbyterians who feared that the Prayer Book's introduction was a step towards making the Kirk not just more like the Church of England, but also (horror of horrors) more Catholic. Nothing daunted, two years later Charles ordered the Privy Council to issue a proclamation about the new Prayer Book – it was coming, whether wanted or not. The text had been altered from the original English version, but only the King's religious advisor William Laud, Archbishop of Canterbury, and the Scots bishops had been consulted about these alterations, and not the rank and file of the Kirk. Inevitably there was opposition to the Prayer Book from the very start; many Scots believing that this departure from the pure Protestant faith was inviting divine retribution against God's chosen people. Eventually it was imposed upon the Kirk by Royal prerogative.

The differences between the Scots Presbyterians and the English Church under Laud's direction were not restricted to matters of church government, nor even liturgy. There was a fundamental, and widening, theological divide. Where the Scots Kirk was Calvinist, Arminianism (called after the Dutch teacher Jacobus Arminus) had the support of the King and was increasingly influential within the Anglican Church. Arminianism taught that salvation was open to all, thus rejecting the fundamental Calvinist belief in election. To the Scots this was not just heresy, but uncomfortably close to Roman Catholicism. Even within England there were very many within the Church unhappy about where Laud was taking things and who had strong leanings to Presbyterianism, and many others – Independents – who thought that the King should have no role in the Church at all.

The interference of Charles in religious affairs in Scotland in this blundering fashion merely added to the suspicion in which he was held by the Scots nobility. Charles had made very little attempt to engage with them in the running of the realm. There was a perception that government was distantly located in England without any input from north of the Border, and Charles seemed only interested in English affairs (it was eight years after his accession to the throne before he even visited his northern Kingdom). Policies in Scotland seemed to be no more than a reflection of what was being implemented down south. From the perspective of nearly 400 years later, it is remarkable how little some aspects of the political debate seem to have altered in the intervening period.

Charles remained insensitive to the concerns of the Scots nobles. He proposed an Act of Revocation whereby all gifts of both Royal and Kirk property to subjects made since 1540 would be revoked. An enormous amount of land was affected by this, perhaps approaching half of all income-generating property. The big losers were the nobility. As it happened Charles intended to allow the Scots nobles to retain most of the lands that they had been granted, and pay compensation for those which were revoked. But this had been made insufficiently clear at the outset, and the result was that he put himself at loggerheads with the most powerful families in the land. At the same time their political power was sidelined with the appointment of the Archbishop of St Andrews as Lord Chancellor of Scotland, the first time since the Reformation that elevated position had been held by a cleric.

On both a political and a religious level grievances against the King were building up. Charles was oblivious to the discontent in Scotland at his actions. The imposition of the new Prayer Book became the key issue on which this unhappiness was focused, but Charles claimed that 'no symptoms of any considerable opposition did appear'[12] to it. Yet, behind the scenes, groups of Scots ministers were meeting and corresponding about how best to prevent its introduction. It was only a matter of time before things would come to a head, and they would do so in dramatic fashion.

Charles I

2

Revolution

1637–38

On a bright summer's morning, 23 July 1637, the drunkards, pickpockets and wife-beaters locked up in Edinburgh's Tolbooth prison gaped through the narrow grilles of their cell windows at the crowds coming early to Sabbath service. All classes of folk gathered, nobility and commoner, townsfolk and peasant, jostling each other to get through the great west door of St Giles High Kirk. Inside they pushed past the wide pillars soaring roofwards, towards the front, eyes adjusting to the relative darkness. A group of 'the meaner sorte of the people, most of them waiting maides and women, who use in that towne for to keepe places for the better sorte'[1] occupied space near the pulpit, some of them seated on folding stools (a few may have been young men disguised in women's clothing). Everywhere there was talk; conversation in low whispers; the atmosphere tense with anticipation. *Something* was due to happen that day, and for the past week Edinburgh had talked of little else.

The previous Sunday, 16 July, the Bishop of Edinburgh had ordered intimation that the new Prayer Book would be used in all churches around the city on the following Lord's Day. Edinburgh was to be used to test public reaction – if the Prayer Book went down well then it would be rolled out across the rest of Scotland. In his ignorance, the King believed that it would be well received: many Scots visiting England had participated in services with the English equivalent without any fuss; the English Service Book had been read in the Chapel Royal of

Edinburgh every day since 1617; it was in use by the bishops and at St Andrew's University; and had been used when Charles visited Scotland. Charles' attitude just demonstrated how out of touch with opinion in his northern Kingdom he had become. And by giving a week's notice, he and his advisors had simply allowed those opposed to the new Prayer Book ample time to plan their protest.

The large congregation at St Giles that July morning included two archbishops, eight or nine bishops, and members of the Privy Council. As soon as the Dean of Edinburgh, Dr George Hanna, started to read from the new Prayer Book, the trouble started. There was a spontaneous outbreak of noise from 'the commone people, especially the women', who 'with clapping of their hands, cursings and outcryes, raised such ane uncoth noyse and hub-bubb in the church, that not any one could heare or be hearde'.[2] Some cried 'Woe, woe!' and some 'Sorrow, sorrow! For this doolefull day, that they are bringand in Poperie among us!'[3] Such was the fury of the congregation that one woman (popularly identified as Jenny Geddes, although her name does not appear in any contemporary accounts) hurled her stool at the Dean, 'intending to give him a ticket of remembrance; but jouking [ducking] became his safegaird at that time.'[4] Another 'good Christian woman', finding herself beside a young man loudly saying 'Amen!' to the Dean's words, 'warmed both his cheeks with the weight of her hand' and gave him a tongue-lashing: 'False theefe! Is there no other parte of the Kirke to sing Masse in, but you must sing it at my lugge?'[5] Suitably rebuked, he deemed it prudent to keep silent.

The Archbishop of St Andrews called for order, but to no avail, and the Bishop of Edinburgh struggled through a 'verie short'[6] sermon. On leaving the church 'the confused multitude rushed violentlie upone him, and furiouslie pursued after him with railing and clodding; and if their hands could have beene as active as their minds were willing, they had doubtlesse demolished the great butt which they aimed at'.[7] The poor bishop, 'a corpulent man'[8] was bundled into the Earl of Roxburgh's coach and taken home, still pursued by the stone-throwing mob, and 'in danger of his lyfe'.[9]

One unnamed nobleman joked that he would write to the King and tell him of a change in the Court, that 'Lord Traquair, Treasurer, used ever before to gette greatest backing, but now the Earl of Roxburgh and the Bishop of Edinburgh have the greatest number of followers.' The Bishop would not have seen the funny side. 'Hee never in his lifetyme got such a laxative purgation', and his terror was such that when he exited the coach no man could endure 'the stinking smell of his fatt carcage'.[10]

A soiled surplice pretty well summed up what a disastrous day it had been for the King's policy in Scotland. An equally negative, if less tumultuous, reception had been given to the reading of the new Prayer Book in other Edinburgh churches.

The Privy Council wrote to Charles advising him of the reaction, blaming it on the 'imprudent precipitation'[11] of the bishops in imposing the Prayer Book, but downplaying the seriousness of the riots. There were fears as to what Charles' reaction would be – 'the towne and country did quake till the return of the King's pleasure',[12] wrote the Reverend Robert Baillie (Minister of Kilwinning in Ayrshire, and later to be Principal of Glasgow University) – but no-one was brave enough to continue the use of the new Prayer Book until his response was received.

Charles was furious when he learned how his subjects had reacted. He replied to the Privy Council stating that those responsible for the riots should be tried and punished, and that the bishops had to be supported. The Privy Council thought better about ordering the reintroduction of the Prayer Book immediately, and met again on 25 August to write to the King in more detail about the seriousness of the situation. The Councillors stated to Charles that they were faced with 'the clamour and fears of your Majesty's subjects, from diverse parts and corners of the Kingdom',[13] and it was suggested that the King should meet with some Councillors and bishops to understand how serious the situation was. A further meeting was planned for 20 September to hear the King's subsequent reply.

Charles was not for turning. He was insistent that the rioters should be punished, and the Prayer Book imposed. How that was to be achieved in practice was not his problem, but one for the authorities in Scotland. Charles' intransigence simply had the effect of driving away the remaining Privy Councillors who still had sympathy for his position.

The political situation was becoming extremely serious and there were even suggestions that civil war was a possibility. From September 1637 to February 1638 correspondence between the King and the Privy Councillors to-ed and fro-ed, with the King maintaining his position that the Scots had to fall into line, and thus increasing dissent amongst Scots nobility and clergymen. Baillie observed: 'there was in our Land never such ane appearance of a sturr; the whole people thinks Poperie at the doors . . . no man may speak any thing in publick for the King's part, except he would have himself marked for a sacrifice to be killed one day. I think our people possessed with a bloody devil . . .'[14]

Amongst those prominent in opposition to the King was the 25-year-old Earl of Montrose. As an elder of the Kirk his sympathies were naturally with those who valued Presbyterianism and resisted Royal interference in the Church's affairs, and his one encounter with Charles had left him feeling under little obligation of loyalty to the monarch. Moreover he was a young man with political ambition looking to make his mark on the world, and here was a righteous cause he could champion. He thrust himself to the forefront of the new crusade. Recognising his abilities and his enthusiasm, his peers elected him as one of four representatives of the nobility on the 'Tables', committees which also contained representatives of lairds, burgesses and clergy, established by the rebels to report on dealings between the King and the Privy Council. Here he served alongside Lord Lindsay of the Byres (later Earl of Crawford-Lindsay), John Campbell, Lord Loudon, and Montrose's friend and mentor James Leslie, 6th Earl of Rothes. Loudon and Rothes were committed to the rebellion, and they saw in Montrose a kindred spirit.

Eventually the rebels took the view that they had to put their grievances in writing in a form to which they could all subscribe, and thus came into being the extraordinary document that was the National Covenant of 1638. The notion of a covenant had clear parallels with the ancient Israelites' Covenant with God, and would have appealed not just to the clergy, but to a people well schooled in the Old Testament. The protestors felt it was no longer enough simply to write to the King with their grievances, but that they had to band together with a clear statement of what they stood for, with an agreement between them, and between them and God, just like the Israelites of old. This was agreed to be a new version of 'the old Covenant for religion',[15] namely the confession of faith of James VI of 1581, the subscribers to which had pledged to uphold the true religion of the Kirk and oppose popery and superstition.

The new Covenant was drawn up primarily by a brilliant and fanatically devout young lawyer, Archibald Johnston of Warriston, and the minister of Leuchars in Fife, Alexander Henderson. It was presented to a gathering of the great and good in Grey-friars Kirk in Edinburgh on 28 February. The Scottish nobles were the first to subscribe. As one of the most committed to the cause, Montrose was at the front of the queue – on at least one copy his was the very first signature. The day after, close on 300 ministers and the commissioners for the burghs signed up, and over the next two days it was the turn of the ordinary people of Edinburgh. Copies were then produced and dispersed all around the country for the entire population to sign. It was a remarkable national bond swearing to defend the King, but also to uphold and defend 'true religion' and protect the existing system of Kirk government. The Covenanters (as those who signed quickly became known) swore not to suffer themselves to be divided or withdrawn by whatsoever suggestion, allurement or terror, and to suppress any divisive motion. They truly were firmly bound together in this new adventure.

There were those around Montrose who feared that his zeal would end up costing him dear. On 22 February he had led, along with Johnston of Warriston, a public protest in Edinburgh against the Royal proclamation on the Prayer Book. The crowds were packed in around the Mercat Cross at the east end of St Giles, and the young Earl had hoisted himself up to stand on a barrel so that he would be above their heads. It was a risky position to put oneself in, and not just on the practical level. Montrose might think that he owed little to his King, but Charles was a dangerous enemy to make. The older and wiser Earl of Rothes remarked, prophetically as it would turn out, 'James, you will never be at rest til you are lifted up above the rest in three fathoms of a rope.'[16] It was Rothes who had influenced Montrose to throw in his lot with the Covenanters, but it was a popular cause. This was not simply about internal Church government and the role of bishops, it was about something much more fundamental – whether the King had unfettered power, or whether he could govern only with the consent of the people. The Covenant was clear in asserting the King's authority, and so it was not a revolution that was being proposed, or at least not yet.

The National Covenant was an astonishing success. It was greeted with enthusiasm across the country, the only exceptions being the Highlands and parts of the North-east where there were still large numbers of adherents to Catholicism and episcopacy (the rule of bishops). Throughout the Lowlands the people were delighted at the opportunity to reassert their support for the Reformed faith, and demonstrate their belief in Scotland as a nation in covenant with God, just like Israel. The signing of the Covenant was often accompanied with scenes of high emotion, people queuing for hours for their turn, some appending their names in blood, some adding the words 'till death'. The national mood was summed up by a breathless entry in Johnston of Warriston's diary referring to 28 February 1638 as 'that glorious marriage day of the Kingdom with God'.[17]

The King's concern about developments in Scotland led him to invite members of the Privy Council to meet in London to provide advice on how he might respond. Charles was particularly anxious that Lord Lorne, who was regarded as having great power and influence and was as yet publicly uncommitted to the Covenanting cause, should attend. He was warned against this by the staunchly Royalist Earl of Traquair, who wrote: 'If the King's Majesty be pleased to hear any of his servants, before he conclude fully what course to take in the prosecution of his business, I remit to your own consideration, if it shall not to be necessary to send for Lorne.' Traquair added cryptically: 'I need not enlarge on this point, the reasons are sufficiently known to yourself.'[18]

Lorne, always more considered and less rash than Montrose, had had little involvement in the various meetings that led to the creation of the National Covenant. He displayed no interest at this stage in signing the Covenant, notwithstanding its popular appeal. But, as Traquair's letter suggests, he was suspected of having private sympathy for the Covenanters. Demonstrating the caution that came to characterise his political approach, Lorne may simply have been keeping his options open, waiting to see how things might develop. Even with the great bulk of the Scots nobility and people signing up to a document that put them on a collision course with the King, it would have been rash for him to have burnt his boats with Charles until it was clearer how matters would develop. And so he made the long journey to London, playing over in his mind what the King might ask of him, and how he should best respond.

In the meantime, a plot had been devised by the Archbishop of St Andrews, also Lord Chancellor, and the Bishop of Ross, to bring together the Highland clans and those remaining loyalists in the Lowlands opposed to the Covenant, to defeat the Covenanters militarily. The forces of the mighty Clan Campbell joining with either side might have proved crucial, and accordingly the architects of this plan suggested to Charles that Lord Lorne be kept as a hostage in London to secure either the Campbells' support, or at least their neutrality. This scheme was thwarted by the actions of the Covenanters in signing up many of the clans to the Covenant, including the Campbells themselves, who accepted it enthusiastically. In any event Charles did not heed the suggestion to hold his visitor captive, despite the urgings of Lorne's own father, the 7th Earl of Argyll, who had no love for his son, and told the King that he should not let Lorne return to Scotland or else he would 'wind him a pin' (cause him a difficulty). Charles thanked the Earl for his counsel, but said that 'he behoved to be a King of his word'[19] and as it would be a breach of faith to detain Lorne, he agreed to allow him to leave.

On 8 April 1638 Lord Lorne arrived at the Court of St James for a private audience with Charles, which would last for an hour and a half. Dressed in the popular style, with doublet, cloak and knee breeches, and with neatly trimmed moustaches and goatee beard, only Lorne's accent would have distinguished him from the courtiers who made it their businesses to be constantly in the Royal presence. There was no doubt as to the scale of the crisis engulfing Charles' northern Kingdom, and the King was serious about talking through the issues with someone who he believed could be useful to him.

Lorne was frank in his opinions about the difficulties that the King's bishops had caused within the Kirk and the nation. Baillie reported: 'The plainnesse of Lorne is much talked of; nothing he is said to have dissembled of all he knew of our countrie's greevances, of his own mislyke of the Books, of the Articles of Perth, of the Bishops' misgovernment, of his resolution to leave the kingdom rather than to the consent to the pressing of any other, let be of himself or his servants, with these burdens, which were against conscience'.[20] That the King was prepared to spend so much time with Lorne is an indication of how highly he was regarded, possibly because, as someone known to have sympathy with the Covenanters' complaints, but not yet publicly an adherent to the Covenant, he had the capacity to be a middle man between the warring parties.

Lorne's reluctance to commit himself publicly to the Covenanting cause would have been influenced, at least in part, by the fact that the King still had, while the 7th Earl was alive, the power to cancel the transfer of family estates to Lorne. It may also have been a product of Lorne's natural caution. He was undoubtedly privately sympathetic to the Covenanters, and had assisted the leading minister and theologian Samuel Rutherford when he was being harassed by the authorities for writing against episcopacy. But it would have been unwise to commit wholeheartedly to one party in a dispute where the stakes were so high until it was clear who was likely to gain the upper hand. Unlike the impetuous Montrose, Archibald Campbell liked to take time to weigh his options before deciding on a course of action.

If Charles had contemplated appointing Lorne as his man in Scotland he clearly thought better of it, perhaps having realised that he was unlikely to be an enthusiastic champion for the

Royalist cause. Instead the Marquis of Hamilton was appointed as the King's Commissioner, and duly despatched north with orders from Charles to bring the Covenanters to heel.

James Hamilton, 3rd Marquis of Hamilton, was Scotland's premier nobleman. It was he who had introduced Charles to the young Earl of Montrose, while warning the King of his ambitious nature. Hamilton had no great history of activity in Scottish affairs, and therefore was a credible appointment as an honest broker with no baggage from the Covenanting cause. But it was clear from the instructions that Charles had given to him that neither man appreciated the strength of feeling that existed amongst the people or nobility. Hamilton was given the power to raise an army in the King's name, any protests against his actions were to be met with force, and any opponents were to be considered rebels and to have their leaders arrested. Hamilton was also given authority to state that the King would bring an army from England to enforce his will should his initial efforts be unsuccessful. In the background Charles had already set about raising the necessary forces, either as an insurance policy against Hamilton's failure, or possibly to strengthen his hand in negotiations.

The Covenanters were represented by the Tables, the previously established committees of nobles, lairds, burgesses, and ministers, where members were known as 'Commissioners'. On Hamilton's arrival in Scotland the Tables appointed a committee of three ministers and three nobles to meet him, amongst their number being Montrose. They presented Hamilton with a series of demands which included the calling of a free General Assembly of the Kirk and a meeting of Parliament to decide issues in dispute. Hamilton protested that these were unacceptable. In truth he had come unprepared for the level of opposition which now faced him. It was clear that there was no likelihood of common ground being found between the demands of the

King and those of the Covenanters, and that negotiations were likely to go nowhere. It dawned on Hamilton that Charles had sent him only to buy time to allow military forces to be raised to crush the rebels.

Hamilton privately told Montrose and the other Commissioners that they should stand their ground as they were likely to be successful if they did. But he must have known that the King had no intention of backing down. He was therefore playing a dangerous game which would make a negotiated settlement almost impossible to achieve. In all Hamilton's dealings over the years he continually tried to be too clever by half. He may have thought himself a Scottish version of Machiavelli, but his blunderings displayed a political ineptitude which was to cost his Royal master dear.

Negotiations continued over the summer of 1638 with Hamilton futilely shuttling between London and Edinburgh with various proposals and counter-proposals. The more Charles dissembled, the more hardened the Covenanters' demands became. Both parties started preparing for battle, Charles raising troops in England while the Covenanters were sourcing arms in the Netherlands. Meantime there were discussions with the Earl of Antrim, a leading Catholic nobleman, about him raising an army loyal to the King in Ireland to join with the Clan MacDonald, hereditary enemies of the Campbells, to invade Argyllshire, with a promise that if successful, Antrim would be granted a share in the Campbell lands. As it happened nothing came of this proposal, but Lord Lorne must have become aware of it, and it could not have endeared him to the Royalist cause.

The Covenanters continued to try and win support. The one area of the Lowlands thus far unpersuaded by the Covenanters' charms was the North-east, largely due to the influence of the powerful, and Catholic, Gordon family led by the Marquis of Huntly. George Gordon, the 2nd Marquis, was married to

Lorne's sister, but having spent most of his life in France was not well known in Scotland. The Covenanters sent Colonel Robert Munro on their behalf to try and attract Huntly to their side, offering him leadership of their cause and the vast sum of £100,000 sterling if he would defect, and at the same time threatening him with ruin if he held out against such a popular movement. But Huntly was a principled Royalist; he thanked Colonel Munro and stated that his family had always been one which had been loyal to Scotland's kings and would remain so: 'if the event proved the ruin of this King, he was resolved to lay his life, honours and estate under the rubbish of the King's ruins'.[21] He would, in time.

Notwithstanding this rebuff, the Covenanters dispatched Montrose, as one of their principal assets, northwards to evangelise for their cause. His family connections with the North-east made him the obvious choice, and he was keen to show his usefulness. Montrose arrived in Aberdeen on 20 July along with three ministers, Alexander Henderson, David Dickson and Andrew Cant, his flowing hair and fine clothes distinguishing him from his austere, soberly-clad companions. The aspiring statesman may have hoped that his personal charm would have been enough to win over the sceptical Aberdonians, but he found them resistant to his advances. While the visitors were greeted cordially by the Provost and the city authorities, it was obvious that they had reservations about the Covenant. Fired with righteous indignation, Montrose refused to participate in the banquet prepared for him and his retinue by the Provost, unless or until their hosts agreed to sign. The poor of Aberdeen were the beneficiaries of this principled stance, becoming the willing recipients of the City fathers' wine which the delegation had rejected.

Having met little success in the city, Montrose and his followers visited neighbouring settlements where they were more warmly received. Discussions with the ministers of Aberdeen continued, but to little effect, with the Aberdonians refusing to condemn episcopacy. Despite Montrose protesting his and his companions' loyalty to the King, he was ultimately unsuccessful in winning Aberdeen for the Covenant, and returned to Edinburgh with his tail between his legs; his mission a failure. It was an early setback to a promising political career.

One of the concessions which Charles had made to the Covenanters was to call a General Assembly of the Church of Scotland, to meet in Glasgow Cathedral on 21 November. The General Assembly was then, as it is today, the supreme governing court of the Kirk. It consists of not just the clergy, but also of lay representatives – elders – from all across the country. As a representative body for members of the Kirk, each Presbytery across the country had the right to elect commissioners from amongst the local ministers and elders to attend the Assembly. The Tables took control of the system of election of commissioners to the Assembly, against the wishes of Hamilton representing the King. Hamilton was in no doubt that it was the intention of the Covenanters to use the Assembly to end episcopacy within the Kirk, and that the Covenanters would be careful to stack the cards in their favour in advance of the event. For once, he was right.

What was proposed at the General Assembly was undoubtedly radical: that the whole system of church government and liturgy which had been established by Royal command be set aside, and a return made to the simple structures which existed post-Reformation. In advance of the Assembly being convened, Charles had already made a number of concessions, agreeing to drop the liturgy and deal with some of the worst abuses of the bishops. But it was already too late for the Covenanters. The time for compromise had passed; it was time for a fresh start for the Kirk, free of Royal control.

The Covenanters, supported by crowds of enthusiasts, made their way to Glasgow, travelling fully armed in defiance of an order from the Privy Council. It was reported that even some of the clergy carried swords and pistols. The Assembly meeting at Glasgow Cathedral was so packed that it was only with difficulty that those attending could find their seats. Present were 240 commissioners, of whom 142 were ministers and 98 elders, and in addition the Privy Council attended. Finely-dressed noblemen, their retainers in tow, rubbed shoulders with stout burgesses from far-flung towns. Row after row of black-gowned ministers squeezed in to hard pews, lined up like crows on a dyke. The Earl of Montrose sat as an elder representing his home presbytery of Auchterarder, while Archibald Campbell, now the 8th Earl of Argyll following the recent death of his father, sat with the Privy Councillors. Seated amongst them too was Hamilton, who as the King's representative held the position of Royal Commissioner, and who was under strict instructions not to allow proceedings to get out of hand.

The Covenanters had agreed in advance that Alexander Henderson should be elected as Moderator to oversee proceedings, ably assisted by the lawyer Johnston of Warriston, Henderson's co-author of the National Covenant, as the Clerk. Hamilton started proceedings by questioning the appointment of many of the commissioners present, among them Erskine of Dun, who had been appointed by the Tables to replace Lord Carnegie, Montrose's brother-in-law, who had been put forward by his home presbytery of Brechin. With his zeal for the Covenanters' cause Montrose was vigorous in defending the appointment of Erskine, and consequently had cross words with both his father-in-law, the Earl of Southesk, and the minister David Dickson: 'the contest betwixt Montrose and Southesk grew so hot, that it terrified the whole Assembly, so that the Commissioner took upon him the Moderator's place, and commanded them all to peace.'[22]

The Assembly proceeded with its business with the clear intention of ending episcopacy and with it Royal interference in the Kirk's affairs. Hamilton was dismayed. He realised that his mission was failing and wrote to the King regretting that he had let his Sovereign down. At the same time he made clear his feelings towards Scotland in unequivocal language: 'next Hell I hate this place'.[23] But he still had a duty to the King to try and put a stop to the Assembly by whatever means at his disposal. No bishops had appeared in Glasgow, but they had submitted a letter refusing to acknowledge the legality of the gathering. This was the cover that Hamilton needed, and on the morning of Wednesday 28 November he announced that he would, as Royal Commissioner, dissolve the Assembly and declare its meeting illegal. As the gathering could not proceed without his presence as the King's representative, Hamilton then rose from his seat and made for the door, under the disapproving gaze of the commissioners. The dramatic effect of his gesture was rather lost when the Marquis arrived at the Cathedral door only to find it locked against him. Worse still, the key could not be located, so the King's representative had to wait patiently, with all eyes on him, while the door was burst open so that he could complete his exit.

This was a crucial moment. The King had withdrawn his authority for the Assembly to meet, and for it to continue to do so would be an act of defiance amounting to treason. Up stood David Dickson, who with a brilliant speech roused his fellow commissioners to continue in the Assembly's work, 'that the nobleman [Hamilton] was very much to be commended for his zeal and faithfulness to his master the King, and sticking close by what he thought for his credit and interest; and he craved leave to propose his example for the Assembly's imitation: they had a better master, Christ the King of Kings, to serve; and his credit and honour to look after, according to their commission in trust;

and therefore he moved that, having this in their eye, they might sit still and do their Master's work faithfully.'[24] And, so encouraged, the Assembly resolved by an overwhelming majority to continue about its business in the face of Royal opposition.

Before departing for London, Hamilton called together the members of the Privy Council. Amongst them was of course the new Earl of Argyll, who had only just declared his hand now that the King no longer had the power to prevent his inheritance of the family estates. Up until this point he had refrained from signing the Covenant and had publicly maintained his neutrality between King and Covenanters, but just before Hamilton's dissolution of the Assembly he had made a bold speech to the gathering stating his support for the Covenanting cause. Argyll said that he had been present at the General Assembly at the King's command, he called on all those present to testify to the impartiality of his actions, and he stated that nothing would induce him to render a flattering obedience to the King or to be one to advise him to enter on a violent course. He further stated that he was surprised at Hamilton's decision to dissolve the Assembly (intention of which had already been intimated) and that there were not sufficient grounds for doing so. His firm view was that the Assembly was lawful and should continue.

The following morning, 29 November, in strict defiance of Hamilton's instructions, the Assembly met again and proceeded with its business. The only Privy Councillor present was Argyll, much to the delight of those gathered. The Covenanters had a huge prize; the King's favourite was now their champion.

It was now clear to all that Argyll had held private sympathies with the Covenanters all along, but had waited for his moment to declare his hand. Breaking with the Royal party when he did proved to be a masterstroke in terms of political timing. Immediately he became the hero of the hour and was accepted as the de facto leader of the rebel cause. It may have been that Argyll was waiting until his father's death, when he would be free of any control that the King had over his estates, before declaring his loyalty. Whatever the reason, he could not have chosen his moment better. Had he been with the Covenanters from the start, as Montrose had been, it was unlikely that he would now have been so influential. By declaring for the Covenanters when he did, in their hour of need, he ensured his own leading role.

Argyll's bold move may well have catapulted him to the head of the popular cause, but it was still not without risk. He had put himself at the forefront of an unprecedented uprising against Royal authority. For all that Charles seemed to have little support amongst the nobility and people, at least in Lowland Scotland, he had the resources of the British Crown at his disposal and the ability to raise an army far superior to anything that the Covenanters could put in the field. Victory for the Covenanters was by no means a foregone conclusion, and the consequences of defeat, and the prospect subsequently of a conviction for treason, would be disastrous. It would be wrong to interpret Argyll's move as simply political opportunism; it was surely driven by conviction and a fundamental view that the Covenanters were in the right. But it was in the timing of his action that Argyll demonstrated a political nous that ensured the advancement of his own interests.

There was another factor in Argyll's decision – a spiritual one. While in Glasgow he had attended prayer meetings conducted by Alexander Henderson, and it was during this time that he experienced a religious conversion and became a committed Christian. Argyll's loyalty from this date to the Covenanting cause was as much about his personal spiritual leanings as about any political judgements, and he never wavered in his commitment to the Reformed faith and Presbyterian Kirk for the rest of his career. Indeed throughout his life he was noted for his personal religious devotion, spending time in private prayer and writing sermons to be preached at the local kirk in Inveraray. If Montrose's career was to be marked by his loyalty to his King, then Argyll's would be distinguished by his devotion to God.

Amongst the stricter Presbyterian clergy, Argyll was now to be regarded as one of their own. In an environment where this group wielded considerable political power, having such loyal, sometimes fanatical, backers would prove a major advantage. This personal connection would mean that they would be more ready to forgive any political failings on his part in the future, and trust him when he took positions which they instinctively distrusted. Despite his late conversion to the Covenanting cause, Argyll had immediately acquired a hardline group of loyalists to watch his back.

Montrose must have welcomed Argyll as a powerful new asset for Covenanters, but it would have been a poor politician who would not have been aware that here was a serious and significant rival for national leadership of the revolution. Hamilton recognised Argyll's new position of power, writing to the King: 'The Earl of Argyll is the only man now called up as a true patriot, a loyal subject, a faithful councillor, and above all, rightly set for the preservation of the purity of religion. And truly, Sir, he takes it upon him. He must be well looked to; for it fears me, he will prove the dangerousest man in this State'. Hamilton added that the Earl of Perth 'should be encouraged, because he may contribute to the curbing of Argyll'. In the same letter he noted dismissively that, amongst the Covenanters, there was 'none more vainly foolish than Montrose'.[25] Hamilton never had much time for the young nobleman, and the feeling was mutual.

The General Assembly continued about its business, and purged the Kirk of all trappings of episcopacy. The Prayer Book and the Book of Canons were condemned as 'full of popish errors', all archbishops and bishops deposed, and for good measure the majority excommunicated. All this was done in strict defiance of the King's wishes. The revolution was gaining momentum.

From his new platform of leadership Argyll was keen to promote moderation. He warned against criticism of the King and his authority, and said that Charles was a 'good and gracious . . . Prince'. In this he won the support of Henderson as Moderator, who in his closing speech to the Assembly gave thanks to Argyll by whose presence and counsel they had been so much comforted and strengthened. Argyll spoke at length in reply, requesting all those present not to misconstrue his late conversion to the Covenanters' cause, protesting that he had always privately been on their side but had delayed to profess it in order that he might be of more use to them by keeping his views a secret, but 'now of late matters had come to such a pass that he would have been proven and made had he not joined himself openly to their society'. In closing he exhorted all those gathered to keep in good harmony with each other, and consider that it was pride and avarice that had brought the bishops to ruin, and that they should therefore 'shun these rocks as they would eschew shipwreck'.[26]

With that the historic General Assembly of 1638 concluded. From the Royal Palace of Holyroodhouse in Edinburgh, Hamilton, at the King's command, issued a proclamation annulling all its acts. Charles authorised him to make the Marquis of Huntly his Lieutenant in the north of the country, and either the Earls of Traquair or Roxburgh in the south, should it be thought necessary. The King was outraged when he heard of Argyll's actions; especially the revelation that he had been on the Covenanters' side from the start. Charles did not care to be taken for a fool. He denounced Argyll for his deceit, writing that if he had secretly been on the side of the King's enemies then 'he must openly joyne with them or be a knave; what he proved himself to bee by this close and false carriadge, lett the world judge'.[27] Baillie referred to 'the wrath his Majestie since has kythed towards him [Argyll], whom before he did singularlie respect: also betwixt the Commissioner [Hamilton] and Argyle there passed words of high enough disdayne, little from threats and personal challenges.'[28] There was now no way back for the one who had so recently been a candidate for the role of the King's man in Scotland. The new Earl of Argyll had burned his bridges.

The King encouraged Hamilton to continue to string the Covenanters along until an invasion force would be ready in the spring. Having risen in revolution against the Crown, the Covenanters, with both the Earls of Montrose and Argyll now amongst their ranks, must have known that they would soon have to go to war to defend their new liberties.

3

Allies against the King

1639

'Now about this tyme, or a little befoir,' wrote John Spalding of Aberdeen, 'thair cam out of Germany fra the wars, home to Scotland, ane gentleman off bass birth borne in Balveny, who had servit long and fortunately in the Germane warris, and callit to his name Felt Marshall Leslie his Excellence. His name indeid was [Alexander] Leslie, bot by his valour and good lvk attaned to this title his Excellens, inferior to none bot the King of Swaden, wnder whome he servit amongis all his cavallerie. Well, this Felt Marschall Leslie haueing conquest fra nocht, honour and welth in gryte aboundance, resoluit to cum hame to his native countrie of Scotland.'[1]

The 'Germane warris' Spalding referred to was the Thirty Years War, which for two decades had devastated Germany and the Low Countries as Protestants and Catholics fought for supremacy in the Holy Roman Empire. The Swedish King Gustavus Aldolphus came to the aid of the German Lutherans fighting the Emperor Ferdinand II, leading a successful campaign until he fell at the Battle of Lutzen in 1632. His forces had a large mercenary contingent, and many of these hired guns were Scots soldiers (like Walter Scott's comic creation Dugald Dalgetty) looking to earn a living in support of a religious cause they could sympathise with. Chief among them was Alexander Leslie, a small, bent man with a magnificent set of whiskers, but an outstanding general, who had attained the rank of Field Marshall in the Swedish army. He had now come home to aid the Covenanters, and he was made most welcome. The Royalists were well aware of his reputation, and the asset that he would be to their enemies: Baillie reported: 'The King's ships also on our coast a while troubled us. It is thought their maine design was to have catched Generall Leslie by the way, bot he, for fear of them, came over in a small bark.'[2]

As the new year of 1639 dawned the Covenanters were making ready for battle. The Earls of Montrose and Rothes and the other leading lights in the Revolution met in Edinburgh to draft a letter to be sent around the country. This stated that the country was being menaced by armies being raised to convert liberty into slavery, and that all lawful means had to be used to prevent this. A new system was to be put in place to make it easier for orders from the centre to be disseminated throughout the nation, with the appointment of Shire Commissioners who would gather in Edinburgh to meet every day for discussions, and to pass news and orders back to their home territory.

Amongst those present at the Covenanters' meeting, and signing the letter, was the Earl of Argyll, who at this stage had still not actually subscribed to the Covenant. Given his public statements to date it is hardly credible that this delay in subscribing was a deliberate act seeking to preserve the impression that he was still uncommitted, but it was not until April that he eventually signed.

In every Shire, Committees of War were to be established to raise troops and ensure adequate training. Due to the general lack of military experience amongst the population, Scots serving in Holland and Germany with a history of command were requested to return home. Many, like Leslie, were happy to have the opportunity to earn a living a little closer to family than their previous field of service. Leslie had first contemplated signing up to support the King, and there were plenty of Scottish professional soldiers serving in Continental armies who were ambivalent about which side they joined. The majority, however, signed up with the Covenanters, probably due to greater sympathy with their religious stance. A few, the purest mercenaries, would first join one side and later support the other if the financial rewards were better (most notoriously Sir John Hurry, who would command the Covenanter army at the Battle of Auldearn, and who switched sides some three times – it cost him his head in the end).

While preparations for war went on, the Covenanters continued to try to negotiate with Charles. George Winrame of Libberton was sent to London on 7 January with a supplication to the King. Despite waiting in the capital for weeks he was unable even to get a hearing. Charles had other plans. On 26 January he summoned the English nobility to meet him at York on 1 April with an army, to prevent a Scottish invasion of England. His aim was to raise 30,000 men to launch a counter-invasion. 5,000 troops under the Marquis of Hamilton were to be sent by sea to Aberdeen to join up with the forces of the Royalist Marquis of Huntly. The Catholic Earl of Antrim was to land in Argyllshire and directly attack the Campbell lands with 10,000 or 12,000 men from Ulster. And Thomas Wentworth, later Earl of Stafford, was to take a fleet from Ireland to land at Dumbarton to attack west central Scotland, using the Isle of Arran as a base. Secret commissions were issued to Sir Donald Macdonald of Sleat and the Earl of Antrim to be joint lieutenants in the Western Isles and Highlands, and to attack rebels against the King's authority. The rebellion was to be crushed with an iron fist.

In need of a military commander, and having been turned down by Huntly, the Covenanters approached Alexander Leslie, who agreed to take on the position. It was to be an inspired appointment, not least because selecting an outsider meant that proud noblemen were not required to take orders from those whom they might have considered political rivals. Baillie observed that: 'such was the wisdom and authoritie of that old, little, crooked souldier, that all, with ane incredible submission, from the beginning to the end, gave over themselves to be guided by him, as if he had been Great Solyman.'[3]

Leslie immediately set to work neutralising the Royalist forces in Scotland. Edinburgh Castle was surrendered to the Covenanters without a blow being struck. The Royalist garrison of Dumbarton Castle, who rather foolishly had a habit of attending church on a Sunday morning outside the castle walls, were ambushed one Sabbath on their way to worship and taken prisoner. The skeleton crew left behind the castle walls had no alternative but to admit defeat. Dalkeith Castle then fell, and with Stirling Castle already in the hands of the Covenanting Earl of Mar, that meant that every fortress in the country south of the Tay was held by the Covenanters, excepting only Caerlaverock Castle, which lay too close to the English border.

There remained the serious problem of Huntly's forces to be dealt with. Having failed the previous summer to win over Aberdeen to the Covenant, Montrose was keen to prove himself in the field for the cause. It was an opportunity to demonstrate his worth to his colleagues, and ensure that he was not eclipsed by the recently-recruited Argyll. With Leslie, 'whose counsall General Montroiss follouit in this business',[4] he summoned the northern families loyal to the Covenant to meet him at Turriff in Aberdeenshire, and set off with an army of between 3,000 and 4,000, 'weill armit both on horses and futt, ilk horseman having five schot at the leist, quhairof he had ane carrabin in his hand, tuo pistollis be his sydis, and vther tua at his sadill torr. The pikmen in thair rankis [with] pik and suord; the muskiteiris in thair rankis with mvscat, staf, bandileir, suord, ball and matche.' It was a formidable and well-equipped force, and carried before it were the Earl of Montrose's personal colours, emblazoned with the motto: 'FOR RELIGIOUN, THE COVENANT, AND THE COUNTRIE'.[5]

Word of the rendezvous at Turriff reached Huntly, who was determined to put a stop to it. He gathered 2,000 men to march on the town. Montrose was quicker, riding through high mountain passes with an advance party of 200 horsemen and joining up with a local contingent of 800 Covenanters. On reaching their destination Montrose's men dug in, defending the churchyard walls. When Huntly arrived it was obvious that they could only be dispersed with a fight. The King's orders were to avoid open battle with the Covenanters, unless provoked, until such time as the Royal invasion force was ready, so Huntly had no alternative but to withdraw. Montrose then turned back towards Aberdeen to meet Leslie and the rest of the army who had been proceeding on foot. They met no opposition. The city's staunchest Royalists fled before the Covenanters could reach its walls.

Montrose and his army entered Aberdeen on 30 March. Now the Covenanter ministers, having been sent away the previous year without the opportunity to preach, 'enter the pulpits of Aberdeen triumphantly . . . and begine to sing a song to the townsman of a farr other tune then they had learned from ther owne ministers and doctors'.[6] It was not just in the kirks that there were signs of change. It had been the custom of the young Gordons who followed Huntly to wear ribbons of red to show their support for the King, and to distinguish themselves Montrose ordered his men to wear ribbons of blue, a tradition which the Covenanting armies continued with long after Montrose had severed connections with them. It was a characteristically flamboyant gesture from the dashing Cavalier.

Flushed from his success in Aberdeen, Montrose marched for Inverurie 'with resolutione to discusse and fynde out Huntlye'.[7] The two met on 5 April. Montrose was under orders to get Huntly's signature on the Covenant. It was obvious that this would not be forthcoming. After 'a long privat discourse together',[8] Montrose, in defiance of his instructions, instead received from the Marquis a signed undertaking that he would defend the authority of the King and the liberties, religion and laws of the kingdom, and allow his followers to sign the Covenant. It seems that this document was one of Montrose's own invention and represented a compromise between the Covenant, and what Huntly was likely to accept. Montrose took the initiative to secure an agreement with Huntly on the best terms that could be achieved, presumably taking the view that if his principal aim was out of reach, then something was better than nothing. But he acted without authority from above, and it would land him in trouble.

When Montrose returned to Aberdeen he soon realised that the other Covenanters regarded his approach as too lenient, and that they were unwilling to ratify the deal that he had struck. Huntly was summoned to Aberdeen under the rules of safe conduct, which Montrose vouched for. On his arrival a number of demands were put to him including payment of a large sum towards the Covenanters' expenses, and when he refused to agree to these he was told that he must go with his opponents to Edinburgh. If he did not agree to go voluntarily, he would go as a prisoner. Faced with this miserable choice, Huntly reluctantly consented. In due course he was taken to Edinburgh Castle where he was incarcerated along with his son and heir, Lord Gordon. The threat of a potential Royalist uprising in the north was deemed to have been removed, and Montrose's mission on behalf of the Covenanters could therefore be counted as a success.

But Montrose himself does not come out of this episode well. In trying to reach an agreement with Huntly he had overreached his authority. He had overestimated his own influence amongst the Covenanters' leadership, carelessly assuming that they would ratify his unauthorised actions. It would not be the only occasion on which the 'vainly foolish' (as Hamilton had described him) young nobleman would make the same mistake. Montrose then compounded his error by effectively tricking, either deliberately or inadvertently, the Gordon chief into giving himself up as a captive to the Covenanters. It is unclear whether he was actually acting in bad faith, or whether, having personally opposed the breaking of trust with Huntly, he had been over-ruled by his more political colleagues. Huntly himself was in no doubt – he held Montrose personally to blame for what had happened, and forever after 'could never be gained to joyne cordially with him, nor to swallow that indignitye'.[9] This split, entirely a consequence of Montrose's naivety and over-confidence, would have far-reaching consequences for the Royalist cause in Scotland.

While all this was happening Charles had not been idle south of the Border. He had reached as far as York with his army; a large force of 2,000 cavalry and 14,000 infantry, but lacking experienced captains or troops, and sufficient weapons, equipment or provisions. Without Parliament meeting to authorise the levy of taxes to pay for a war (it had not met since 1629), Charles had had to resort to funding the military simply by donations. Inevitably, insufficient sums had been forthcoming. There was little enthusiasm in England for Charles' actions. His invasion force was seen as being primarily designed to support the bishops in Scotland who had been deposed by the Kirk.

On 7 April Charles issued a proclamation to the rebels stating his intention to stand by the position taken by Hamilton on his behalf at the Glasgow Assembly. The first draft of this document threatened 19 leaders of the Covenanters, including the Earl of Argyll, that if they did not submit themselves to the King's mercy within 24 hours a price was to be set on their heads. The King's advisors counselled against this encouragement to assassination. So the final version of the proclamation stated that all rebels who did not lay down their arms within eight days would be declared traitors, and forfeit their estates and property. All tenants of the rebels were ordered to make no further payments to them, with one half of the amount to be paid direct to the King and the other half to be retained by the tenants – a substantial inducement. There were further promises made to those who would take the King's side.

Argyll wrote directly to the King defending the actions of the Covenanters and taking issue with Charles' resort to military action against them. Charles was enraged, and tore the letter to pieces, leaving those present in no doubt that he was resolved to have the writer's head. He may have known about Argyll's latest activities in support of his enemies. While Montrose had been busy bringing Huntly to heel, Argyll had been campaigning on the other side of the country. Aware of the threat from Ireland to the Campbell lands in Argyllshire, he had raised 900 men, some of whom he stationed in Lorne against threat of attack from the Royalist Clan Macdonald, with the remainder sent to Kintyre to protect the coast from invasion. Argyll himself took a force to the Isle of Arran and seized Hamilton's castle at Brodick to prevent the island being used as a landing place for the expected Irish forces. As it happened there seemed no realistic prospect of the Earl of Antrim being capable of gathering the army that the King had hoped for.

Charles' hopes of an Irish invasion were not being fulfilled, and the imprisonment of Huntly and the Covenanters' occupation of Aberdeen had thwarted Hamilton's intention to land men in the North-east to join up with the Gordons. So the King changed his plans and instead ordered Hamilton to take his fleet to the Firth of Forth to attack Edinburgh. On 1 May the Marquis arrived with 19 ships and 5,000 men, but found that the Covenanters had fortified the port of Leith and indeed both sides of the Forth, so that there was nowhere safe to land. Even Hamilton's own mother, the old Dowager Countess who lived at Kinneil House near Bo'ness, turned up with a pistol and stated that she would shoot her own son if he set foot on shore. Unable to reach the mainland, Hamilton took over the two islands of Inchkeith and Inchcolm in the Forth, and awaited further orders.

Back in Aberdeenshire there was a skirmish which became known as 'the Trot of Turriff', when the Gordons and their allies routed the Covenanters' garrison in the town, and then took Aberdeen. With both Huntly and his heir Lord Gordon under lock and key it was left to the second son, Lord Aboyne, to take the initiative. Aboyne travelled to meet Charles at Newcastle to offer his service, whereupon the grateful King sent him back to Scotland to ask Hamilton for support for his efforts in the North-east. Sadly for the Royalist cause, the hapless and unimaginative Hamilton failed to seize the opportunity to extend what could have been a significant second front against his enemies.

The Covenanters, who had assumed that with Huntly impris-oned the threat of a Royalist uprising had been removed, were taken by surprise with what was happening in Aberdeenshire. They had to react swiftly, and it again fell to Montrose to take action. At the head of 4,000 men he arrived in Aberdeen on 25 May, where he found that the Royalist forces had already left to try and join up with sympathetic Highlanders. Deprived of a fight, the Covenanter troops entertained themselves by slaugh-tering the city's dogs, whose owners had decked them with blue ribbons in a calculated insult to the invaders. Montrose pursued the enemy eastwards, moving to attack the Gordon stronghold of the Castle of Gight. Then news reached him that a large force of Royalists was on its way by ship to Aberdeen. This was actu-ally led by Aboyne, but Montrose was lacking in the necessary intelligence and feared that it was Hamilton with the bulk of his army. Not wanting to be cut off from the rest of the Covenanters he took his men south. On 5 June Aboyne arrived at the port of Aberdeen to be greeted by his younger brother, Lord Lewis Gordon, and 1,000 clansmen. Quickly this grew to an army of 4,000, which presented a serious Royalist threat that had to be addressed.

Montrose, who was by now at Stonehaven on the coast, turned and marched his men to meet Aboyne at Aberdeen. The city was protected to the south by the River Dee which was in flood, and control over the narrow, single bridge, with its seven stone arches, became the fulcrum of the battle that developed. The Royalists were determined to prevent Montrose crossing the river and accessing the city. They put up a barricade of earth and stones across the bridge, behind the gate house at the south end, both to hamper the attackers and provide protection to the defenders. The Covenanters' musketeers fired volley after volley across the deep, fast waters, but their opponents were well dug in, and took too few casualties to weaken their position sufficiently to allow an infantry charge to break through. Despite heavy fighting, Montrose's men could make little progress throughout the first day.

Overnight Montrose decided on a change of tactics. He brought up his heavy cannon from Stonehaven so 'they might brashe the gates of the porte and scoure the bridge all along'.[10] He also realised that he needed to do something to reduce the enemy's strength at the bridgehead. At dawn he dispatched a detachment of cavalry upstream in a feint, hoping that the Royalists would be fooled into thinking that their adversaries were attempting to cross the Dee upstream and attack them in the flank. The plan worked, with the Gordon cavalry setting off along the north bank of the river to shadow the enemy, leaving the bridge defences weakened. Montrose's gunners turned fire with cannon shot on the bridge's north end, crushing the spirit of the defenders. The Royalist cavalryman Seton of Pitmedden was an early casualty, the top half of his body blown clear off his horse by a direct hit with a cannon ball. The blue-ribboned Covenanter infantry, wielding their formidable long pikes, made a rush across the bridge, scattering the demoralised Royalists. With the way open, the day turned into a rout, Montrose's cavalry having the space to use carbine, pistol and sword on the fleeing defenders. It was the young soldier's first battle as a general, in which he had demonstrated both initiative and tactical awareness, and he had scored a resounding victory. The Earl Marischal, who was with Montrose at the head of the Covenanting army, was all for taking revenge on the city of Aberdeen for its support of the Gordons, but Montrose argued for restraint. Whatever the provocation, punishing innocent civilians was not the action of a Christian warrior.

While Montrose had been dealing with the King's forces in the North of Scotland and enhancing his reputation as a military leader, the bulk of the Covenanting army had been heading south. The King had reached Newcastle on 14 May, and from there issued another proclamation stating it was his purpose 'to give his good people of Scotland all just satisfaction in Parliament as soon as the present disorders and tumultuous proceedings of some there were quieted and would leave his Majesty a fair way of coming like a gracious King to declare his good meaning to them'.[11] The document added that if all civil and temporal obedience were shown to him he would not himself invade Scotland with his army, but that he would not allow the Scots to invade England. Should anyone without his authority raise soldiers and bring them within ten miles of the Border he would consider this to be an invasion, and would instruct his army to proceed against them as rebels and destroy them. Although still strident in tone this was a lot more conciliatory than the previous proclamation of a month before.

The Covenanters replied that their preparations were merely for self defence, that they were still loyal to the King, and that they would be happy to obey his order not to come in within ten miles of the Border if he were to withdraw both his own army and his fleet from the Scottish coast. Charles made no effort to respond. So the great Covenanter army of 20,000 infantry and 500 cavalry under the command of Alexander Leslie, that grizzled veteran of wars in Europe, marched from Leith to Dunglass on the coast of Haddingtonshire (East Lothian) heading for England. Although he commanded a force smaller than the King's army, Leslie's men were better led, better equipped, better disciplined and much better motivated.

Charles sent troops on forays across the Border, one body of which read out his latest proclamation at Duns. Leslie continued to move his army closer to the Border, eventually occupying a commanding position at Duns Law. According to contemporary reports the Scots army was well-provisioned and well-equipped with tents, and every company flew new colours with the Scottish arms and the motto 'For Christ's Crown and Covenant' in golden letters. In the morning and evening could be heard the sound of men reading the Bible, others praying, others singing psalms. But lest anyone think that this was simply the Kirk going to war, there were also reports of the inevitable cursing, swearing and brawling which occur wherever large numbers of soldiers are quartered in close proximity.

In contrast to the plentiful provisions and high morale found amongst the Scots, Charles' army was in a poor state. His men had no tents to protect them from the weather, food was in short supply, and the camp was riven with disease and vermin (with predictable soldiers' humour, the Royalist troops christened the horrible beasties 'covenanters'). Many deserted. The King knew he had not the strength to defeat Leslie, and Leslie had no particular wish to take the battle to the King. It was in the interest of both parties to go back to the negotiating table, but neither side could be seen to be losing face.

Argyll had not originally been with Leslie's army, having stayed at Stirling with his own forces to protect against attacks from the north and on the coasts. Once it became apparent that Charles was likely to treat, his presence on the Border was deemed essential. He was already too important a player amongst the Covenanters to be absent when there were important decisions to be taken. 'Argyll was sent for to the treatie of peace; for without him none would mint [mind] to treat',[12] wrote Baillie. (It did not seem to occur to anyone that Montrose should also be present, presumably because, unlike Argyll, his strength was viewed as being in the field rather than the stateroom.) Argyll duly arrived with a retinue of Gaelic-speaking clansmen, whose dress and weaponry were the talk of the camp. Many Lowland Scots were not accustomed to the sight of Highlanders in blue woollen waistcoats and blue bonnets, a great mantle of plaid wrapped around them, some carrying swords and targes, some muskets, and many with bows and arrows. To English visitors these 1,000 warriors with their outlandish attire, speaking an alien tongue, must have seemed like they had come from another planet: 'It was thought the countrey of England was more afraid for the barbariete of his Highlanders than of any other terror: these of the English that came to visit our camp, did gaze with much admiration upon these souple fellows, with their playds, targes, and dorlachs'.[13]

On 6 June Robert Leslie, a Scottish page of the King, visited the Covenanters' camp and suggested that they should send a supplication to the King seeking a settlement. It is very likely that this suggestion originated from Charles himself, but he wanted it to appear that the Covenanters were making the first move. The Scots had no real wish for war and were enthusiastic at the prospect of a negotiated resolution. The following day the Earl of Dunfermline went to the King asking him to appoint some Englishmen 'well affected to the true religion and to the common peace'[14] to meet with the Scots. Charles, keen to do a deal but recognising that he had to be seen acting from a position of strength, responded that he would comply with the request but only if the Covenanters first published his April proclamation, the one which had denounced the Covenanting leaders as traitors. With some ingenuity the Covenanters satisfied this requirement by reading over the King's proclamation in a tent at Duns in the presence of Argyll and other nobles who were named in it. Sir Edmund Verney, the King's representative, then advised Charles that his condition had been fulfilled, although whether all the circumstances were disclosed is unclear. In any event this was enough for progress to be made, and discussions began on 11 June about the terms of peace.

After some protracted negotiations, which the Covenanters' representatives were surprised to find were conducted on the other side by the King personally, it was agreed that henceforth all Church matters would be decided by the General Assembly of the Kirk, and all civil matters by Parliament and the courts. A free General Assembly and a free Parliament would meet in Edinburgh the following month. Both armies would be disbanded, all prisoners set free, and the royal castles which had been captured by the Covenanters would be returned to the King or his representatives. Such were the terms of 'the Pacification of Berwick' (or, alternatively, of Birks), settled on 18 June 1639. Following the agreement being concluded, a number of leading Covenanters, Argyll amongst them, crossed over to the Royalist camp to kiss the King's hand. According to Baillie they 'were bot coldie welcomed'.[15] Charles had not forgiven his former favourite.

Montrose was still in Aberdeen when the news reached him of the peace treaty. He did as instructed in releasing the Royalist prisoners in his care and dismissed his troops, but not without first imposing another fine on the long-suffering citizens of

Aberdeen. Then he and the Earl Marischal headed south to Duns to join their colleagues in the celebration of peace, and the end, after very little bloodshed, of what would later become known as the First Bishops' War.

4

An Uneasy Peace

1639–40

The grand coach creaking and bouncing its slow way over the refuse-strewn stones of the High Street was always going to attract attention. Edinburgh's main thoroughfare was crowded with folk buying and selling, going about their business, and always looking for a diversion. The city mob, excitable at the best of times, were in a state of agitation at King Charles' actions towards his Scottish subjects, and every passing dignitary was closely scrutinised to see where his allegiances lay: with the King, or with the people. At the sight of this liveried carriage approaching, the fishwives and water-caddies pressed forwards, up against the windows, thrusting their heads inside to see who this was: friend or foe. The cry went up that this was a King's man, indeed one of the most prominent – John Stewart, 1st Earl of Traquair. Shrinking back in his seat, the Earl shouted at his coachmen to keep going, while the women outside clambered over one another to reach into the carriage and hit him with their punches. Bruised and shaken, Traquair made it out of the city, thankful he had not suffered a worse fate. He would later tell his friends that the attack was welcome, as it would enhance his reputation with Charles as a loyal subject.

It had soon become apparent that the Pacification of Berwick was little more than a face-saving exercise, designed to avoid conflict at all costs by papering over the very wide cracks between the Royalist and Covenanter positions. The General Assembly of the Kirk was scheduled to meet on 6 August 1639, and on 1 July

Royal proclamation of the meeting was made in Edinburgh. At that point it emerged that the bishops, whom the Covenanters had assumed they had driven from office, were to attend. The King believed he was legally entitled to invite the bishops as the action of the Glasgow Assembly in removing them from office still had not been confirmed by him or by Parliament. The Covenanters felt he was acting in bad faith, having secured the disbandment of their army on the basis of false expectations.

Traquair was not alone amongst the King's supporters in facing the frustration of the Edinburgh mob. On both sides there was a sense that the terms agreed in the Pacification were not being adhered to by the other party. The Covenanters did not feel that they could disband their army nor dissolve the Tables as had been agreed. The King summoned fourteen of the leading Covenanters to Berwick to meet him, including Argyll, with 'letters full of alluring and kind expressions', but most of them 'smelling the rat from afar off', were secretly advised by their friends to look to themselves, and to come no nearer to Berwick at this time, as they wolde euitt and eschew an whfallable and most certain destruction.'[1] In the end six attended, including Rothes and Montrose. The conference in Berwick was a disaster, with Charles taking offence at Rothes' attitude towards him. The King gave up in exasperation, abandoned what had been his intention to visit Edinburgh, and returned to London where the public hangman was ordered to burn a paper outlining the Covenanters' claims.

But there was one consolation for Charles. At Berwick he had his first proper meeting with Montrose since they had seen each other in London briefly many years previously. The contrast with the previous encounter could not have been more stark. Charles was at his most gracious and charming, and the gallant young nobleman came under his spell. Montrose pledged his loyalty to his monarch, and from that day established a direct line of communication. Even before arriving in Berwick he had been under suspicion for having Royalist sympathies (perhaps caused by his lenient treatment of Huntly), and some hard-line Covenanters had threatened to prevent him from making the journey, by force if necessary. After his meeting with Charles, there was found stuck on his chamber door a paper with the legend '*invictus armis, verbis vincitur*' (invincible in war, conquered by words), a reference to his encounter with the King. The bold Covenanter had been perhaps too obviously enchanted by his Sovereign.

Charles required to appoint a Royal Commissioner to the General Assembly in Edinburgh, and with Hamilton reluctant to continue in the role, Traquair (fresh from his beating) was appointed in his place. The King gave him strict instructions as to what was to be permissible. Charles also told the bishops that they were not to attend. With David Dickson appointed as Moderator to replace Alexander Henderson, proceedings at the General Assembly began on 12 August. Both Argyll and Montrose were appointed as Assessors amongst the other leading Covenanting nobles.

The Assembly proceeded, at breakneck speed, to endorse all that had been passed at the previous year's Assembly in Glasgow. Thus episcopacy was abolished for a second time, to great rejoicing from some of those present. Traquair, as the King's Commissioner, assented to the Act abolishing episcopacy, but failed in his attempt to add a clause declaring that episcopacy was not in itself unlawful and that there was no implied censure for England and Ireland, as Charles had specifically instructed him to do. The Assembly then censured a publication supporting the Royalist cause by Dr Balcanquhal, the Dean of Durham, known as the 'Large Declaration', which also happened to contain a derogatory reference to Argyll for his supposed double-dealing in the run-up to the Glasgow Assembly.

Argyll himself made regular contributions to the Assembly, generally taking a conciliatory tone towards the King and Traquair. Montrose, meanwhile, was part of a committee along with Henderson putting forward a request to the Privy Council that the Covenant should be signed by every Scot regardless of rank or quality. In due course this was agreed by the Council on 30 August. Addressing the Assembly, Traquair promised that the Parliament which was due to meet shortly thereafter would take as its first business a ratification of all of the Assembly's acts. This was greeted with delight by the Commissioners, with clapping and shouts of 'God Save the King'. It seemed that the Covenanters were having it all their own way.

If Montrose was entirely in tune with mainstream opinion amongst the Covenanters at this point, that was a situation which was not to last long. The day after the Assembly dissolved, 31 August, Parliament met. Immediately there was a problem. Having been deposed from office the bishops were no longer eligible to take their seats. Historically Parliament had contained representation from the 'Three Estates' – firstly, nobles and barons; secondly, the clergy (until now represented by the bishops); and thirdly, the burgesses, representing the burghs. The exclusion of the bishops meant that there was a gap to fill. Moreover, their absence meant that the King no longer had a majority amongst the Lords of the Articles who controlled the business of Parliament. So Charles proposed that instead of the bishops there should be fourteen ministers chosen by him, failing which, fourteen laymen. But neither the Kirk nor the nobles were happy with this exercise of royal power. Traquair proposed a temporary compromise whereby he would choose eight nobles, who in turn would choose eight lesser barons and eight burgesses to fill the vacancies. This allowed proceedings to continue, but left open the more fundamental question of how the membership of Parliament would be constituted in the future.

Here a divide amongst the Covenanters started to open up. Montrose championed the view that it should be up to the King to appoint fourteen laymen to take the bishops' places, thus retaining the King's power of patronage and effective control over the Lords of the Articles. Perhaps this was a display of the first fruits of his recent reconciliation with Charles. But a second group, led by Argyll, proposed a much more radical solution. The barons, or lesser nobles, would be classed for the first time as an Estate in their own right, to fill the vacancy left by the clergy. Each Estate – nobles, barons and burgesses – would then elect eight of their own lords to the Articles. This latter proposal was indeed revolutionary, shifting power from King to Parliament. It was hardly democracy in the modern sense, but it was empowering both the nobility and, crucially, the middle classes, at the expense of the Crown. And for the first time the lesser barons and burgesses could potentially outvote the greater nobles. From then on power would not necessarily lie with whoever had the greatest lands or armies, but with whoever was best able to rally the people to his standard.

Cynics might decry this as a crude attempt at a power grab by Argyll, who was conscious of his own support amongst the middle classes as a true believer in the Covenanting cause. But whether he was acting from self-interest or not, the proposal amounted to a major step in the democratising of the Scottish Parliament and the creation of a constitutional monarchy.

Clearly perceiving the threat, Charles moved against Argyll: 'the King beganne to smell him out as his most dangerouse and implacable enemye.'[2] Charles wrote to the Provost and Baillies of Edinburgh with a proclamation announcing that he had decided to deprive Argyll of his post as Justiciary of Argyll, ordering that none should obey him, appear at his court or pay taxes or duties to him until Argyll had appeared before the King and Parliament to answer charges against him. The Edinburgh Magistrates responded that 'in sic troublous tymes (the countrie being in uproar, effrayit with the incoming of sea and land armyis, and also with the daylie thretning of the castell of Edinburgh) they durst scarslie hassard to mak sic proclamationis against the persone of sic ane pryme noble man',[3] and that in any event the action was illegal without the approval of the Privy Council and Parliament. As a result the proclamation was never published.

The Parliament of 1639 in the end agreed by a single vote to support Argyll's motion as to its future constitution. Control of the Mint and the appointment of Great Officers of State were transferred to Parliament from the Crown. It was an extraordinary moment in Scottish history. For the first time real power was no longer in the hands of the monarch and the great landed families, but was held by the middle classes. Just as the revolution in the Church had seen their triumph, so in civil government it was the lesser barons and burgesses who now had the whip hand. And they had as leader the Earl of Argyll, who had astutely positioned himself as their champion and could now reasonably expect their grateful support in return. Montrose, who had defended the position of the King and the great noble families, was left floundering. Events had taken a turn that he had never anticipated, and decisions made that he could never support. His position all along had been that he wanted the King's right to interfere in religious matters to be curbed, but not his temporal power. In his view the Covenanters had over-reached themselves in dismantling Royal authority, and this would lead, he feared, to disorder and chaos, and simply give ambitious men like Argyll more opportunity to expand their influence. From this point, Montrose's interests would increasingly diverge from those of the more radical Covenanters, now in the majority.

Parliament was supposed to ratify the Acts of the General Assembly, but an insurmountable difficulty arose as the King could not give consent to the Act passed on the abolition of episcopacy, which denounced it as unlawful even in England and Ireland. With no room for manoeuvre, the King ordered Traquair to prorogue Parliament until June the next year. Matters had again reached an impasse, and it seemed that a return to the battlefield was now inevitable. The Pacification had been a dismal failure.

The Scots were divided over where to go next. Argyll's victory in Parliament and the radical reform which had ensued left the more moderate nobles in a state of concern as to where all this was heading. Charles, writing regularly from London, was energetic in trying to win over to his cause those who he thought least sympathetic to the new regime. Unsurprisingly, given that he had been on the losing side, Montrose was amongst those thought likely to be tempted to join the Royalists. His cousin, William Graham, Earl of Airth, wrote to Charles: 'Montrose hath carried himself both faithfully, and is more willing to contribute to his uttermost in anything for your Majesty's service, than any of these lords covenanters',[4] while Baillie observed that Montrose was 'not unlyke to be ensnared with the false promises of advancement'.[5]

The King was furious at the conduct of his Scottish subjects. He told Hamilton, in terms which with hindsight appear almost prophetic: 'I will rather die than yield to their impertinent and damnable demands'. But Charles needed money to fund his army, and called what became known as the Short Parliament in London to raise the necessary sums. Unfortunately for him, the Parliamentarians present were more interested in bringing up concerns about the actions of his government in England than they were with dealing with rebellious Scots. The meeting of the Short Parliament was dissolved after three weeks.

In the meantime the Covenanters had not been idle. Funds were raised from across the country to establish and equip an army ready to face Charles again. The reliable Alexander Leslie was once more appointed as Commander-in-Chief. When the Scottish Parliament eventually met on 2 June 1640, it was in defiance of an order from Charles to postpone the meeting for a month, and there was immediately a dispute as to whether Parliament had the power to meet without the King's permission or his Commissioner's presence. In the architect James Murray of Kilbaberton's magnificent new Parliament Hall in Edinburgh, under its oak hammerbeam roof, Montrose spoke up for his Royal master. The events of the last year had made him determined to defend openly what he believed to be right. Montrose argued that so long as there was a King, Parliament could not sit without him. In this he was opposed by Argyll, Rothes, Johnston of Warriston and others, and the majority view was for continuation of proceedings. In response to Montrose's protest, Argyll stated rather cryptically that 'to do the less was more lawful than to do the greater',[6] by which he seems to have meant that it was better to meet in defiance of the King's orders, than it would be to take the drastic step of deposing the King.

The possible removal of Charles from the throne was no doubt a matter of private discussions amongst the Covenanters. It was certainly in tune with the Scottish constitutional tradition, dating back at least as far as the Declaration of Arbroath, that a despotic king who did not enjoy the support of the people could be removed and replaced with another; a principle which flew in the face of the Stewarts' belief in the Divine Right. There were suggestions at the time that one or more dictators should be appointed (inevitably, Argyll's name was mooted) to oversee the affairs of the kingdom until proper government could be restored, but nothing ever came of these. What is clear is that Argyll's position as a leading light in national affairs was now unchallenged. In contrast Montrose was increasingly isolated and out of step with the majority opinion in the country, which was prepared for ever more radical moves to limit Royal power.

The Parliament now passed an Act stating that the Covenant was obligatory upon all citizens, that the Estates were now deemed to consist of nobles, barons and burgesses (instead of bishops, barons and burgesses as previously), and that executive power was devolved to a Committee of Estates to oversee the day to day running of government in a kingdom in rebellion against its King. While Argyll did not serve personally on the Committee, he made sure that his allies were well represented: 'All saw he was a *major potestas*, and, although not formally a member, yet all knew that it was his influence that gave being, life and motion to these new-modelled governors; and not a few thought that this *juncto* was his invention', observed Gordon of Rothiemay.[7]

The new Committee of Estates had much to do. Leslie was ordered to assemble the army, and within a month 24,000 infantry and 2,500 cavalry were once more encamped just outside Duns. But again there was a threat from the north which the Covenanters had to counter. Argyll was commissioned (Montrose being one of the signatories to the Commission) to raise an army of 4,000 Highlanders to take fire and sword against Royalist clans in Atholl and Angus. The Chief of Clan Campbell would have needed little encouragement to wage war on his hereditary enemies. The Campbells had a long history of expanding their power and influence in the Highlands at the expense of other clans, and to have a Parliamentary authority for extending this was an opportunity not to be sniffed at.

Argyll's first victim was the Earl of Atholl, whose forces were hugely outnumbered by the Campbells. Possibly tricked by Argyll, he and his retinue were captured at the east end of Loch Tay and sent to Edinburgh as prisoners. After making promises not to cause further trouble, and on giving security, they were subsequently released. Among Atholl's associates on this occasion was John Stewart, Younger of Ladywell, the Commissary of

Dunkeld, who would later testify that Argyll had made treason-ous remarks about the King. It was the view of Argyll's enemies that his opposition to the King was motivated by a desire to remove Charles from the throne altogether, and have the Crown for himself, and they claimed that his clansmen sang that they were 'King Campbell's men, not King Stewart's'. A Gaelic song of the time contained the lines: 'I give Argyle the praise, becaus all men sies it is treuth; for he will tak geir from the lawland men; and he will tak the Croun per force; and he will cry King at Whitsonday.'[8]

Argyll was camped with his men at the Fords of Lyon, among the hills and woods of north Perthshire. At the heart of the Campbell territory of Breadalbane, and surrounded by his loyal warriors, he felt perfectly secure. Here, in his tent, he entered a discussion with Atholl and the other prisoners about the nature of kingship, in which, Stewart of Ladywell would claim, Argyll had hinted at replacing the King. He supposedly claimed that the Covenanters 'had consulted both lawyers and divines anent the deposing of the King, and gotten resolution that it might be done in three cases: 1. Desertion, 2. Invasion [by a foreign power], 3. Vendition [destruction of laws and liberties]; and that once they thought to have done it at the last meeting of Parlia-ment, and would do it at the next sitting thereof.'[9] Argyll went on, it was claimed, to state that he was eighth in line from King Robert the Bruce. If true, this was high treason, and carried with it the death penalty. But none of this came to light at the time.

Having dealt with Atholl, Argyll's next target was Angus, where many of the lands were held by the Earl of Airlie as head of the Ogilvie family, whose loyalties had always been to the Crown. Much of the county of Angus was Lowland Scotland, which had enjoyed many years of undisturbed peace, and the sight of Campbell clansmen on the warpath must have struck terror into the local residents. The Earl of Airlie himself was south of the Border, leaving his houses and territories in the care of his son and heir Lord Ogilvie. On arrival in the county Argyll discovered that Montrose, acting on his own initiative, had some days previously secured Airlie Castle and put his own men under a Colonel Sibbald to garrison it. Montrose even wrote to Argyll stating there was no need for him to be in Angus.

Montrose had been given no authority from Parliament or the Committee of Estates to take this action. He had known (having signed the commission) that it was Argyll who had the right to act in Angus, and not him. Montrose's motives for acting in this way are still unclear. He certainly had personal loyalties to the Ogilvies whom he wished to protect – Lord Ogilvie was a close friend. He undoubtedly had growing, but at this stage still mostly secret, Royalist sympathies. Or he may simply have wanted to deny Argyll the opportunity both to extend his influence, and gain from plundering wealthy lands. It was probably some combination of all three. What is clear is that, in line with his earlier dealings with the Marquis of Huntly, the young Montrose was more than happy to ignore higher authority when it suited him (Baillie observed that his 'extraordinary and evil pride made him hard to be guided').[10]

Argyll was furious when he discovered Montrose's action to try and thwart him, and that in support of an out-and-out Royalist. He had Parliamentary authority to act against a rival clan, and he was not about to let Montrose's sensibilities stand in his way. Argyll displaced Montrose's garrison and occupied Airlie Castle, his Campbell clansmen finding to their great annoyance that Lord Ogilvie had, with Montrose's permission, removed most of the valuables. Instead the Highlanders set about plundering the neighbouring lands to the extent that 'there was not left behind even a cock to welcome in the new morning'.[11] The Castle itself was burned and knocked to the ground. Such was Argyll's anger that it was reported that he took up a hammer himself against the walls 'till he did sweate for heate at his worke'.[12] The events are remembered in the famous ballad 'The Bonnie Hoose o' Airlie' (although the notion that Argyll had sexual designs on Lady Ogilvie, who in any event was elsewhere, is simply Royalist propaganda):

> Lady Ogilvy looks oer her bower-window
> And oh, but she looks weary!
> And there she spy'd the great Argyll
> Come to plunder the boonie hoose of Airlie.
> 'Come down, come down, my Lady Ogilvy,
> Come down, and kiss me fairly,'
> 'O I winna kiss the fause Argyll,
> If he should na leave a standing stane in Airlie.'

Argyll's men proceeded up Glen Isla to another of Airlie's properties, Forter Castle, today wonderfully restored, and at that time occupied by the pregnant Lady Ogilvie. Argyll had written to his lieutenant Dugald Campbell of Inveraray with instructions to send all livestock captured back to Argyllshire, continuing: 'Ye shall not faill to stay and demolishe my Lord Ogilbie's hous of Forthar. Sie how ye can cast off the irone yeattes and windows; and tak doon the rooff: and iff ye find it will be longsome, ye shall fyre it weill, that so it may be destroyed.' He added: 'Bot you neid not to latt know that ye have directions from me to fyer it: onlie ye may say that ye have warrand to demoleishe it, and that to mak the work short ye will fyr it.'[13] It was alleged that he treated the expecting Lady Ogilvie with great brutality, turning her out in to the wild despite her condition, but there is no convincing evidence of this. Certainly Archibald Campbell was taking care to protect his reputation being sullied by the actions of his men, while discreetly encouraging them. Like politicians of all eras, he had his image to consider.

His work in Angus being completed, Argyll marched his men westwards to Lochaber to deal with the MacGregors and MacDonalds. He found support amongst members of Clan Cameron who had as their hereditary overlord the Marquis of Huntly, and were happy to side with his chief rival as liberator. When finished in Lochaber, Argyll made his way back east with a smaller force of about 1,200 men to travel along Deeside in what was territory sympathetic to the King.

Having been so successful in carrying out the orders of the Committee of Estates, Argyll was fêted by his countrymen upon his joining the rest of the Covenanters' army at Duns. And he had a score to settle with Montrose, who had by now marched south with between 1,600 and 2,500 men from Stirling and Strathearn. At the camp in Duns Montrose encountered Lord Lindsay of the Byres, a loyal Covenanter, to whom he expressed concern about the current state of affairs, 'and that some were crying up the Earl of Argyle too much'.[14] The rivals eventually came face to face among the tents and fluttering pennants of the encamped Covenant army. In front of the Covenanting leadership, Argyll took Montrose to task for his dealings with Lord Ogilvie, and for supposedly dragging his feet in bringing his men to join Leslie's army. Montrose was defended by Leslie and other members of the Estates, who were anxious to avoid a division in the ranks at this crucial time. But the relationship between the two men deteriorated further when the proposal to create a dictatorship resurfaced, with Argyll to be given command of all Scotland north of the Forth. Inevitably Montrose objected to this huge expansion of his rival's power. To make matters worse, Lindsay then told Montrose of a plan to have a *single* dictator for the whole country. Montrose later said that Argyll's name was mentioned, and although Lindsay himself denied this, there could not reasonably have been another candidate for the role in his mind. It would have been Montrose's worst nightmare.

Whatever the merits of the proposal, in the end there were no dictators appointed. The focus was elsewhere. The Committee of Estates decided unanimously on 3 August that it was time to invade England. A large army required substantial upkeep, not to mention payment, and there was no point in having Leslie's men sitting twiddling their thumbs on the Border waiting for Charles to act. There was a risk in a pre-emptive strike, that the English would rise up against a Scottish invasion and bolster Charles' forces. But that had to be countered by the prospect of the King's many enemies within England supporting the Scots if they invaded, and indeed there were many sympathisers amongst the English nobility who were encouraging them to action.

All this was too much for Montrose. He called together those he knew to be of like mind at the Earl of Wigton's house at Cumbernauld, and they signed a covenant of their own, 'The Cumbernauld Bond', pledging continuing support for the National Covenant, but stating that the country and cause were now suffering because of 'the particular and indirect practising of a few' (presumably meaning Argyll) and that they would bind themselves together to do all tending 'to the safety both of religion, laws and liberties',[15] and to protect each other's interests against all others. Those who signed included the Earl Marischal, the Earls of Wigton, Kinghorn, Home, Atholl, Marr, Perth, Galloway and Seaforth, along of course with Montrose himself, and various others including Lord Almond, who was Leslie's second-in-command of the Covenanting army. Quite what the full purpose of the Bond was it is impossible to know, but it signalled the creation of a caucus with an identifiable leader, determined to pursue a particular political path different from the one being chosen by Argyll and the majority group within the Covenanters.

Montrose had come to the point where he realised that loyalty to his Sovereign was more important to him than adherence to the Covenant, and as the two now seemed to be in competition he could not ride both horses for much longer. For the time being, however, he and the other signatories to the Bond deemed it prudent to keep the matter secret. The powerful Earl of Argyll already had an eye on his younger rival, and for Montrose to provoke him and his allies further at this stage would have been unwise indeed.

5

King Campbell

1640–41

On 20 August 1640 James Graham, 5th Earl of Montrose, arrived on the banks of the River Tweed at Coldstream at the head of a Scots army invading England, in a cause in which he no longer entirely believed. The privilege of being in the vanguard of the army was one for which the senior nobles drew lots, and on this occasion the lot fell to Montrose. He had serious doubts about the direction being taken by the Covenanters' leadership, but he hid it well. Gordon of Ruthven comments that his 'cheerfulnesse was but seeminglye', as he had 'fallen in dislycke with the Covenanters acting and was now waiting for the first opportunity to crosse them'.

The blue-bonneted soldiers drew up on the river's north bank, looking anxiously at the fast-flowing dark waters separating them from their destination. Arriving at the Tweed in flood, they were reluctant to move. With their weapons, armour and gear burdening them down, a river crossing at the best of times was a tricky business, but even more fraught with danger in deep, fast waters. It was a moment for a dramatic gesture, and Montrose was just the man to provide it. Jumping from his horse, he waded in to the river, making it across to the far bank, and then returning. Thus reassured by their bold captain, the men made their way slowly across, the cavalry going in upstream to provide those on foot with some protection from the current. One poor fellow was swept away and drowned, but all the rest arrived safely in Northumberland. Montrose wrote: 'I was, of all myself the first that putt my futt in the watter, and led over ane regiment in the view of all the armie.'[1]

Montrose may have been first across the Border, but the General of the Army was Alexander Leslie, and it was an impressive force that he commanded. There were 22,000 infantry armed primarily with pikes – up to 15 feet long – which individually were of little effect, but presented in a mass were highly dangerous used offensively, and extremely useful defensively even against cavalry. At close quarters these weapons were useless, and many pikemen therefore also carried a short sword. Amongst the infantry were musketeers with their bandoliers of ammunition. The Highlanders, including Argyll's Campbells, carried broadswords, Lochaber axes and targes, and even bows and arrows ('the nakedest fellows that ever I saw', one observer described them).[2] There were 3,000 cavalry with carbines, swords and pistols. Before the regiments went a banner bearing the words 'Covenant for Religion, Crowne and Country'. Behind came the baggage train, with tents, supplies, cooking equipment, spare weapons, artillery, and great herds of cattle and sheep to feed the army. There were armourers, smiths, farriers, cooks and surgeons. There were ministers to meet the spiritual needs of the army, and whores to satisfy more earthly requirements. And with them all, many of the wives, sweethearts, and even children, of the men on the march. Not since King James IV's expedition of 1513 which had ended so tragically on the field of Flodden had such a great Scottish army crossed the Tweed.

King Charles was in a hopeless position. His attempt to raise an army to take on the Covenanters had come to nothing. He had appealed to the City of London, to Spain, to France, and even to the Pope, all to no avail. There was no appetite in England for going to war with the Scots, not least because there were many south of the Border who had sympathy with the Scottish cause and little affection for episcopacy. Even amongst the

King's army, Roman Catholic officers who had been appointed were rejected by the men, and in at least one case an officer was killed. Against a motivated, well-equipped and well-led Scottish force, the Royalists had no chance.

With Charles at York it was left to Lord Conway to defend the North of England. He made a stand on the River Tyne at Newburn, just outside Newcastle, on 27 August. Leslie turned his artillery on the English, and after a day they abandoned the field. Conway fled south, leaving Newcastle at the mercy of the Scots. The city surrendered, and with the expenditure of very little effort the Scots had secured a substantial victory, gained one of the great cities of England, and now controlled the vital coal supply to London and the South. It was a devastating blow for Charles.

The King had no choice but to recall Parliament, and what became known as the Long Parliament was therefore constituted on 3 November. The Scots were invited to send commissioners to London to negotiate a settlement. Far from being conciliatory in his approach, Charles opened proceedings at the Long Parliament by denouncing the Scots as rebels who should be chased out of England. This call met with little sympathy from the Parliamentarians present, chief amongst them the Member for Calne in Wiltshire, John Pym, long a thorn in the King's side. Many considered that the Scots had done them a huge favour in weakening Charles' position and giving them the opportunity to strip him of some of his powers.

The Scots commissioners received a warm welcome from the Puritans (fellow Calvinists) in England, and the ministers in the Scottish delegation were given the use of a church in which they preached to large congregations. There were many who were sympathetic to the Scots' position that episcopacy should be rooted out in all three Kingdoms. Parliament was petitioned to this effect, and Alexander Henderson, amongst others, believed that the establishment of Presbyterianism in England was essential if it was to be safeguarded in Scotland. Moreover, the Covenanters believed that there would only be a lasting peace between the two Kingdoms if there was uniformity of church government. Throughout the seventeenth century in all parts of Europe religious divisions were a major cause of war, so their removal was necessary if future conflict was to be avoided. The visitors' ambitions enraged Charles; Baillie reported: 'The King was so inflamed as he was never before in his tyme for any other business; for the keeping up of Episcopacie in England, which we strove to have down, is the verie apple of his eye.'[3] The Scots' demands were not limited to spiritual matters; they also wanted closer political union with England, with a free trade area.

Argyll, as the leading player amongst the Covenanters, was actively involved in the negotiations taking place, shuttling between the Scots' base in Newcastle and London, and keeping a close eye on the commissioners' moves. He was also granted a commission to raise 10,000 men to invade Ireland, although it is not clear how seriously this was intended, and in the event no invasion took place. It may simply have been proposed to dissuade Royalists in Ireland from planning their own invasion in the other direction.

In the meantime Montrose had written to Charles from Newcastle, and purely by accident this communication was intercepted by the Covenanters. The letter simply protested his loyalty to the King, but led to Montrose being accused of 'having intelligence with the enemy'. For Covenanters who had started to doubt his loyalties, it confirmed their suspicions. 'Montrose, whose pryde was long agoe intolerable, and meaning verie doubtful,' wrote Baillie, 'was found to have intercourse of letters with the King, for which he was accused publicklie by the Generall [Leslie], in the face of the committee.'[4] Montrose replied, rather cleverly, that given the Articles of War stated the

Scots' loyalty to the King he could hardly be classed as treacherous. While this got him off the hook – according to Spalding, 'this mater, thogh suspitious, wes wyslie supprest' – lingering suspicions remained.

Things were to get worse for Montrose when the Bond of Cumbernauld came to public knowledge. One of its signatories, Lord Boyd, was dying young from fever, and on his deathbed hinted that such a document existed. So concerned was he as to this news that Argyll immediately set himself to enquire further. If a rival faction had been established he needed to know who was in it, and for what purpose. Argyll interrogated Lord Almond, second-in-command to Leslie, and was able to discover from him the full details of the Bond.

The Committee of Estates immediately called together all the subscribers to ask them to explain their actions. Some ministers present were so concerned that they called for their execution, but Argyll and many others were aware that the subscribers represented too powerful a force to take serious action against, so instead settled for a promise that they would do nothing against the public good, and that the Bond would be surrendered and burned.

Although escaping any more severe punishment, Montrose and his allies were exposed and humiliated. Charles had to write to Argyll, distancing himself from Montrose's actions, and pledging his good intentions: 'I meane, so to establishe Peace in State, and Religion in the Churche, that there may be a happie harmonie amongst my Subjects there.'[5] But the fissures within the Covenanting movement were widening, personified by the growing divide between Montrose and Argyll.

Increasingly sidelined and jealous of Argyll's influence, Montrose and his colleagues decided to act independently of the Covenanting leadership. Their plan was to invite Charles to Scotland to make concessions to the Covenanters' more reasonable demands. In a letter to the King, Montrose urged him to agree to freedom of religion, warned him against absolute authority and called for 'temperate government'. Montrose also advised Charles that he had evidence – based on the testimony of John Stewart of Ladywell as to what was supposedly said at the Fords of Lyon – which would convict Argyll of treason for seeking to overthrow the King and take his place.

In his enthusiasm Montrose allowed too much careless talk. Reverend John Graham of Auchterarder, Montrose's local parish, was heard discussing openly Argyll's alleged treason. As soon as Argyll was told, he had to act on this serious threat to both his position and person, and he had Reverend Graham brought before the Committee of Estates. It assembled on Thursday 27 May 1641 in Edinburgh to hear the matter. Montrose had not expected the explosive information he had collected about his rival to be publicly revealed so soon, but, regardless of the timing, this was his longed-for opportunity to do serious damage to Argyll, or perhaps even to destroy him.

Members of the Committee sat in rows facing one another, the unfortunate minister nervous and sweating before them; Argyll outwardly all peace and reason but inwardly furious at this affront, and, sitting opposite him, Montrose, calm, detached and collected, awaiting the revelations that he knew were coming. Reverend Graham was asked to repeat the account that he had heard of Argyll's treasonous comments at the Fords of Lyon; he did so. Then he was asked: where had he heard them? With Montrose sitting just feet away, he was 'loth to reveill his author'. But Montrose came to his rescue; he 'spak boldlie', saying, 'Feir not, tell your author.' The minister, hugely relieved at being given permission to reveal his source, replied, 'Then, my lord, it is your self that is my author'. All eyes turned on Montrose. Whom, it was asked, was *his* source? Montrose named Stewart of Ladywell. At this point Argyll, sitting with his sister, could keep his peace no longer; he 'wes netled, and becam offendit with Montross, betuixt whome fell out sum querrellous speiches.'[6] They were both ordered to desist, while a summons was prepared for Stewart.

Four days later the Estates reconvened with Stewart present as a witness. The atmosphere was alive was anticipation, the members gathering in groups, all talk of the remarkable scenes they had witnessed previously and what they might hear today. The young Montrose was taking a huge gamble, so publicly confronting the country's most powerful man. If he could establish that his claims were true, then Argyll was in serious trouble. If, however, the evidence did not support him, then James Graham would live to regret this challenge. All hung on what Stewart of Ladywell would have to say. The vital question was put to him: was Montrose's account true? To gasps from those present, he confirmed every word. Addressing Argyll directly, Stewart said, 'My Lord, I hard yow speik these wordis in Atholl, in presens of a great many people, quhairof yow ar in good memorie.'[7] Argyll exploded. Jumping to his feet, he 'broke into a passion and with great oaths denied the whole or part thereof'.[8] Members of the Estates, nobles, barons and burgesses, many of them Argyll's own men, looked at each other in wonder. This was a grave threat to the position, perhaps even the life, of their patron. All were in confusion, so to give time for further consideration, Stewart of Ladywell was committed to prison for the night, and the Estates agreed to reconvene the following morning.

The next day Montrose arrived at Parliament House in high spirits; the tables having been turned on his enemy. But one look at the sombre faces of Montrose's friends gathered in the great Parliament Hall was enough to send a chill to his bones. Something was very wrong. Sitting before the members of the Estates was Stewart of Ladywell, slumped in a chair, head down, face pale and drawn, unable to make eye contact with anyone around him, a very different man from the one who had so confidently stood and testified against Argyll the previous day. Just how different became clear when he was asked to speak. With a great effort, hardly managing more than a whisper, Stewart spoke of 'the infirmitie and weiknes of my bodie and spreit'[9] which meant that he could neither stand nor walk. He retracted his statements from the day before, claiming that he had invented them out of malice against Argyll, and went further, stating that he had been acting on the orders of Montrose and his colleagues in sending a copy of the fabricated remarks of Argyll to the King. Suddenly Argyll was in the clear, and Montrose the one facing accusations.

What lay behind this remarkable volte-face by such a key witness? Stewart of Ladywell may simply have had a fit of conscience overnight and decided to tell the truth after all, but the combination of his dramatic U-turn and the sudden deterioration in his physical condition suggest a more sinister explanation: torture, either on Argyll's orders, or at least by those acting in his interests. In seventeenth-century Scotland, the preferred instruments of torture, used to extract information or confessions, were the thumbscrews and the Boot. Both operated on the same principle of applying extreme pressure to parts of the body. The Boot was an iron cylinder, fixed round the leg of the victim, into which would be hammered wedges of wood or iron between kneecap and casing, crushing flesh, muscle and sinew, and ultimately splintering and shattering bone. The pain would have been excruciating, and the victim (if he survived the ordeal) left weeping and broken, unlikely ever to recover. There is no direct evidence to support the view that Stewart of Ladywell was tortured into retracting his original story, but as a credible explanation for his behaviour it makes a great deal of sense.

Whatever motivated Stewart of Ladywell to change his story, was his original account accurate? Even Montrose's biographer and great admirer John Buchan accepts that it is not likely that it was true. If he did have designs on the Crown for himself, for which there is no other evidence, a politician as astute as Argyll surely would not have been so foolish as to have spoken of them in front of 'a great many people', some of whom were antipathetic to his ambitions. It is possible that Argyll was discussing the theoretical grounds on which Parliament could depose a King, and when Stewart of Ladywell reported to Montrose he embellished the story (or Montrose did himself) so it appeared that Argyll had greater ambitions than were in fact revealed.

There was worse to come for the unfortunate prisoner. He was charged and convicted of the old Scots law of 'lease-making', stirring up resentment between a king and his subjects, which was a capital crime. The Committee of Estates were determined to make an example of him and, notwithstanding that there was no record of anyone previously being condemned to death for this offence, they decided on execution. Argyll actually fought for a more lenient sentence, given that Stewart had confessed his crime (which again suggests Argyll's innocence in the matter), but to no avail.

One of the advantages of noble birth in the seventeenth-century was that a death sentence was carried out not by hanging, which in the days before the introduction of the Long Drop meant slow strangulation, but by beheading. In England this function was performed by a headsman with a sharp axe, and it was as late as 1747 that the last such execution took place, that of Simon Fraser, Lord Lovat, for his part in the Jacobite rebellion (to the sound of the large crowd at Tower Hill singing at him the cheery ditty, 'Don't you love it, Lord Lovat, Lord Lovat?'). A problem with this method was that horrible mistakes could occur. With a leather hood causing his head to sweat and partially obscuring his view, even a skilled axeman could easily fail to land his first blow at precisely the right point to ensure a clean decapitation, with hideous consequences for the victim. As a result, motivated as much by the demands of efficiency as humanity, the Scots had introduced the Maiden, an early form of guillotine, which ensured a swift and supposedly painless end (the original instrument can be seen today in the National Museum of Scotland, still kept in working order lest some future generation should decide that errant politicians deserve a fate worse than retirement on a generous pension). So it was the Maiden which, on 28 July 1641, took off the head of Stewart of Ladywell, as a salutary lesson to anyone else who might seek to defame the most powerful man in the kingdom. There was to be a lot more work for this lady in the coming years.

Argyll was determined not to be taken by surprise for a second time. 'Now, Argile, seing Montross thus set against him, strives by all meinis possibill to haue ane watchful eye over his ways.'[10] A messenger carrying correspondence from the King to Scotland was intercepted and found to have in his possession letters from Charles to Montrose, together with other papers which had the look of being written in code. It was enough for the Committee of Estates to imprison Montrose and his allies in Edinburgh Castle.

For the Covenanting leaders the matter had become very serious. There had been a direct threat against Argyll, and now it looked like Montrose and his faction were working secretly with the King. Montrose was brought before Parliament three times, but said nothing that would incriminate himself or his friends. He remained defiant; the Parliamentary Register for 27 July 1641 records: 'The Earl of Montrose declared that albeit some great imputations be laid to his charge, yet he is so confident of his own innocency that he will not deprecate but supplicate for justice and trial.' On hearing the news from Edinburgh, Charles wrote to Argyll denying his part in any plot. The last thing the King needed when he was building a relationship with those in power was to be undermined by Montrose's excessive enthusiasm for Royal interests. Not for the last time, James Graham was to be treated as expendable.

In London, negotiations were concluding. On 10 August a Treaty was finally signed and the Second Bishops' War was over. Charles had had to make substantial concessions, although he had not gone as far as the Covenanters had wished. All Acts passed by the Scots Parliament without his authority were now to be approved, there was a sum of £300,000 sterling to be paid for the Scots army, and Parliament was to deal with the 'incendiaries' who had been causing trouble.

Four days later, with peace now agreed, Charles arrived in Edinburgh, believing there would still be public sympathy for his position. On his way north he had stopped at Newcastle to meet the Covenanters' army, and was warmly greeted by Leslie before inspecting the troops.

On Sunday 15 August, Charles listened to Alexander Henderson preach in the chapel at Holyroodhouse. Two days later the King assembled Parliament, making his way in procession up the High Street preceded by Hamilton carrying the crown, Argyll with the sceptre and the Earl of Sutherland with the sword of state, folk coming from far and wide to throng the street and the windows of the overhanging tenements for a glimpse of their distant sovereign. Charles was conciliatory in his remarks to Parliament, referring to 'unlucky differences' and 'unhappy mistakings'. He pledged that he had come to settle the religion and just liberties of the country, and referred to the Covenant which bound its subscribers to loyalty to their sovereign. Speaking in reply, Argyll compared the Kingdom to a ship in a stormy sea with the King at the helm, who had steered her through rocks and shallows to safe anchor. And continuing the nautical allusion, he made reference to the need for the ship's safety, and that the King had consented to cast overboard some of 'the naughtiest baggage to lighten her',[11] by which presumably he was referring to Montrose and his allies.

So complete had been the Covenanters' victory that none were permitted to attend Parliament until they first subscribed the Covenant. Even Royalists like Hamilton, Lennox and Perth, who had previously resisted, now had no alternative but to sign, given that it was the King's command. In no position to negotiate, Charles had little choice but to accept the Covenanters' demands, putting up only token resistance. He accepted defeat in a gracious manner, at least outwardly, calculating that he would need the support of the Scots in future to deal with a growing threat from those in England who were now challenging his authority.

The positions of the principal officers of state had to be filled, starting with those of Chancellor and Treasurer. The Covenanters put forward Argyll for Chancellor and Lord Loudon as Treasurer (who were both Campbells). The King was prepared to accept Loudon as Treasurer, but for Chancellor proposed Argyll's father-in-law, Morton, who was more sympathetic to the Royalist cause. Argyll was energetic in his opposition to this, and there was a lively slanging match between him and Morton, with Argyll alleging that his father-in-law was unfit to hold such an office as he was nearly bankrupt, and with Morton retorting that as he was Argyll's tutor and mentor, his son-in-law would have been nowhere without his guidance.

Morton then withdrew, at which point Charles nominated the Earl of Almond, but again Argyll objected, in this case on the basis that Almond had been a signatory to the Bond of Cumbernauld. Eventually it was agreed that Loudon would be Chancellor and the Treasurer's position shared between five commissioners, of whom Argyll was one. One of the consequences of these disputes was that any rapprochement between Charles and the Covenanters was short-lived. The King's opposition to

Argyll holding senior office was clear, and was not well received by the Campbells' allies.

Montrose still languished in prison. On 15 September Sir Patrick Wemyss wrote that Charles had promised Montrose that he would not leave Scotland until Montrose was brought to trial, in order to try and safeguard his life. Twice Montrose wrote to the King seeking a meeting, and suggesting that he had information 'which not only concerns his Honour in a high degree, but also the standing and falling of his crown'.[12] He wrote a third time on 11 October, stating that he had proof that Hamilton was guilty of treason. This was too much for Charles, who took the letter to the Privy Council, amongst them Argyll.

Argyll had concerns of his own by this point. He had just been warned of a plot against himself and the other leading Covenanters, including Hamilton (who, having now signed the Covenant, was developing a working relationship with the Campbell chief). The staunchly Royalist Earl of Crawford was accused of having planned to kidnap both Argyll and Hamilton, to take them onto a ship on the Forth well out of public gaze, and there cut their throats. News of this plan reached Alexander Leslie, who on hearing it took the immediate precaution of leaving Edinburgh, taking with him Argyll, Hamilton, and Hamilton's brother, the Earl of Lanark, and removing to Kinneil House near Bo'ness. Lanark wrote, rather gallantly; 'I was not so much troubled with the hazard of losing a life, wherein, God knows, these many years I have not taken great pleasure, as with the great prejudice I saw this would bring to his Majesty's affairs, and the peace and quiet of this poor kingdom.'[13]

This episode became known as the 'Incident'. It is not clear how seriously the alleged plot should be taken, or the extent to which Charles was involved. At a time when Hamilton was threatened with allegations of treason, which might well implicate Argyll, it would have suited them both as a diversionary tactic to be seen as the targets of a planned assassination attempt. This allowed the Covenanters to take the moral high ground, and inevitably suspicion would fall on the King and his allies. It is very probable that there was indeed a Royalist plot, but its discovery could not have been better timed for the supposed victims.

✳

Charles ordered an immediate investigation into these events, conscious that he could not allow his own good name to be linked with a conspiracy against leading Covenanters. He spoke passionately to Parliament of his concern as to the situation, and how wounded he was that Hamilton in particular felt that he was no longer safe in the King's company. But the appearance of Charles, accompanied by 500 armed men, did little to calm fears. 'It grieved my soul,' wrote Lanark, 'to see his Majesty take this course.'[14] In the end, the inquiry of the Committee of Estates into the matter was inconclusive, but the King at least was absolved of any responsibility. Argyll and his associates were free to return to Edinburgh in safety, indeed in triumph, their public standing in relation to that of the King greatly enhanced.

Whether blameless or not, Charles had bridges to mend, and immediately set about with enthusiasm rewarding the leading Covenanters. Argyll was elevated to a Marquis with a pension of £1,000 sterling per year. There was, apparently, an ancient prophecy which said that the last Earl of Argyll would be red-haired and squinting, and as this described the current holder of the post only too well it was prudent for him to accept the marquisate in order to defeat the curse. Leslie, who had defeated the King's armies, was made the Earl of Leven. Loudon was also created an Earl, and even Johnston of Warriston, the architect of the Covenant, was knighted. Charles then agreed to a distribution of the income due to the now deposed episcopal bishops, passing some on to the universities, but most to the leading Covenanters. Argyll was the beneficiary of the income that had fallen to the Bishop of Argyll and the Isles. He had, like so many of the other Scottish nobles, incurred substantial expense in prosecuting the war against the King.

On 28 October Charles was playing golf on Leith Links when word reached him of rebellion against his rule in Ireland. He had already spent too much time in Scotland to the neglect of his other Kingdoms, so, having concluded his business, he left Scotland on 18 November, never to return. The day before he left, Montrose and his associates were at last released from prison, on probation, thanks to Argyll's merciful intervention. There were no further proceedings against them for the plot in which they were accused of being part.

Charles left Scotland for the last time having secured peace in his northern Kingdom, but at a huge price. He had been forced to abandon his plans to impose episcopacy on the Scottish Church and had seen his secular power substantially restricted by the parliamentary reforms pushed through by the Covenanters. Largely through the efforts of Argyll, Scotland had become a country which had substantially shifted the balance of power between King and Parliament, and while nowhere near a modern democracy, the King's authority was now subject to control not just by the nobility but by the middle class. In addition the Covenanters now had a close relationship with Charles' enemies in the English Parliament, a development which was to prove crucial in the future.

In three years Scotland had undergone a revolution. The principal beneficiary had been Argyll, now not just the 8th Earl but a Marquis, and the leading power in the land, a remarkable advancement for one who had come only late to the Covenanting cause. For Archibald Campbell it was a time of political triumph. He might not be King Campbell in name, but few could doubt his pre-eminent position. He could even afford to demonstrate magnanimity towards those, principally Montrose, who had made accusations against him. Such was the scale of his victory that he no longer had anything to fear.

In contrast Montrose, who had been an enthusiastic Covenanter from the very start, had been pushed aside. He had watched as Argyll's influence and power had overtaken him. His attempts to build alliances with the King against the more radical elements leading the Covenanters had come to nought, he had spent five months in jail, and he had received nothing while his enemies had been fêted and rewarded. His political career had turned to dust. For one so ambitious, and who had once been seen as the coming man of Scottish politics, it was a galling turn of events.

Montrose had one consolation. In January the King wrote to him from London, referring to 'your sufferings for me'. Charles was, at least, aware of what Montrose had been through in defence of his interests. He went on to write: '. . . the same generosity which has made you hazard so much as you have done for my service, will at this time induce you to testify your affection to me as there shall be occasion; assuring you that for what you have already done I shall ever remain, your assured friend.'[15] The next occasion would come soon enough.

Charles had told the Scots Parliament that he was leaving 'a contented Prince and a contented people'. But his Royal authority had been dramatically weakened. Scotland might be at peace, but Ireland was now in rebellion, and in England he faced a new threat which was soon to overwhelm him.

6

Drawing Swords

1642–44

Three o'clock on a cold January afternoon in Westminster, the sun already sinking in the sky, the winter chill seeping along stone floors. Seated on rows of wooden benches are members of the House of Commons, stout city merchants, sturdy shire knights, grateful for the blazing fires bringing some warmth. A whisper creeps into the room, winds its way past the Speaker's chair, around the seated clerks with their leatherbound law books, and settles at the ear of John Pym, the King's arch-critic. Pym turns to his neighbour, in quiet but anxious and urgent conference. Around the room the whisper reaches others, and one by one they rise from their places and gather by the door – five there are, Arthur Haselrig, John Hampden, Denzil Holles, William Strode and Pym himself, all sought by the King for treason. They huddle in discussion, then, abruptly, conversation ended, decision made, as one they take their leave, and are gone.

It is barely a moment too soon. There is a hammering at the great door, it flies open, in pour the King's officers, all fine clothes, proud hats and jingling swords. They take up position by the entrance and around the walls. And then, who comes in but Charles himself – the King! In the Commons! In breach of every principle of Parliamentary privilege! Elegant, dignified Charles, walking slowly up to the Speaker, William Lenthall, removing his hat as a gesture of respect, and politely demanding: 'Mr Speaker, I must for a time make bold with your chair.' Mr Speaker, amazed, wordlessly makes way for his monarch, here usurping his place. Charles scans the room, the stunned faces gaping his way, and asks for his enemies, first Pym, then Holles. There is silence. It dawns on the King that his quarry has escaped him. He addresses the remaining Members of Parliament: 'I must declare unto you here that albeit no king that ever was in England shall be more careful of your privileges…yet you must know that in cases of Treason, no person hath a privilege . . . since I see all the birds have flown, I do expect from you that you will send them unto me as soon as they return here. But I assure you, on the word of a king, I never did intend any force, but shall proceed against them in a legal and fair way.' The MPs present would be forgiven for doubting the truth of that last statement, given the evidence before them.

Charles asks Lenthall directly, where have the five traitors gone? The Speaker's reply is a classic reassertion of Parliamentary independence: 'May it pleasure your Majesty, I have neither eyes to see nor tongue to speak in this place but as the House is pleased to direct me, whose servant I am here.' And not *yours*, he could have added, but Charles gets the message. Realising there are no gains here for him, the King retires with as much dignity as he can muster, but as he leaves, one MP after another rises to his feet to shout 'Privilege!' The Royal entourage depart with the reproachful cries following them into the chill outside air, and the gathering dark.

No sooner had Charles returned to London the previous autumn but he had to face the growing agitation from Parliament against his rule. There was no single reason for the division. Amongst members of the House of Commons there were concerns about the abuse of civil powers (one MP, a country squire from Huntingdon by the name of Oliver Cromwell, raised the issue of corruption in the Commission of Sewers), while the increasingly vocal Puritans were worried about religious developments, and wanted the King's Catholic advisers removed.

They had all seen what the Scots had achieved by standing up to Charles, and now it was their turn to put the King in his place. To help protect themselves, leading Parliamentarians made an attempt to take over control of the militia to prevent its use by the King against their interests.

Charles had come back to his capital with information, some of which had been provided by Montrose, that Pym and his allies had encouraged the Scots to invade. This amounted to treason, and was the excuse the King needed to strike. This is what led him, in a foolish miscalculation, to enter the House of Commons on 4 January 1642 in an attempt to capture Pym and his colleagues in order to take them to trial. Such was the outrage caused that the King was forced to leave London, never to return as a free man. Just as the King's disputes with the Scots had ended up being resolved by war, so his growing divisions with the English Parliament looked increasingly like they would only be settled in the same manner.

Whatever setbacks his career had suffered, no-one could accuse James Graham, Earl of Montrose, of lacking self-belief. Desperate to find a role, he was quick to offer the beleaguered King his support. But Charles knew that accepting assistance from that direction might well alienate his new friends amongst the Covenanters, and politely declined. Instead he wrote to Argyll in flattering terms, saying, 'it is well known that your power wants not to serve me . . . I cannot doubt of your readiness.'[1] Argyll had enough experience of the King's ways not to be fooled.

The most pressing business for Charles was to deal with the rebellion in Ireland. The marginalised and dispossessed Catholic population had risen up against their overlords, and terrible atrocities had been committed against Protestants. Charles told the English Parliament and the Privy Council in Scotland that he wished to raise an expeditionary force and equip it from the armoury in Hull. The English Parliamentarians were suspicious that the King would use such a force, not in Ireland, but against his political opponents in England, while the Scots, who were generally sympathetic to the Parliamentary cause, told Charles he first needed to resolve his differences with Parliament. When Charles took his men to Hull he found that Parliament denied him access to the weapons and ammunition located there.

Believing that his relations with the Scots were still good, Charles appealed to the Privy Council to support him against Parliament. All of the senior Scots nobles were therefore called to Edinburgh, and came well-protected with bodies of men. 'There was a great rumour raised of a wicked designe against Argyle's persone',[2] and so Edinburgh was soon filled with the supportive gentry and ministers of Fife and the Lothians, which deterred any move against their champion. With so many of Argyll's backers in town, the Royalist sympathisers on the Privy Council had no option but to tell Charles that he was on his own if it came to war with Parliament. Notwithstanding the set-back, on 22 August Charles raised his standard at Nottingham, calling on his loving subjects to assist him in suppressing the rebellion against his authority.

While not wishing to play any part in a war in England between the King and his subjects, the Scots had nevertheless seen the need for intervention in Ireland. There were many Scots settlers in Ulster who had close family ties to the Covenanters, and the Covenanting leadership did not wish to leave them to their fates. In July the English Parliament had agreed to fund a Scots force of 10,000 men to cross the North Channel to put down the rebellion, with Sandy Leslie, the new Earl of Leven, as General, and Robert Monro as Major-General.

The Scots army based itself in Carrickfergus and was successful in securing the northern counties against the rebels. Although Argyll played no personal part in the war in Ulster,

1,500 of his Campbell followers under the command of Sir Duncan Campbell of Auchinbreck were actively engaged from a base in the Rathlin Isles (where they were accused of a massacre of the inhabitants), at his own considerable expense. The Marquis also ordered a successful raid on the Isle of Man, controlled by the leading Royalist the Earl of Derby, utilising the considerable naval power which he had accumulated. Although not yet formally allied with the English Parliamentarians, Argyll was certainly assisting their cause.

In England, without the Scots actively supporting either side in the civil war, the King enjoyed early success. The first major clash of his forces and those of Parliament was at Edgehill on 23 October, which neither side won decisively, but the outcome of which was viewed as favouring the King. Finding themselves on the back foot, it was the turn of the Parliamentarians to ask the Scots for help. Charles still had his supporters in Scotland; in August he had written to Montrose from Nottingham telling the Earl that he was the one whom the King had found most faithful, and in whom he reposed greatest trust. But it was still Hamilton who was Charles' closest confidant north of the Border, and so it was Hamilton who set about countering the efforts of the English Parliament to win the Covenanters to their side.

Charles was wise enough to know there was little prospect of the Scots intervening in the English civil war to support him, but at least he could try to prevent them joining with his enemies. With the aid of Hamilton and Traquair, Charles asked the Scots Privy Council to stay out of the war, but he was competing with an appeal from Parliament for military assistance. In the Privy Council, Hamilton's brother, the Earl of Lanark hotly disputed with Argyll as to whether or not the King's will should be followed. Many moderate Covenanters were resistant to an alliance with the Parliamentarians. Baillie wrote to Johnston of Warriston, 'If yow think that any considerable partie in the West will be gotten to move for the Parliament of England, I fear you shall be altogether deceaved . . . to dream of any assistance from us to England at this tyme will be a meer fancie.'[3] But the majority view was clearly sympathetic to a deal, if, and only if, they could get the English to agree to their terms.

While the Covenanters were moving towards war in England, they did not need to face a threat at their own backs in Scotland. It was important to try and neutralise the Scottish Royalists, and so an approach was made to Montrose to win him over, recognising both his military skills and his ambition. He was offered the Lieutenant-Generalship of the army if he would join with the Covenanters. This olive branch must have come from Argyll, realising that Montrose would make a dangerous enemy. Argyll may have been a man of firm principles, but he was always a pragmatist, prepared to make deals with whomsoever if they would advance his interests. But Montrose had too many differences with his rival's camp to take the bait.

In February 1643 Montrose travelled to England to see the King at Oxford, accompanied by Huntly's son Lord Aboyne, and Lord Ogilvie. En route he heard that Queen Henrietta Maria, who had gone to the Continent with the crown jewels to sell to raise money for her husband's war, was returning by ship from Holland. Montrose met her at Bridlington and tried to persuade her of the merits of a Royalist uprising in Scotland. The Queen, who was suffering from seasickness, wanted time to consider the matter, and said she would speak to him further at York. Hamilton and Traquair got to her first, and persuaded her that such a radical move was not necessary. Neither would Charles himself heed Montrose's urgings. He believed Hamilton's advice that the way to prevent the Scots entering the war was to string out negotiations with them while looking for a swift military victory against his enemies in England. Such was the King's regard for Hamilton that he elevated him to the title of Duke. Once again sidelined, Montrose was angry and frustrated, and from then on treated Hamilton as an enemy. Time would prove Montrose's advice to be right, but the Royalist cause in Scotland was left fatally divided, to Argyll's benefit.

Montrose's disdain for Hamilton is summed up in a few lines of poetry he penned, as an epitaph to a dog belonging to the Earl of Newcastle's son. The unfortunate creature was in a scrap in the Queen's garden in York, when up came Hamilton. For some unknown reason (perhaps it was getting the better of its adversary), the Marquis whipped out his sword and ran the dog through. Montrose was contemptuous – was this the extent of Hamilton's military prowess?

> Here lies a Dog, whose qualities did plead
> Such fatal end from a *renowned* blade, –
> And blame him not that he succumbed now,
> For Herc'les could not combat against two, –
> For while he on his foe revenge did take,
> He *manfully* was killed behind his back.
> Then say, to eternize the Cur that's gone,
> He *fleshed the maiden sword* of HAMILTON.

While the Royalists were falling out with each other, the Covenanters were advancing their plans, Argyll as ever at the centre. By now the Covenanters had become convinced that the only way to secure Presbyterianism in Scotland was to export it. The experience of history told them that any monarch, and particularly a Stewart, would have as his aim uniformity of religion in all parts of his Kingdoms. For so long as the Scots Kirk ordered its affairs differently from those of the Church in England, it would be at risk from meddling monarchs trying to reimpose episcopacy against the public will. Only by establishing Presbyterian church government in England would the future of the independent Scots Kirk be secured, and the prospect of future wars between the two Kingdoms significantly reduced.

Today this might seem a far-fetched ambition on the part of the Scots, but at the time there was a great deal of distrust of bishops within the English Church, and many English Reformers looked on Scots Presbyterianism as a model which should be followed in the larger Kingdom. Meantime there were many Independents who equally deplored both Episcopacy and Presbyterianism, but were theologically more sympathetic to the Reformed faith of the Scots. With all this in their favour the Covenanters negotiated with the King with the aim of establishing religious unity on the basis of Presbyterianism. Argyll might be agitating for a deal with the Parliamentarians, but this was no time to close down options.

Charles had the upper hand in the war for the time being, but he knew that the intervention of the Scots on the side of Parliament could easily tip the balance against him. He was anxious to maintain negotiations as long as possible in an effort to maintain Scottish neutrality, but without making any significant concessions. Argyll was shrewd enough to understand the game that Charles was playing. He also knew, as did the other Covenanters, that should Charles be successful in his war against the English Parliament then it would only be a matter of time before he would turn his attentions again to Scotland and reassert his Royal authority. The English poet John Milton summed the situation up with what would prove to be prophetic words: 'Woe be to you, Presbyterians especially if ever any of Charles' race recover the English sceptre. Believe me you shall all pay the reckoning.'[4]

The victory of the English Parliament forces, and the establishment of a political system with a limited monarchy similar to that which had been established in Scotland, appeared more and more to be in the Scots' interest. But public opinion had still to be won over to the idea of a Scots army once again taking arms against their King, and this time in someone else's dispute. If the Scots were to ally with the Parliamentarians, it needed to be clear what was in it for them. And there remained the risk of Scots loyal to Charles rallying to his cause north of the Border and threatening the unity of the Kingdom.

Argyll knew that if there were to be a Royalist rising in Scotland the candidate for leadership presenting the greatest threat was Montrose, who had established for himself a strong reputation as a general following his successful North-east campaign four years before. Argyll tried again to win his rival over to the Covenanting side; Montrose was once more offered the post of Lieutenant-General of the army under Leven, and payment of debts that he had incurred. Alexander Henderson, with whom Montrose had always had a good relationship, was sent to conduct negotiations. The two met near Stirling, where Henderson laid out to Montrose the enthusiasm there was amongst the Covenanters to have him on their side, and their belief that he would bring with him many of the moderate Royalists. Montrose did not immediately decline the offer, but on quizzing Henderson as to whether he came with the Estates' full authority, Henderson had to say no, which gave Montrose his out. He said that he would have to take time to consider the matter, and the issue was left unresolved. Baillie wrote of Montrose: 'The man is said to be verie double, which in so proud a spirit is strange. Argyle and our Nobles, especiallie since Hamiltoun's falling off, would have been content, for the peace of the countrey, to have dispensed with that man's bypast demeanours, bot private ends misleads manie.'[5] In the end Montrose did not accept the offer of reconciliation, and his response to Henderson was probably good manners to a man he respected rather than any serious indication that he was considering abandoning his loyalty to the King and switching sides. He had long since made up his mind as to where his heart lay.

The Covenanters had asked Charles for the right to call a Parliament to discuss the dangerous situation the country was now in, as the next sitting was not due until the following year. Charles refused, so Argyll encouraged his colleagues to arrange for a meeting of the Convention of Estates. There was certainly serious business to be dealt with, not least the situation of the Scots army in Ireland and how funds would be raised to pay for it. It was a bold move to meet without the King's authority, but Argyll was determined that the Convention should happen. Always looking to protect his Royal master's interests, Hamilton attempted rather half-heartedly to block the meeting taking place, but when it was clear that it was to proceed he persuaded Charles to allow it, but under protest. Hamilton was anxious that the King should do nothing which would raise the temperature and precipitate the Covenanters into entering the war on Parliament's side.

The King's cause was not helped by belated news from Ireland. The Royalist Earl of Antrim was captured in May 1643 and found to have in his possession letters from the Earl of Nithsdale and Lord Aboyne making reference to preparations for war, which implicated both Huntly and Montrose. The real threat of an invasion by Irish Catholic troops in support of the King caused great alarm. As it happened Montrose had refused to have anything to do with Antrim's plots, but public exposure of them further strengthened Argyll's position.

When the Convention of Estates met, Archibald Campbell was in full control. He was determined to press on with agreeing a deal with the English Parliamentarians for Scots military assistance in return for key concessions. The House of Commons sent four commissioners to conduct negotiations, asking for the withdrawal of the Scots army from Ireland in the hope that this would be redirected to England. The cost of this would be met by Parliament, which would also guarantee the protection of Scotland in the event of invasion or Royalist uprising, and there would be no peace treaty between the King and Parliament without Scottish interests being protected.

With matters temporal under discussion, spiritual issues also had to be addressed. The General Assembly of the Kirk met on 2 August in St Giles with Alexander Henderson again as Moderator; the crucial item for discussion being the proposed alliance with the Parliamentarians. The four commissioners from England wished to restrict the alliance to civil matters, but the General Assembly wanted to go further – 'The English were for a civill League, we for a religious Covenant' – and the English were in no position to argue. For the Scots there was no point entering the war in England unless the prize of a Presbyterian church, north *and* south of the Border, could be secured. This had been Argyll's objective all along, and he worked tirelessly to achieve it. Even Baillie, who had serious misgivings, had to concede, 'I admired the industrie of Argyll.'[6]

The terms of any alliance with Parliament had to be documented, and it was at this point that Henderson and Johnston of Warriston jointly produced the Solemn League and Covenant. This was based on the National Covenant of 1638, and while pledging to preserve and defend the King's majesties, person and authority, was an even more revolutionary document than its predecessor. By its subscription both Scotland and England would bind themselves together to protect their religion and to seek to secure church uniformity across three kingdoms, 'according to the word of God, and the example of the best reformed churches'. Both popery and episcopacy were to be extinguished, the rights of the English and Scottish Parliaments upheld, and those hostile to these ends to be punished. Johnston of Warriston called it 'God's dishcloth' – about to cleanse the three Kingdoms of popery.

The General Assembly greeted the Solemn League and Covenant rapturously: 'it was received with the greatest applause that ever I saw any thing, with so heartie affections, expressed in the tears of pitie and joy by very manie grave, wise, and old men.'[7] And no wonder. Here at last was the opportunity to safeguard the Reformed Kirk from meddling by Charles or any subsequent monarch. The Convention of Estates agreed it enthusiastically, and it was dispatched to London for signature by the English Parliamentarians, which duly occurred in St Margaret's Church in Westminster on 25 September. Whatever reservations the English might have had, not least those of the Independents who opposed the imposition of Presbyterian order on the English church, they were prepared to swallow them in order to secure vital Scots military help in their struggle with the King. The Covenanters were at war with Charles again.

Terms of engagement being agreed, the Scots could now deal with the practical side of providing aid. An army was to be raised of 18,000 infantry, 2,000 cavalry and 1,000 dragoons, with artillery. The costs were to be met initially by the Scots, but they were to be paid £30,000 sterling a month by the English Parliament, and the balance of arrears of pay settled in full when the war was concluded. Leven was again appointed in charge of the army, and David Leslie, another veteran of the Thirty Years' War, was made his Lieutenant-General.

The Solemn League and Covenant was a triumph for Argyll, the pinnacle of his political achievement. For Montrose it was both a betrayal, and the opportunity that he had been waiting for. The Covenanters had gone too far, finally breaking faith with their King. Charles had, however reluctantly, made substantial concessions to the Covenanters, and had taken no overt steps to have these overturned. Unlike in the Bishops' Wars in which Montrose had played a leading part, there could be no excuse for taking arms against the King. As a loyal monarchist, James Graham felt that he had no alternative but to throw his lot in with Charles wholeheartedly. He departed immediately for Oxford where he hoped to find the King, eventually catching up with him overseeing the Royalist siege of Gloucester, and begged for authority to act on Charles' behalf in Scotland. But the King was still being told by Hamilton that everything was under control, and refused to authorise action.

Montrose was deeply frustrated that Charles had no response even while the Covenanters were raising and equipping an army. Eventually Charles realised that matters were much more serious than Hamilton had originally led him to believe. In December Hamilton was called to Oxford along with his brother Lanark, and there they were both accused of foolishness falling little short of treason. Hamilton was arrested and imprisoned in Pendennis Castle in Devon, while Lanark escaped and eventually made his way back to join the Covenanters. At last Montrose could feel vindicated, and hopeful. With his enemy Hamilton no longer poisoning Charles against him, surely the King would start putting trust in his most loyal subject?

By the new year of 1644 the Scots army was ready once again to invade England. On 19 January it crossed the Tweed at Berwick on a frozen river offering safe passage on the ice even for the artillery. Scotland in the mid-seventeenth century was in the depths of 'the Little Ice Age' with bitter winter temperatures and deep snow lying on upland areas for many months, making travel extremely difficult (despite what we might think, climate change is not a modern phenomenon). With the troops rode Argyll, in military command of part of the cavalry, but in addition the *de facto* leader of a national cause now entirely aligned with his own political and religious outlook. This was Archibald Campbell at the height of his powers, a major player on the British stage. He was acting not just in his own and the national interests, but as an instrument of God doing His work, and defending His Kirk.

The Scots army headed for Newcastle, but unlike at the time of the previous invasion Leven found it well defended. Argyll and Sir William Armyne called on the city to surrender, sending a conciliatory message: 'Our Appearance here in this Posture, through Mis-informations and Mis-understandings, may occasion strange thoughts in you. If we had the opportunity of speaking together (which hereby we offer and desire) it is not impossible, that as we held forth the same Ends, viz., The Preservation of Religion, the King's true Honour and Happiness, the publick Peace and Liberty of his Dominions, so we might agree upon the same way to promote them.' Unimpressed, the Mayor replied that he and the other residents intended to hazard their lives and fortunes in the city's defence.

The last thing the Scots wanted was to tie up their forces in a prolonged siege, so Leven divided his troops, leaving some behind at Newcastle and taking the rest south across the Tyne. He took Sunderland easily, entering on 4 March. The Royalist Marquis of Newcastle had assembled a large army of 10,000 men to confront the Scots, but in wintry weather they did not come to battle and the Royalists retreated to defend Durham.

Leven continued to capture forts and towns around the Tyne and maintained the siege of Newcastle, but it would not be until October that the city eventually fell. There was frustration at home at the lack of progress, Baillie complaining, 'That our armie, after two moneths abode in England, had done so little . . . that their provision of victuals is so extreamlie small, that their moneys and munition is so inlacking . . . and that so much misorder among the sojours . . .'[8]

Argyll left the Scots army at Sunderland on 20 March to return by ship to Edinburgh to help deal with a national emergency. The inevitable Royalist uprising in Scotland had occurred, led by Huntly. From Montrose's perspective, this was a missed opportunity. Still in Oxford with the King, he had been pleading, unsuccessfully, for permission to take the war north of the Border. Always the man of action, he itched to be up and doing, but Charles was reluctant to commit. This was understandable; Montrose was personally unpopular with many Scottish Royalists who recalled his early enthusiasm for the Covenant and regarded him as a self-serving *arriviste* with no history of loyalty to the King, and as someone undeserving of the King's favour. Moreover, there was little sympathy for Charles' cause outside of the traditionally Royalist families such as the Ogilvies and Gordons and some of the Highland clans. If Montrose were to make any impact then he would need an army, and it was not clear from where this would come.

It was the Earl of Antrim, who had escaped from imprisonment for a second time, who came to the rescue. He offered to raise 10,000 Irish troops to fight in England and 3,000 to invade Scotland. On 20 January Charles had commissioned Antrim to act, giving him instructions to take 2,000 men to invade Argyllshire by 1 April. Concurrent with this Montrose would lead a Royalist uprising within Scotland from those still loyal to the King. Charles offered to appoint him Captain-General of the Royal forces, but Montrose declined and instead accepted the Lieutenant-Generalship, under the King's nephew Prince Maurice. Charles had eventually been persuaded of the sense of taking the war to Scotland. The Scots army in the North of England were doing real damage to his prospects of success against Parliament, and the opening of a second front at their backs must have seemed like good sense.

From the start nothing went according to plan. Antrim was not able to raise the army he required in anything like the intended timescale, and 1 April came and went without the Irish invasion. Montrose had set out from Oxford accompanied by Lords Ogilvie and Aboyne to seek the Marquis of Newcastle. He found him at Durham on 15 March, but Montrose's hopes of acquiring either men or finances were quickly dashed. Newcastle had enough to do facing Leven's army. All he could spare were two small brass cannon and 100 mounted troopers, but he also asked for the Cumberland and Westmoreland militia to join with Montrose. So the King's Lieutenant-General managed to assemble a small army of 1,300 men to take to Scotland. But by the time he had made it as far as Dumfries, already more than half his force, principally the local militia, had given up and gone home.

Montrose met no opposition at Dumfries and was warmly welcomed by the Provost, but there was little sympathy in that part of the country for the Royalist cause. Montrose grandly declared that he had 'taken up arms for the King for the defence and maintenance of the true Protestant religion, his Majesty's just and sacred authority, the fundamental laws and privileges of Parliament, the peace and freedom of the oppressed and enthralled subject.'[9] But no one was listening. Even the local nobles like Roxburgh and Traquair, staunch Royalists both, refused to join him. With a Covenanting force coming south to meet his little army, Montrose had no alternative but to retreat back across the Border, even leaving some of the cannons behind. Montrose's consolation was that as a reward for his service to the King he was elevated to the rank of Marquis, as Argyll had been two years before.

Argyll had arrived in Edinburgh determined to stamp out his brother-in-law Huntly's rather ineffectual Royalist rising in the north. Huntly was a poor war leader, indecisive and lacking in funds. He was acting in expectation both of the Irish invasion under Antrim and of support from England from Montrose, but neither materialised. Nevertheless Huntly took Aberdeen, and his troops went on to sack the town of Montrose on the Angus coast.

The Convention of Estates met on 10 April to discuss how to deal with the threat, and commissioned Argyll to lead the forces to oppress the rising 'with fire and sword and in all other hostile manner', praising his 'fidelity, affection and abilities'. He was given the power to raise three regiments from Fife, Angus and Perthshire to join with his own men, making a total command of 5,200. It was expected that these would be joined by another 800 from the Scots army in Ireland. On 26 April, riding in advance of the main forces, Argyll arrived at Dunottar just south of Aberdeen. With his brother-in-law's forces assembling, and with no sign of assistance from Ireland or England, Huntly realised that he was engaged in a lost cause. He fled, firstly to Strathbogie, and then on in a boat to Sutherland, where he would remain holed up at the home of Lord Reay, the Royalist chief of Clan Mackay, who was away with the King's troops under siege in Newcastle.

Argyll's army moved through the Gordon territories of Aberdeenshire and Banffshire, taking revenge as they went on those who had risen for the King. Not even Argyll's own niece, married to the eldest son of Irving of Drum, was spared, with her house being sacked as a reward for her husband's conduct.

Argyll's task was to prevent any future repeat of the Royalist rising. He offered rewards for the capture, dead or alive, of its leaders, and left a regiment of his own Campbell Highlanders stationed in the district to discourage any future Royalist activity. The city of Aberdeen itself, which had suffered so much in previous conflicts, was fined £1,000 sterling towards costs. Notwithstanding this burden, the Magistrates of Aberdeen conferred on Argyll and his associates the freedom of the city, celebrating with liberal quantities of wine. Unlike on the previous occasion when Montrose visited, this time the poor were not to be the beneficiaries. When Argyll took his leave of Aberdeen he was treated to a proper civic send-off, 'so highly was he in their days exalted, little inferior to a king'.[10] His victory was complete; the Royalist threat, for now at least, had been suppressed; and Argyll was able to return to Edinburgh as a hero. The Kirk took this opportunity to excommunicate a number of leading Royalists, among them the new Marquis of Montrose. Those who took up arms for the King were setting themselves up not just against Scotland and its Covenanted people, but against God himself.

Montrose was back in England preparing the ground for a fresh Royalist uprising in Scotland. Having been thoroughly outmanoeuvred by his rival in the political arena, he could now see his conflict with Argyll moving to a different setting, away from the world of politics and onto the battlefield. It was on this new stage that Montrose would have, at last, the opportunity to prove his superiority.

7

Annus Mirabilis

1644-45

Around a table strewn with empty glasses is huddled a discon-
solate group, deep in urgent debate, while a large white poodle
rests its face on the floor amidst their mud-splattered boots.
Under the low roof-beams of this Yorkshire inn in Richmond,
the Royalist high command is at council of war. A messenger
enters and approaches the youngest man at the table, whispering
in his ear. He nods assent, the messenger departs, then returns
moments later with a visitor: James Graham, Marquis of Montrose, here with a request. As the young man rises slowly to his
feet, the dog, suddenly alert, raises its head from the floor to
look adoringly at its master: Prince Rupert of the Rhine, the
King's nephew, and his finest commander in the field. Prince
Rupert greets the visitor warmly, and Montrose notices how tall
he is – at 6 feet 4 inches he has to stoop to avoid hitting his head
on the roof – and the sadness and weariness in his eyes. He and
the King's army have just suffered a terrible defeat, and while the
Prince has escaped the battlefield with 6,000 men, the Royalist
cause has taken serious losses.

The principal Royalist effort in the North of England had
been focused on the relief of York, the city being besieged by a
Parliamentary army of which the Covenanting forces comprised
a significant part. Prince Rupert's army of 12,000 men relieved
the city on 1 July, and the following afternoon met the Parliamentary forces – under Sandy Leslie, Earl of Leven – at Marsden
Moor, and were crushed. Significant factors in the Parliamentary

victory were the performance of their cavalry, commanded on the left flank by Oliver Cromwell, already proving himself to be an outstanding battlefield commander; and the contribution made by the Scots, notably David Leslie. Scottish intervention in the English war was proving crucial.

Montrose had not been present at Marsden Moor, instead busying himself elsewhere in northern England on the King's behalf. Now he wanted help to take the fight across the Border. 'Give me a thousand of your horse and I will cut my way into the heart of Scotland,' he promised Prince Rupert. The Prince could only shake his head sadly. He had none to spare; indeed, he was also in need of the few whom Montrose himself commanded.

It was the last thing that Montrose wanted to hear. With the Royalist cause now in retreat in England and with no army to take into Scotland, there seemed little hope for the Scottish captain. The best option available was to report to the King at Oxford, and thereafter perhaps even depart for the Continent to await developments. But Montrose determined on a different course of action: he would take the King's fight to Scotland, if necessary by himself, confident that there were those there who would rise to the Royal banner. It was a bold move, perhaps a reckless one, but typical of a man who was a gambler by nature.

Accompanied only by Sir William Rollo and Colonel Sibbald, Montrose crossed the Border, his two companions dressed as members of the Covenanters' army and the Marquis himself disguised as their groom. There was better news from his home country. Antrim's invasion had finally occurred, albeit on a much smaller scale than he had promised. Alasdair MacDonald had taken three regiments, comprising 1,600 men, of experienced Irish warriors across the sea to Kintyre, where he was ravaging the Campbell lands between there and Ardnamurchan.

MacDonald, or MacColla as he is often known, was a giant of a man and a remarkable soldier. His father was a MacDonald of Colonsay, nicknamed 'Colkitto' (Coll who can fight with either hand), and this title is sometimes also applied to the son. Like many in the West Highlands he shared ancestry with those in Ulster and was closely related to the MacDonnells of Antrim. MacDonald was just 21, but already had substantial military experience and a reputation for great courage. He was also an outstanding battlefield tactician who perfected the Highland Charge, which was to prove devastatingly successful in conflicts against Lowland or English troops for the next 100 years. Irregular Highland troops would discharge their firearms, or even arrows, and then immediately rush at their opponents with swords, targes, axes and clubs, and the very sight of the attack was enough to strike fear even into the most hardened soldiers. It would be another century before the Duke of Cumberland would devise a successful defensive tactic for regular infantry facing such an onslaught.

MacDonald had hoped that his invasion of Scotland would instigate an uprising amongst Highland clans against the Campbells, his clan's hereditary enemies, but he was soon disappointed. There were few recruits to the cause, and the Campbells were quickly on his trail seeking revenge. MacDonald had no choice but to try and return to Ulster, but he found that his foes had burnt his ships and that he was trapped. He then decided to make his way to Aberdeenshire to join up with the Gordons loyal to the King. In this he had some success, adding 500 men to his numbers, but his position became increasingly precarious. MacDonald eventually found himself in Atholl facing a threat on three fronts: Argyll and the Campbells, fresh from the ravaging of Aberdeenshire, were approaching from the west; Lord Elcho commanded a Covenanting force based in Perth to the south; and in the east another hostile army was assembling in Aberdeen.

MacDonald's greatest problem was that he was distrusted by the Highland clansmen whom he needed to assemble under the

Royalist flag. His Catholic Irish troops, accompanied on their campaigns by a rabble of women and children, were regarded even by the Highlanders (strange enough themselves to their Lowland cousins) as untrustworthy aliens. MacDonald needed a general who could unite the Royalist forces, and he had only one candidate in mind. He wrote to Montrose, desperate for assistance.

The new Marquis was making his way northwards in disguise with his two companions, on one occasion being recognised by a traveller who fortunately turned out to be sympathetic to the Royalist cause. They stopped at Tullybelton, just north of Perth, a safe house and home of Montrose's relative, Patrick Graham of Inchbrakie. It was here that MacDonald's letter reached Montrose, and it must have been wonderful news for the Marquis to learn that an army was being put at his disposal, and that it was not many miles away. The gamble was paying off. So Montrose, with only Patrick Graham the Younger for company, and dressed as a Highlander in trews and plaid, set off for Blair Atholl where he met up with MacDonald.

Alasdair MacDonald was delighted to pass the responsibility of command on to the King's Lieutenant-General, and Montrose must have been equally pleased to have a decent contingent of troops at last. With the King's commission, Montrose was a figure of authority to whom Royalist clans could rally, and the Stewarts and Robertsons joined the Irish in pledging their swords to him. Having spent the night at the house of Lude, the following morning Montrose raised the Royal Standard on Truidh Hill, among the mountains of Atholl, 'for the defence and maintenance of the trew protestant religion, his Majestie's just and sacred authoritie, the fundamentall lawes and priveledges of Parliaments, the peace and freedom of the oppressed and enthralled subject.'[1] Around him his new Irish troops cheered their noble leader, with his 'flaxin haire' and eyes 'sparkling and full of lyfe'.[2] It felt like the start of a great adventure.

Montrose now commanded an army of 3,000 men, and was ready to take the fight to the Convenanters. Everything was working out as well as he could have hoped for. He even sent a defiant message to Argyll, encouraging him to make up with the King, but warning: 'if you shall continue obstinate, I call God witness that through your own stubbornness I shall be compelled to endeavour to reduce you by force. So I rest, your friend if you please.'[3] His friend Argyll did not reply.

While MacDonald's military genius was to prove crucial to Montrose's chances of success, and the 1,600 troops he provided were to be the core of the Royalist army in Scotland, from a political perspective, incorporating the Irish contingent into his forces was a questionable move by the King's General. It was bad enough taking a Highland army into the Lowlands, but the Irish were viewed as bestial: 'too cruel; for it was everywhere observed they did ordinarily kill all they could be master of, without any notion of pity or any consideration of humanity . . . for they killed men ordinarily with no more feeling of compassion and with the same neglect that they kill a hen or capon for their supper; and they were also without all shame, most brutishly given to uncleanness and flighty lust.'[4] Worse still, they were Catholics, and as such an affront to God's Covenanted people. To have some sense of the Covenanters' horror, imagine the reaction today if an Israeli army were to attack the holy cities of Islam in Saudi Arabia. Using the Irish might help Montrose win battles for the King, but they would make it much harder for him to win the affection of Lowland Scots. And the men were poorly equipped, the Irish having only a few muskets, and clubs and axes rather than swords or pikes. The Highlanders were little better off, mostly carrying only broadswords or pikes, or even bows and arrows. Many could only throw stones, and fight with their hands. When it came to cavalry, things were even worse: just three horses, described by Wishart as *omnino strigosos et emaciatos* – all string and bone. But Montrose could not afford to be choosy – he needed an army, and he had nowhere else to turn. And with three separate forces threatening him, he had no time to delay.

Montrose decided to take the offensive against the nearest Covenanting force, that of Lord Elcho at Perth. Elcho's army was drawn from the citizens of Perth and the surrounding counties, assisted by local gentlemen who provided the cavalry. Though he had perhaps twice the numbers under his command than his opponent, Elcho's men were untrained and inexperienced, and up against Montrose's battle-hungry Irish and Highlanders. The two armies met in the fields at Tippermuir, just to the west of Perth, on a warm Sunday morning, 1 September. The sun was shining bright, and Elcho's troops were in good spirits. Despite sweltering under heavy coats and padded jerkins, they were encouraged by a number of local ministers promising that God was on their side and that He would grant them an easy victory. The Lord would scatter their enemies, just as He had those of the ancient Israelites (the claim that the Covenanters flew a banner with the appalling legend 'Jesus and No Quarter', is however undoubtedly an invention, a piece of black propaganda intended to damage the reputation of the Covenanters originating from the seventeenth-century equivalent of a political spin doctor.)

Elcho set out his forces with the infantry in the centre supported by seven light pieces of artillery, and the cavalry on the flanks. Elcho commanded the right, Lord Murray of Gask the centre, and the professional soldier, Sir James Scott of Rossie, took the left. With his forces better armed, better fed, and in far greater numbers than the enemy, Elcho thought he had every reason to feel confident. Montrose drew up his men in a long line to match the Covenanters' front. MacDonald took command of the centre and Montrose the left, while on the right was a contingent of 500 'bowmen' (probably musketeers), under the command of Lord Kilpont. Kilpont had joined with Montrose's army on their march south, having originally been raised to oppose MacDonald's troops.

It was customary, prior to a blow being struck, for the two sides in a conflict to set out terms to each other, and Montrose dispatched David Drummond, the Master of Madderty, under a flag of truce to tell Elcho that he was acting on the King's behalf, that he wished to avoid bloodshed, and in any event that there should be a truce so that the fighting would not take place on the Sabbath. Elcho's response was that it was the Lord's Day for doing the Lord's will, and he summarily apprehended the messenger, who for good measure was told that he would be hanged after the battle ('but God was more merciful,' reports Wishart, 'and saved this worthy young man, by ordering matters otherwise than they expected').

The conflict when it came was short and bloody. Elcho sent forward Lord Drummond to attack Montrose's centre, but the Covenanters were met with a volley of shot which made them break and turn. Seeing the opportunity, Montrose ordered the charge. The inexperienced local levies in Elcho's army, many of them shop boys and farm lads who had never been near a battlefield in their lives, were now faced with a shrieking horde of half-naked savages running at them full pelt waving swords, axes and clubs, and they did what any reasonable person would do in the circumstances. They dropped their weapons, turned and fled, rushing from the dreadful killing ground, all hopes of divine favour forgotten, each man forgetting his fellows and single-mindedly seeking his own immediate salvation from the forces of Hell pursuing him. Only Sir James Scott on the Covenanters' left made any sort of a stand, but even that was not to last long.

The broken Covenanter army was pursued all the way back to Perth, with Montrose's men killing and plundering as they went. In the rout perhaps 2,000 of Elcho's men fell, and it was said that 'men might have walked upon the dead corps to the town'.[5] Some were killed by the Royalists, while many simply expired from exhaustion, among them ten Perth burgesses who died from their exertions in fleeing the battlefield, rather than by any blow struck by the enemy. With nothing now to stop him, Montrose took control of Perth, fining the burgesses £50 sterling but preventing his exhilarated troops from harming the citizens. The ministers of Perth decreed that the occupation by 'a company of the worst men in the earth' was divine judgement for the sins of the faithful. Such was the antipathy towards Montrose that the Minister of Tippermuir, Alexander Balneaves, was defrocked by the Presbytery of Perth for giving the Marquis a refreshing cup of cold water on what had been a warm September morning (his defiant, and not unreasonable, response to his fellow clerics was that there was not a man amongst them who would not have kissed Montrose's arse that day).

It was a feature of the battles won by Montrose and Alasdair MacDonald that the Covenanter troops they faced could not withstand the sudden charge of Irish and Highlanders against them, even when they had substantial numerical superiority. The weapons used by the infantry of the time are key to understanding why this could happen. Musketeers were armed only with their firearm, and given the range – and the time it took to reload – they would be lucky to fire off more than one shot against fast-advancing opponents. Once discharged, they had only the butts of their muskets to defend themselves with, and relied on pikemen for protection. The bulk of the infantry were armed with 12 or 15-foot long pikes, heavy and unwieldy, highly effective defensively in a mass, but virtually useless used singly. The strength of a foot formation therefore depended entirely on all its members holding their ground and supporting one another. It would not take many individuals to lose their nerve, turn, and run, for the integrity of the formation to be lost and those remaining to be left vulnerable, which would naturally encourage them to follow suit. A trickle of deserters would soon become a torrent until, like a dam bursting, the entire company would collapse.

At Tippermuir and elsewhere many more men died in the rout than on the battlefield itself. An enemy soldier, even unarmed, fleeing from a conflict was fair game. For combatants on both sides (but particularly so for the Highlanders and Irish) the prospect of plunder from defeated opponents was a major inducement to participation in war. The weapons, gear and clothes of the enemy were all of value (even underwear was worth collecting). It would be a fortunate member of a defeated army who would escape the battlefield naked and bleeding, but with his life intact. Montrose's victory was a great opportunity for his poorly clothed and ill-shod Irish soldiers to improve on their dress and equipment. More importantly, it gave many of them access to modern weapons for the first time.

Tippermuir was the first battle in what would become known as Montrose's 'Year of Miracles'. It caused shockwaves amongst the Covenanting leadership. They had not for a moment considered that there was any real threat of a successful Royalist uprising after Argyll had satisfactorily put down the Gordons earlier in the year. But there were still two Covenanting armies in Scotland to deal with Montrose, one of them being led by Argyll himself, and it would surely only be a matter of time before the rebels would be brought to heel.

As for Montrose, he had no wish to be trapped in Perth with a small force when Argyll was advancing from the west. He left Perth on 4 September heading north-east, and seven days later his adversary reached the city and occupied it in his place. Writing from Elswick by Newcastle, Leven urged the Committee of Estates to have Argyll 'to make sure the hills, and cutt off their retreat, and follow the enemie close, and carefully watch over all his motions, and fall on them before they acquire strength in their march northward; for that course may prove dangerous, and it is more easy to stop the spring in the beginning then afterward when it comes to be a flood.'[6] It was good advice, but it required a bolder commander than Argyll to follow it.

If Montrose had hoped that his victory would rally more men to his cause, then he was to be disappointed. As Charles Edward Stewart was to find out to his cost a century later, Highland clansmen did not favour long campaigns. Going to war was a short adventure which, if successful, would be rewarded with booty from the vanquished. The Highlander aimed to return home to his family as soon as he could, the better to enjoy his new-found wealth, before the next opportunity for glory and gain came his way. So far from adding to his numbers, Montrose saw many of his Highland troops drift away, though he was joined by some new recruits from Angus and the Mearns.

If morale in Montrose's camp was high following the victory at Tippermuir, it was rocked by a shocking incident which happened on the night of 6 September at the Kirk of Collace in Perthshire. Lord Kilpont, who had joined with Montrose's army just before the battle, was stabbed through the heart by his tentmate, James Stewart of Ardvoirlich, who then murdered two sentries and escaped. The reasons for Stewart's actions are unclear. It may have been that he was trying to persuade Kilpont to leave with him and join with the Covenanters, or perhaps more likely that he had told Kilpont of his intention to desert and then killed Kilpont in self-defence when he had tried to stop him. Stewart made his way to join with Argyll's forces in Perth, where in due course the Committee of Estates believed his story, granted him a pardon, and appointed him a Major in Argyll's army.

The loss of one of his principal supporters in such a fashion must have been a serious blow to Montrose. To add to his woes the Estates put a price of £20,000 Scots (£1,666 sterling) on his head, dead or alive, denouncing him as 'having casten off all feare of God, respect and loyaltie to his Native Kingdome, and regard of his Oath in the Covenant . . . now joined with ane Band of Irish Rebels, and Masse-Priests . . . and in a traitorous and perfidious maner, has Invaded this Kingdome, Tane possession of some of the royall Burrowes thereof, Apprehended, killed, and cruelly murdered diverse of his Majesties good Subjects; Presseth new Oaths, contrary to the Covenant, and for establishing of Poperie.'[7] The sum offered was substantial, and doubtless intended to induce those close to Montrose to betray him.

Montrose had by now heard that Balfour of Burleigh was waiting in Aberdeen with the third Covenanting army, and decided to go north to meet him. His small force had gained a little detachment of cavalry, comprising 45 horsemen under Lord Airlie, and 30 Gordons under Nathaniel Gordon of Ardlogie. But with two of Huntly's sons, Lord Gordon and his brother Lord Lewis Gordon, in Burleigh's army, few other members of that Royalist family were going to join Montrose. Burleigh was a weak and indecisive commander and Lord Gordon would have been a better choice as leader, but as his loyalties were in question given his family background, he was made to play second fiddle.

Montrose took his army across the Dee at Mills of Drum and turned east down the north bank of the river to approach Aberdeen. Burleigh's men had taken up a defensive position around the road which is now the Hardgate, making good use of the houses and garden walls which provided cover. He had at his disposal perhaps 2,000 infantry and 500 cavalry, the latter made up mainly from the Crichton, Forbes and Fraser families. Montrose drew up his men on Willowbank with the Irish regiments in the centre under his direct command, the left under

Colonel Hay with 30 horse and 100 musketeers, and the right under Sir William Rollo, again with a party of musketeers and Sir Thomas Ogilvie's horse.

In advance of the engagement Montrose sent a messenger, accompanied by a drummer boy, to the Magistrates of Aberdeen offering terms of surrender. He told them they should send away their women and children to safety, and that there would be no quarter given to those who remained. The Aberdonians misinterpreted his offer, perhaps deliberately, replying that they understood that there was to be no quarter except to old persons, women and children.

Montrose's dealings with Aberdeen in previous campaigns had left him with little love for its citizens. In wars on the Continent, cities which refused to surrender suffered brutality towards their civilians, but it had been many years since non-combatants in Scotland had faced such a threat. Perhaps Montrose was simply trying to turn up the heat on his opponents and force a surrender, or perhaps the precariousness of his situation combined with the murder of Lord Kilpont had rattled him. But worse was to come. The drummer boy who had accompanied Montrose's messenger was sent back to the Royalist army with a silver coin, but fell to a shot in the back from one of the Covenanting troops. This affront was enough to tip Montrose over the edge. In a rage he promised Alasdair MacDonald and his Irish troops that they would have the right to sack the city if the battle were won. Whatever difficulties Montrose had had with the citizens of Aberdeen in previous years, nothing could excuse this monstrous offence against his fellow countrymen. It was Friday 13 September – Black Friday, indeed, as it would turn out both for the folk of Aberdeen and for the romantic hero's reputation.

Battle commenced with Colonel Hay taking his men to attack the Covenanters holding the Justice Mills. They drove back the defenders towards Burleigh's main line. There was a counter-attack under Lord Forbes, but Hay was able to repulse it. Alasdair MacDonald then took the Royalist centre forward up the hill on the attack.

The brave Sir William Forbes of Craigievar led a cavalry attack against the Irish infantry, but showing great discipline MacDonald's soldiers opened ranks to let the horses through and then fired at them as they passed. The cavalry charge ended disastrously for the Covenanters, and was Burleigh's last throw of the dice in the battle. In a hard-fought encounter, Montrose's men were slowly gaining ground. Eventually the Covenanters' centre broke and, as at Tippermuir, many of the inexperienced levies simply turned and ran.

No quarter had been promised and none was given, with hundreds killed in the rout. The Royalists claimed that they lost merely seven men, while the Covenanting dead were put at between 500 and 1,000, the great majority of whom died in bloody battles in the streets of the city. They were killed without mercy and in cold blood, and many having been disarmed were then made to remove their clothes so these would not bear bloodstains from the final killing blow.

The rape of the city lasted three days. For the folk of Aberdeen, cowering in their homes, their doors smashed in by these filthy, hairy aliens, the men held at knifepoint having to watch while their goods were ransacked, their shrieking, sobbing wives and daughters violated before their eyes, or carried off as prizes, it was as if Hell had come to Earth. How many defenceless citizens died is unclear, but it was probably between 100 and 200. It was an appalling war crime carried out against innocent civilians, but sadly all too typical of civil wars then and now. Perhaps, in a perverse sense, brutality against fellow countrymen who have the misfortune to be associated with a rival cause – and can therefore be denounced as traitors – is more easily justified than criminal acts against the citizens of a foreign land who are just being loyal to their rulers.

The order for the sacking of Aberdeen by Montrose must forever be a stain on this hero's character. The Thirty Years' War in Europe had seen many brutalities against civilians, and in England both sides had been guilty of similar abuses (the Royalist sack of Bolton that same year being just one example), but this was the first – and worst – such atrocity in Scotland. The irony was that Aberdeen had always been a city with sympathy for the Royalists rather than a hotbed of the Covenanters. But whatever judgement history would make, Montrose's actions had a more immediate effect. News of what had occurred, doubtless embellished by Covenanting propagandists, enraged Lowland Scotland and made it harder yet to win converts to King Charles' cause.

With Argyll approaching from the south, Montrose could not afford to dally in Aberdeen no matter what the attractions were for his unrestrained men. On 16 September he moved to Kintore on Donside, and three days later Argyll occupied the ravaged city. The Covenanting General had a large force with him consisting not just of Campbells but also of experienced regular troops under the command of the Earl of Lothian. He may have had up to 4,000 infantry and 1,000 cavalry. With a smaller force, and facing experienced troops unlike the raw levies it had been his fortune to encounter so far, Montrose decided not to seek further battle at this point but rather to use the relative speed of his army to put space between himself and his pursuers. Although he hoped that his two successes would draw more Royalist sympathisers to his banner, he needed time to build up his forces before he was ready for another pitched battle, particularly against as strong a force as Argyll's.

Montrose moved east hoping to raise the Gordons, but found little sympathy. The Marquis of Huntly had not forgiven Montrose for his treatment years before, and without his support the

Gordons were not to come out *en masse* to join the Royalist army. Montrose headed for Speyside with Argyll in plodding pursuit. He got as far as Badenoch where Alasdair MacDonald decided it was time to take his forces to the west to support their comrades in Ardnamurchan and try and raise more men. Montrose, left with perhaps just 500 troops, took ill (it may have been exhaustion). He recovered after several days, but not before rumours of his demise had already caused celebrations amongst the Covenanters.

Throughout October, Montrose with a small force crossed through the Highlands at the centre of Scotland, from Badenoch to Atholl, to Angus, to Deeside, and back to Donside, always with Argyll, with a much larger force, following slowly behind. 25 October found him at Fyvie in Aberdeenshire thinking that Argyll was still far away, when in fact the Covenanting army was almost upon him. At Fyvie, for the first and only time, Montrose and Argyll met in battle head-to-head. Argyll had the much larger army and the element of surprise. Montrose was ill-prepared for a fight and had so little ammunition his men had to melt down the pewter they found in Fyvie Castle to make bullets (one Irishman was reported as saying on firing his pistol at the enemy, 'There goes another traitor's face spoilt with a pewter-pot').

The stout castle was an obvious defensive point, but Montrose was sensible enough to realise that once inside its walls he and his forces would be trapped, and all Argyll would have to do would be to sit and starve him out. Instead he picked his ground with the River Ythan protecting the Royalist right and some woodland on their left. He drew up his men on the top of a hillside, the slope below with ditches and dykes offering some protection from frontal attack.

Argyll had an early boost when some of the Gordons from Strathbogie deserted his adversary's force. He ordered an attack from one regiment up the hill where they encountered the

Royalists and started to win ground. Montrose commanded a counter-attack led by Magnus O'Cahan, one of MacDonald's Irish lieutenants, which successfully drove the Covenanters back. Argyll then ordered Lothian's cavalry to charge. Montrose's men fell back, but it was a trap – they hoped to draw the Covenanters further on and attack them from behind. Unfortunately for Montrose the men from Atholl fired too soon, giving the game away. Realising the danger, Argyll's horse withdrew.

For a third time Argyll tried an attack, this time with both cavalry and infantry, but again Montrose was too well dug in. Despite superior numbers the Covenanters were getting nowhere. After two days, having made no progress, Argyll gave up. It had been no victory, but neither had he suffered defeats like those of Elcho or Burleigh. For all that Argyll's detractors claimed he had no ability as a soldier, of all the Covenanting Generals, Argyll was the only one, apart from David Leslie, to meet in battle with Montrose and not be crushed by him.

Montrose knew his own position was weak and withdrew his own forces after night fell, heading for Strathbogie. Argyll followed, cautiously. His aim was to keep Montrose in check and look for an opportunity to take his army by surprise and defeat it decisively. He also sought to undermine Montrose's command by offering free passage to any of his officers who wished to give up the campaign and go home, an offer which had enough appeal to attract at least one defection. Morale in Montrose's camp was low. It was now getting into winter, no time for military campaigning in inhospitable country. The Lowland officers in the Royalist army were a long way from home and must have been concerned about the fate of their families and properties. Although they had seen two marked successes over the Covenanters, they were really in no better place than they had been when Montrose had first raised the King's banner at Blair Atholl three months before.

Montrose wanted to invade the Lowlands to strike a blow at the heart of Covenanting country, but there was no appetite amongst his men to take such a small force onto territory which might favour a larger regular army against them. With no settled plan of action, key lieutenants such as Sir James Drummond, Colonel Hay and the Earl of Kinnoull left the army to make their way home. After so much early promise the Royalist rebellion seemed to be fizzling out.

Argyll had taken his army to Dunkeld, aiming to settle in for the winter. Scenting an opportunity, Montrose took his troops through the Drumochter Pass and made it as far as Blair Atholl, when word of his approach reached Argyll. The Campbell chief decided it would be too risky to face a conflict, particularly with the Covenanting cavalry having been previously dispatched to winter quarters, and instead withdrew to Perth which was strongly held. Argyll continued to Edinburgh accompanied by Lothian, and there both resigned their commissions, complaining that they had not had adequate support with men or money. Although not without talent as a soldier, Argyll's priority was the world of politics. He had no interest in playing an interminable cat-and-mouse game with Montrose which would keep him away from the corridors of power for months at a time, when there were others better qualified for military command.

Both commanders were formally thanked, although it was noted rather wickedly that the gratitude was the greater because so little blood had been shed. There was no great queue of volunteers to take up the vacant position of commander-in-chief, and with both Lothian and the Earl of Callander (who as Lord Almond had previously been Leven's second-in-command) declining the position, it was given to William Baillie who had served both in the Swedish army and under Leven in England.

Although thwarted in his plan of attacking Argyll, Montrose had a substantial consolation when at Blair Atholl he was reunited with Alasdair MacDonald, who had come with fresh recruits. Alasdair had been successful in raising 500 MacDonalds from Keppoch, Glen Garry, Glencoe, Glen Nevis, Clanranald and the Isles; and in addition there were MacLeans, Stewarts, Farquharsons and Camerons of Lochaber. Montrose had a new army, but a new problem. In the depth of a severe winter he had to find supplies for his troops, and he had to find a way of continuing the war without losing more momentum. With an assault on the Lowlands ruled out, there was one course of action open to him that would ensure the provisions he desperately needed and which would be enthusiastically endorsed by the gathered clansmen, and that was to invade the heart of Campbell country in Argyllshire. It was an idea of genius from Alasdair MacDonald, adopted by Montrose. For the hereditary enemies of Clan Campbell it was a delicious prospect, and for the Royalist cause, a strike at the territory of the leader of their opposition was all too tempting to refuse.

The Campbell lands in Argyllshire were well settled and prosperous. Under the patronage of *MacCailein Mor* the Campbells and their confederates had enjoyed peace, trade and civilisation, the long sea lochs giving easy access by ship to Lowland Scotland and further afield. In Inveraray there was a stoutly built town watched over by the castle of the clan chief. Argyllshire was deemed vulnerable only to invasion by sea, as where it linked with the rest of Scotland in the north and east, the way was blocked by high mountains and difficult passes which, all believed, made the territory impregnable in winter (the Campbell slogan 'It's a far cry to Loch Awe' summed up the sense of security enjoyed by the clan). The Marquis of Argyll himself had returned to Inveraray to await better campaign weather in the spring, and at home he felt entirely safe.

But he had reckoned without Montrose. The Royalist General left Blair Atholl on 11 December, taking his band of now around 3,000 men south and west through Breadalbane and Glen Dochart, along to Loch Awe, crossing difficult terrain in dreadful weather conditions. They slaughtered and plundered as they went. Any man they encountered bearing arms, or of an age capable of doing so, was killed. While the women and children were spared, every house was burned and all livestock or supplies stolen. For the Argyllshire residents, accustomed to years of settled peace and order, it was horrific.

Word had reached Argyll that Montrose's men were on their way, but he had no idea how close they were. When terrified shepherds and cowherds ran from the hills into the town of Inveraray to bring news that the MacDonalds were upon them, Argyll was both shocked and taken utterly by surprise. With no time to prepare a defence he boarded a boat and fled down Loch Fyne to his other house at Roseneath, and out of harm's way. The citizens of Inveraray evacuated, as many as they could, in boats across the loch to the relative safety of Cowal. Montrose entered the town without opposition. The capital of Campbell territory had fallen to their sworn enemies, and it was a day of humiliation for Clan Diarmid.

Local legend tells that when Montrose's Irish troops occupied Inveraray Castle they found amongst the staff a young Irish boy who had been employed to play the harp for Argyll's family. So furious were they that one of their countrymen would work for their sworn enemy that they murdered him and left his quartered body on what is now known as the Duke's Bed. Although the old castle was demolished and replaced by the current building in the eighteenth century, it is claimed that the boy's ghost became so attached to the bed that when it was moved into the new castle the spirit came with it, and today the poor lad can still be seen, and more often heard, playing his harp in different parts of the building. The story is a good one, but unlikely to be true; Gordon reports that Montrose did not in fact take the castle: 'because the general thought it not worth his paines to waire out a lingering seidge for gaineing of the castell, the toune and all the countray round about is consumed with fyre.'

For some six weeks from the middle of December 1644 until about the end of January 1645 the Royalist troops sacked Argyllshire, enriching themselves at their enemies' expense. In total nearly 900 Campbells were slaughtered. Infuriated, embarrassed and deeply frustrated, Argyll made his way to Dumbarton where he met Baillie, the new general of the Covenanters, and plotted his revenge. Montrose, who up until now had been more of an irritant to him than a serious threat, had stung *MacCailein Mor* much worse than he could ever have expected. James Graham and the MacDonalds would be made to pay for their affront to the reputation of Clan Campbell.

8

Montrose the Master

1645

The Committee of Estates was quick to respond to Montrose's latest success, meeting in Edinburgh on 7 January 1645 to pass an 'Act anent the putting of the kingdom in a posture of war for defence'. This regretted the advances made by the enemy, 'especially James Graham, sometime earl of Montrose, the Irish rebels and other degenerate and perfidious countrymen who have cruelly killed and murdered great numbers of the subjects, depopulated and wasted many parts of the country and are going on with full resolution to undo the whole nation and overthrow the liberties of kirk and kingdom so happily established by God's providence'. The response was to call for a general muster of arms, and 'if any fencible persons between 60 and 16 are not already provided with arms, it is hereby statute and ordained that they shall arm themselves sufficiently against the said muster day respectively under pain of £20 to be paid by each person who shall be found by the committee to lack a musket and sword who is able to buy the same, and 10 merks by each person able to buy a pike and lacking the same . . .'[1] The whole nation was being called on to face down the threat from Montrose, and there were consequences for those not prepared to play their part.

No-one could accuse Argyll of shirking his responsibilities. Smarting from the humiliation of having his home and clan lands despoiled by his great rival, he had lost no time in planning a retaliation. At Dumbarton he had met up with William

Baillie, the Covenanters' new General, whom he was determined would take his orders. Baillie was not so keen, and he reported later that, 'because I would not content to receave orders from the Marquess of Argyle . . . my Lord seemed to be displeased, and expressed himself so unto some, that if he lived, he should remember it; wherein his Lordship indeed hath superabundantly been alse good as his word.'[2] Argyll was not a man without a sense of his own importance, and he was used to getting his own way. He wanted to command personally the army which would take its revenge on Montrose, and the Estates agreed, ordering Baillie to provide him with 1,100 men, mainly new recruits from the Lowlands, to supplement the Campbell clansmen. Argyll's hopes of leading in the field were dashed when he suffered a fall from his horse and dislocated his arm, meaning that he could wield neither sword nor pistol. Accordingly he called back from Ireland his cousin, Sir Duncan Campbell of Auchinbreck, a doughty and experienced soldier who was outraged that his home and estate had been burned and plundered in his absence, and gave him the command. And so the pursuit of Montrose began.

On leaving Argyllshire, Montrose had entered the Great Glen heading northwards. He had ahead of him one Covenanting army under the Earl of Seaforth, presently stationed in Inverness. Baillie was with another army in Perth, while Argyll was advancing with his forces from the south. Realising the dangers of being caught in a pincer movement, Montrose decided that his best bet was to take on Seaforth and, if he could secure victory there, then worry about the rest thereafter. However precarious his position, James Graham was in his element; answerable to no-one, with an army of fierce warriors loyal to his every command, and fighting for a cause he passionately believed in. Not for him the word play and smoky rooms of politics, where Argyll would always be the master. Here, out in the field, sword in hand, he was having the time of his life.

By 29 January 1645 Montrose was camped at Kilcumin (now Fort Augustus), at the southern end of Loch Ness. Although, inevitably, some of the Highlanders who had joined him in the invasion of Argyllshire had returned home, he still had a force of around 1,500 men at his disposal. Montrose was concentrating on the threat in front of him from Seaforth, and unaware that Argyll was fast on his heels, until Iain Lom MacDonald arrived with news that the Campbells were less than 30 miles away at Inverlochy, barely more than a day's march. Montrose ordered the remarkable mountain march which allowed him to take Argyll by surprise, and deliver another spectacular Royalist victory, on 2 February, Candlemas Day, on the shores of Loch Linnhe. This battle at Inverlochy was a disaster for the Covenanters, who lost between 1,500 and 1,700 men, the great majority of them Campbells. On the Royalist side it was claimed that as few as four men died. The clash saw not just the defeat of a Covenanting army but the blackest day in the history of Clan Campbell, with the Clan Chief, *MacCailein Mor,* watching it all from his galley, powerless to intervene.

Argyll's conduct at Inverlochy in putting himself out of harm's way while his army faced Montrose, led to him being accused, at the time and since, of cowardice. But there were sound reasons for him to be kept away from the battle. He was personally unable to fight and would have been of little use on the battlefield. He had appointed as commander in his place someone who had more experience and was probably more capable. And, if Argyll had fallen, it would have been a huge blow not just to his clan, but to the whole Covenanting cause behind which he was the principal driving force. His decision was in fact made for him by his comrades, who according to contemporary reports forced him to retire to his galley rather than put himself at risk. It was the prudent, and correct, course of action for the leading Covenanter politician. And yet Argyll was more than just a politician, he was also *MacCailein Mor*, Chief of Clan Campbell. It can have done nothing for the morale of his clansmen on the eve of battle to have seen their Chief take himself out of danger and leave them to fight for his cause. At the battle of Inverlochy, in the conflict between Argyll's roles as Lowland politician and Highland chief, it was the former which won out. It is hard to imagine in a similar circumstance Montrose taking the same decision.

In triumph Montrose penned a letter to the King recounting his success, and stating his optimism at the prospects for Royalist victory in Scotland. 'I doubt not before the end of this summer I shall be able to come to your Majesty's assistance with a brave army, which, backed with the justice of your Majesty's cause, will make the rebels in England, as well as in Scotland, feel the just rewards of rebellion',[3] he wrote, rather carried away with enthusiasm. But Montrose had reasons to be cheerful. In his year of miracles he had already defeated three Covenanting armies, he had routed his rival's forces, and increasingly it looked like there was none able to stand against him.

In contrast Argyll must have been devastated by the loss at Inverlochy, not just of his army but of so many of his kinsmen and clansmen. The damage was both personal and political; his own reputation was tarnished, his personal courage derided by Royalists. He made it back to Edinburgh, meeting with the Estates on 12 February, 'having his left arm tied up in a scarf, as if he had been at bones-breaking',[4] to give an account of what had occurred. Argyll was careful not to give full details of the defeat; perhaps he was trying to put as good a gloss as he could on events, or perhaps he could not bring himself to narrate the full horror of what he had witnessed. The Estates were greatly concerned at the news, and confused as to why the Almighty had so punished His most faithful servant (Robert Baillie wrote: 'Behold the indignation of the Lord! . . . This disaster did extreamlie amaze us'),[5] but nonetheless made the point of publicly thanking Argyll in glowing terms: 'the Lord Marquis hath painfully, wisely and diligently, behaved himself in that charge, and, therefore, that his courage therein deserveth public thanks and approbation, and that himself should be entreated and encouraged to continue in the service with that forwardness of affection which in all his actions he hath ever constantly witnessed to religion and the Kingdom'.

The Estates could do little more against Montrose at this stage than make a gesture, and so they declared him a traitor to the realm along with twelve other Royalists, including MacDonald and Airlie, ordering the forfeiture of all their property and honours. Montrose could from now on only be referred to simply as James Graham. He had already been excommunicated by the Kirk, but a move was made by the General Assembly to execute those of his allies who were being held in prison. A delegation of five Ministers was sent with this message to the Estates, whose members wisely 'commended as an Act of great Zeal and Piety in the Assembly; yet deferred the Performance some time, until Montross should be brought lower; lest otherwise if through Misfortune any of their Friends happened to fall into his Hands, he might repay it.'[7]

With the Lowlands in ferment, the best move for Montrose might have been to have capitalised on the situation and headed straight for Edinburgh. Robert Baillie summed up the Covenanters' fears when he wrote: 'I verily think had Montrose come presently from that battle, he would have had no great opposition . . . scarce till he had come to Edinburgh.'[8] But the King's General's forces were still too weak for an all-out assault on the Covenanters' heartlands. He decided instead to head again for the North-east, where he had reason to believe that his recent successes might finally persuade the Gordons and their allies to join his forces. Seaforth was now nowhere to be seen, so Montrose made his way without challenge as far as Elgin, where 300 men under the Laird of Grant first joined him, and then, wonderfully, Lord Gordon and his younger brother Lord Lewis, who had now at last lost faith with the Covenanters. Crucially they brought with them 200 Gordon cavalry. Even Seaforth himself came: never having been an enthusiastic Covenanter, he decided the time was now right to make his peace with the King's representative. With Clan Campbell having been crushed, the whole northern part of Scotland was falling into Montrose's hands.

Of the three armies which had so recently challenged him, one (Argyll's) had been destroyed, one (Seaforth's) had disintegrated, and there now remained only William Baillie's force at Perth to deal with. With more men coming to his aid, Montrose was ready to take the King's Standard against the Covenanters' new Commander-in-chief. He moved towards Aberdeen, but on the way suffered a personal tragedy when his eldest son and heir, the teenage Lord Graham, died of illness and exhaustion brought on from being at his father's side over the past months. In all his battles Montrose had lost few men, and it must have been a particularly dreadful blow to face the death of his own son.

But there was no time to mourn. The Royalist army reached Kintore, planning on this occasion to bypass Aberdeen, which the Covenanters had abandoned. However Nathaniel Gordon rather rashly took 80 mounted men on a raid into the city. News of this reached the ears of General Baillie's Captain of Cavalry, the professional soldier Sir John Hurry, who was a few miles to the south. Rushing northwards, Hurry ambushed Gordon's force, killing a number, amongst them Donald Farquharson of Strathavon, whose loss was keenly felt by Montrose. In addition Montrose's second son, the new Lord Graham, was captured by Hurry and taken as a hostage to the capital.

Montrose headed south through the Mearns and north Angus, skirmishing with Hurry on the way. Baillie's army, now with 3,000 men, was advancing from the south. These were no raw levies but experienced troops, some of whom had returned from the fighting in England or Ireland. The two armies eventually found themselves on opposite banks of the River Isla, at Couttie just outside Coupar Angus, but with neither having the inclination to force the river crossing, a stalemate developed. Montrose gallantly made Baillie an offer that if the Royalists could have the river crossing unimpeded they would happily fight on the south bank, or alternatively they would allow Baillie to cross to the north bank to fight there. Baillie, being well aware of the mettle of his opponent and being no fool himself (Wishart described him as 'an experienced and wary general'), sensibly responded that he would fight at his own pleasure and not to suit his adversary's convenience.

Aiming to make further progress towards central Scotland, Montrose headed west towards Dunkeld, looking to cross the Tay there and then turn south. Baillie retreated southwards towards Fife to protect the Lowlands. By the time he got to Dunkeld, Montrose found that some of his Highland troops, bored with the lack of challenge or more likely the absence of plunder, were already deserting. Even the Gordons were beginning to get itchy feet. To keep them occupied, Montrose led them in a daring raid east against the city of Dundee, whose small garrison was quickly overcome. The Irish and Highlanders then set about the more serious business of looting the town, but were so busy enjoying themselves courtesy of Dundee's citizens that they were almost caught in a trap. Baillie's army, with 3,000 infantry and 800 cavalry under Hurry, had not crossed over into Fife as had been believed, but were now no more than a mile away and advancing fast. With his men spread throughout the town and many asleep or drunk, some of his lieutenants even advised Montrose to save himself and abandon the troops to their fate. With a huge force of will he pulled his army back together and they escaped Dundee to the east by the skin of their teeth, with Hurry in fast pursuit.

As night fell, Montrose marched his men hard in the direction of Arbroath with the Covenanters' cavalry right behind. Baillie sent men to guard the hill passes to the west to block off any escape by the Royalists in that direction, and took his army towards Arbroath and the enemy. But under cover of darkness Montrose changed direction and headed inland, marching his exhausted men as far as Careston Castle, his father-in-law's home, where they could finally stop for breath. As soon as daybreak came Hurry's cavalry caught up with them, inflicting serious injury on the fleeing troops. Only the shelter of the hills of Glen Esk, territory where mounted men were at a disadvantage, saved the Royalist army from further losses. Notwithstanding the casualties, it was another remarkable example of leadership from Montrose to have driven his exhausted, half-drunk army so far in such a short space of time. He may on this occasion have escaped by the skin of his teeth from a larger pursuing force, but just as at Fyvie a failure of intelligence had very nearly led to disaster (the next time there would be a much higher price to pay). What the raid on Dundee also demonstrated was that Montrose, with his small and swift force, was capable of striking fast and hard at enemy targets, but that he was still incapable of holding territory which was won.

So anxious were the Covenanters for good news, particularly to reassure their allies amongst the English Parliamentarians, that they celebrated Montrose's expulsion from Dundee as a great victory. They had to protect the Lowlands from such incursions in the future, but they could not afford just to sit and do nothing while Montrose had the run of the Highlands and Aberdeenshire. So the Estates ordered a substantial strengthening of the army and divided the forces in two, with Baillie remaining at Perth and Hurry being sent northwards after Montrose.

Once again Montrose desperately needed new troops. Lord Gordon was sent back to Aberdeenshire to find more men, while Alasdair MacDonald went westwards. Montrose himself headed for Crieff in Perthshire, too close for comfort to Baillie, who caught up with him on 17 April. With too small a force to do battle, the Royalists retreated west towards Loch Earn, and from there made it to Balquhidder in the Trossachs, where they met up with Lord Aboyne, Lord Gordon's younger brother, who had come from Carlisle with 16 men. Baillie had taken his army to Atholl while Hurry was harrying the Gordon territories in Aberdeenshire. Montrose made his way across the Highlands back to the North-east, where on 30 April he found Lord Gordon, who was no doubt delighted to be reunited with his younger brother. The Gordons had perhaps 1,000 infantry and 200 cavalry, more than doubling the size of Montrose's forces. He now had enough to take on Hurry.

Hurry had had his own success in recruiting. Seaforth had changed sides once again, and his clan MacKenzie had rallied to the Covenanters' banner. With him came other clans from the eastern Highlands who had no love of the Gordons, among them the Frasers, Forbes and Roses. It was already a formidable force and Hurry had the promise of more men from the west. He retreated westwards before Montrose, drawing the Royalists in and waiting for his moment to strike. On 8 May Montrose had got as far as the village of Auldearn, between Nairn and Forres. Believing Hurry to be some way ahead of him, he camped for the night. Hurry had planned to catch the Royalists by surprise with a night attack along the sea shore, but it was pouring rain and a number of his men who were concerned that their powder might be damp fired off their muskets to clear them. 'They wer confident also that the waters, as they usuallie do, would carrie the sound from the land. But the thundering report of this vollie, contraire to ther expectation, was, by a suddain changeing of the wynd, carried throw the aire unto the eares of five or six scouts',[9] and the game was given away. So by the time dawn came, Montrose was ready for battle. He made the most of the resources at his disposal, putting Alasdair MacDonald and his men on the west of the village, and a few amongst the houses to give the appearance of greater numbers. He also gave Alasdair the King's Standard, hoping that Hurry would be fooled into thinking that was where Montrose himself was with the principal force. The balance of the army, including Lord Gordon's cavalry, was kept out of sight to the south.

Taken in by the ruse, Hurry made a bold attack on Mac-Donald's men, sending Lawers' experienced infantry forward. Backed by Seaforth's men they started to push the Irish back. The irrepressible MacDonald fought furiously: 'he was ever in the frount, and his strenth, his curage, and dexterittie let his enemies sie, even with terror, wonderfull feats of armes for his fellowes to imitate, his stronge arme cutting asunder whatsoever and whosoever did him resist',[10] but even he failed to check the Covenanters' advance. Realising that the Irish needed support, Montrose ordered the Gordons forward, with the words, 'MacDonald drives all before him. Is his clan to have all the honours this day? Are there to be no laurels for the House of Huntly?' The Gordon troopers charged into the Covenanters' flank, followed by the Royalist reserve infantry. The shock was enough to turn the battle. There was a bloody carnage of hand-to-hand fighting between the infantry on both sides, but slowly the Royalists gained the upper hand, and the Covenanting line broke. As many as 2,000 of the Covenanting army died either in battle or in the rout that followed, while the Royalists lost perhaps 200.

Auldearn was the hardest fought, and closest run, of all Montrose's victories. Hurry had put up a brave fight, and managed to escape with 100 of his cavalry. His men were tough and experienced. But they still could not match the military genius of Montrose on the battlefield, nor the fighting skill of his Irish and Highland troops. Was there anyone, the Covenanters must have been wondering, who could take on Montrose?

It fell to Baillie, still in command of the bulk of the Covenanters' army, to try to succeed where others had failed in bringing Montrose to heel. If Baillie had been left to his own devices he might have had a chance of success. But the Estates had been wooed by Lord Lindsay, the new Earl of Crawford, who had a high opinion of his own military abilities in comparison to both Baillie and Argyll. The Estates ordered Baillie to give Crawford-Lindsay between 1,000 and 1,200 of the former's experienced troops, in exchange for 400 of Crawford-Lindsay's untried levies. Once more politics was intervening in what should have been purely military decisions.

Throughout May and June the armies of Montrose and Baillie shadowboxed throughout Aberdeenshire, Moray and Badenoch, but not once coming to blows. Montrose suffered a major setback when Huntly recalled his followers from the Royalist army, motivated either by his personal enmity towards Montrose or possibly by a desire to protect his own territories from the Covenanters. With the loss of a large part of his cavalry Montrose was forced to abandon his original plan to strike at Crawford-Lindsay, now in Atholl, and instead decided to focus first on dealing with Baillie. He headquartered himself at Corgarth Castle in Strathdon, seeking to strengthen his army.

Baillie was being plagued with political interference by the Estates, and with unrest amongst his troops begged for permission to resign his command. 'I wes alltogether unwilling to ruine the forces committed to my charge in ways both against reason and common sence; and therefore my humble intreaty was, that I might be recalled, and some one imployed who would undertake more and perform better',[11] he later wrote. Permission was refused and the unwilling Baillie was forced to carry on, with his heart simply no longer in the fight. It was only a matter of time before the two armies would have to meet, and when word reached Baillie, who now had Argyll with him effectively as political commissar, that the redoubtable Alasdair MacDonald and a proportion of his Irish followers were absent elsewhere in search of new recruits, it was the spur he needed to attack. In pursuit of Montrose the Covenanting army finally met him at Alford on Donside on 2 July.

In numbers both armies were closely matched. Baillie had around 1,800 infantry, a mixture of veterans and new recruits ('listed from among the lowest class of people, and fought for pay, having little discipline, and far less honour to excite them'),[12] and around 300 cavalry under the Earl of Balcarres. Facing them, Montrose had around 2,000 foot soldiers and 200 cavalry, the latter led by Lord Gordon and Lord Aboyne.

Battle commenced with a cavalry charge by Lord Gordon on Balcarres' horse, Gordon's fury having been got up by the sight of herds of Aberdeenshire cattle looted from his father's lands penned in an enclosure behind Baillie's ranks. The fighting was fierce: 'at close quarters, fighting hand to hand so stubbornly that none could advance a foot or a nail's breadth but over the body of his foe, while retreat was impossible, so great was the crush of men pressing on behind.'[13] Balcarres was a tough solder, 'one of the bravest men of the kingdome,' wrote Gordon of Ruthven, 'he relyed them diverse tymes in squadrones, standing to it with such hardy and valorous resolutione, as had well neere wronge backe the victorie out of the Royalists' hands.'[14] The melée was indecisive until a detachment of Montrose's infantry went in under Nathaniel Gordon with their swords and dirks to stab and hamstring Balcarres' horses. This was enough to swing the balance in Gordon's favour. The survivors of the Covenanter cavalry fled the field, leaving the flank of their infantry exposed.

Baillie's foot soldiers fought hard, but they were being attacked on three fronts, and were eventually overwhelmed: 'being thus deserted by their horse, continued, notwithstanding, to fight for some time most desperately, and refusing quarter, were almost every one killed on the spot.'[15] The familiar scenario of a bloody rout ensued, with the remaining Covenanters being cut down by pursuing Royalists as they tried to make their escape. Perhaps 1,000 of Baillie's men fell, the General himself managing to escape along with Balcarres and Argyll, the last having had two horses fall under him. Casualties on the Royalist side were much lower, but Montrose suffered the grievous loss of Lord Gordon, his Captain of Cavalry, who was shot while trying to apprehend Baillie. This was not just a personal and military blow to Montrose but a political one; for without Lord Gordon, Montrose's support from that great Aberdeenshire family would be much weakened.

Baillie may have escaped with his life, but he still had overall command of the Covenanters' army. He desperately tried again and again to resign, but the Estates would have none of it. They ordered the raising of 8,800 infantry and 485 cavalry to form a new army to defend the Lowlands against the all-conquering Montrose; passing another Act deploring how the peace of the kingdom had 'been troubled these months bygone by a base crew of Irish rebels joined with unnatural countrymen, who have had the greater success in their traitorous attempts that they have never been pursued with the strength that was necessary, only some weakened regiments and country people raised in the shires being employed against them without the assistance or countenance of the nobility, gentry and strength of these bounds from which they were raised.'[16] You can sense the frustration of the Estates that not enough of the upper and middle classes were pulling their weight in the war against Montrose, and the urgency with which that situation had to change.

The Royalists in Scotland may have been having great success on the battlefield, but south of the Border it was a different story. On 14 June the Royalist army had been crushed by the Parliamentary forces under Sir Thomas Fairfax at Naseby. The contrast with the situation in Scotland could not have been more stark. 'Our spirits are deeplie wounded within us, and broken, by what we hear from tyme to tyme from dear Scotland,' wrote Robert Baillie from London. 'We are amazed that it should be the pleasure of our God to make us fall thus the fifth time, before a company of the worst men in the earth . . . That the Lord should cast them doune here, and sett them up there, it is one of the deeps of divyne wisdome, which we will adore.'[17] Whatever was God's plan, if the King was to have any chance of success in this war then he urgently needed his Scottish general to complete his series of victories and provide assistance to the army in England. Montrose still had work do. His army was strengthened by the return of Alasdair MacDonald who brought with him 1,400 men. With the addition of more Gordon recruits raised by Lord Aboyne, this gave a total force of around 4,500 infantry and 500 cavalry, which marched south to assail the Covenanting Lowlands.

The reluctant General Baillie now had at his command yet another new army of 6,000 infantry and 800 cavalry, but again many were raw levies who had never seen action before. And, as before, Baillie was subject to endless political interference which hampered his capacity for action. So exasperated did Baillie become that he informed the Estates that he considered himself no longer to be in command and that he would simply do what the politicians ordered. It was a recipe for disaster.

Baillie caught up with Montrose at Kilsyth, in the lee of the Campsie Hills, on Friday 15 August. Montrose's army were camped in a hollow of land beside the Colzium burn a little way to the north-east of the town. Baillie drew up his troops in a strong position on higher ground above. If there were to be a battle, the Covenanter's general had chosen the right territory on which to fight. Unfortunately for Baillie, politics again intervened. 'He was obliged to yield to the importunity and authority of the Earl of Lindsay [Crawford-Lindsay], and the other noblemen in the army [including Argyll], who compelled him to draw up his men, and prepare for battle much against his inclination.'[18] Argyll and his colleagues were determined that Montrose would at last be crushed by their much larger force, and were concerned that the way had been left open for the Royalists to escape northwards into the hills. So Baillie was instructed to order his men to move to the right to block off the potential route of retreat and outflank the enemy.

There were sound military reasons for this move in that it would provide the Covenanters with better ground over which to advance and engage with the Royalists, and properly executed it could have been a safe manoeuvre. But it exposed a weakness which Montrose was quick to exploit. With his men in a poor position and with inferior numbers he could scarcely believe his luck when he saw his opponents moving position and presenting their flanks to him. Montrose's Highlanders attacked up the hill, breaking the Covenanters' line in two. The Royalist cavalry attacked Balcarres' horse, driving them from the field. Baillie's Lowland troops could not withstand a fresh Highland charge, and the Covenanting lines broke and ran.

The losses amongst the Covenanter infantry were horrendous – out of 6,000 only a few hundred escaped with their lives. The mounted nobility made their escapes as best they could; Argyll rode 20 miles as fast as his horse could carry him to South Queensferry, reportedly never once looking over his shoulder. There he was able to find a boat to take him to Berwick-on-Tweed and the safety of the Covenanters' army in England. It was the third occasion on which the Covenanters' leader had escaped Montrose by sea. The black galley on the Campbell family coat of arms was proving to be a lucky talisman.

Montrose had not just won another great victory, he had now defeated no fewer than six of the Covenanters' armies in a mere twelve months. There was now no longer a substantial force in the field able to defy him. With the Covenanting leaders all fled the country or gone to ground, he had the mastery of the entire realm. His objective all along had been to force the Covenanters' army in England fighting against King Charles to return to Scotland, or perhaps even to take an army into England to join with the Royalists there, and surely one or both of these would now happen. But while Montrose and his men celebrated, events down south meant that it was perhaps already too late to turn the tide back in the King's favour.

9

The Tide Turns Again

1645-46

John Buchan describes Montrose's Irish troops as: 'cheerful ruf-fians, who loved fighting for fighting's sake, and cracked jokes in the thick of battle,'[1] but their portrayal as loveable rogues would have been anathema to the God-fearing Presbyterian Lowland Scots, who regarded the Irish as subhuman Papist savages. Stories of the atrocities committed by his men against the citizens of Aberdeen, no doubt exaggerated in the telling, made it impossible for Montrose to win over the affections of the common people. While a number of the nobility were now prepared to throw in their lot with him, amongst the burgesses and ordinary folk who were enthusiastic for the Covenant there was little support for his cause. It was not just Montrose personally who was adversely affected in this way – such sympathies that there may once have been for the King had been reduced by the manner in which the campaign on his behalf had been prosecuted. Having won six spectacular victories in an astonishingly short space of time Montrose might now be the military master of all Scotland, but even with arch-enemy Argyll fled to England, his political position was still weak.

Montrose also faced another familiar problem. The Highland-ers in his army, seeing the campaign at an end, started to drift back to their homes. A factor in their decision was an outbreak of bubonic plague which was sweeping across Lowland towns. Montrose had taken his army to Glasgow where, despite strict commands against looting, some of his Highland followers had been unable to resist the temptation. In an effort to restore discipline Montrose had a number of the worst offenders hanged. Winning the peace was proving harder than winning the war had been.

The logical next step for Montrose was to occupy the capital and establish Royalist government in Scotland. But plague was rife in the city, and there were rumours of 200 deaths a day. So instead Nathaniel Gordon and the Master of Napier (Montrose's nephew) were sent to meet with Edinburgh's magistrates at a safe distance away, where the release of Royalist prisoners from the Tolbooth was negotiated. Sadly these did not include Montrose's heir Lord Graham, who was held in Edinburgh Castle, and who bravely declined to be exchanged on the grounds that his father would be better served with another more useful soldier released.

On 1 September 1645 Montrose was camped with his army at Bothwell in Lanarkshire when a letter arrived from King Charles appointing him Lieutenant-Governor and Captain-General of Scotland. The King requested him to support the Earls of Home, Roxburgh and Traquair, and come south with all speed to assist the Royal army in England. Charles, whose position was now perilous after his comprehensive defeat by Parliament at Naseby, was desperate for Montrose's aid, clutching at news of his victories like a falling man grasping for a branch. When the King should have been negotiating peace terms with his English enemies, he hung on to the belief that his Scottish general would be his salvation. 'It seems Montrose shall be fatal to the King,' wrote Robert Baillie from London. 'His victories hitherto hes been powerfull snares to his hard heart: a little more continuance in this disposition is lyke to undoe him.'[2]

Before crossing the Border to come to the aid of his Sovereign, Montrose wanted to put the government of Scotland on a proper footing, and summoned a Parliament to be held in Glasgow on 20 October, 'for settling religion and peace, and freeing the oppressed subjects of those insupportable burdens they have groaned under this time bygone.' But he continued to have problems on the military front. The redoubtable Alasdair MacDonald, newly knighted by Montrose as the King's representative, took his leave with half his forces, heading for Argyllshire to continue the war against the Campbells. It was the last Montrose was to see of his brilliant lieutenant, who would die in battle two years later at Knocknanuss in Ireland, still a young man. The loss of Alasdair was more significant than Montrose could then have imagined – with MacDonald at his side, he had never lost a battle; without him, he would never again win one. At least Magnus O'Cahan stayed with Montrose with 500 of the Irish, accompanied by their women and children as camp followers.

For Argyll, holed up in Berwick with other members of the Estates, it must have been galling to see Montrose claiming the mastery of Scotland. Many years later, at his trial for treason, Argyll would claim he had been in contact with his great rival at this time and that '. . . a treaty past betwixt us'.[3] It is not beyond the realms of possibility that the ever-pragmatic master politician Argyll would have reached out to an enemy who now found himself in a position of such strength, but with no other historical evidence of such an accord the matter must remain a mystery. Whether or not there were any private dealings with Montrose, the Covenanters decided that it was time for the counter-strike against him. This came in the form of David Leslie, the ablest by far of the Covenanters' generals, and one who had proven himself in the Civil War in England. When the disturbing news from Scotland reached Leslie's men at Hereford, they insisted on returning north to deal with Montrose. So, with 4,000 cavalry and around 800 infantry, Leslie made it to Berwick to meet the Estates. This time, however, it was made clear that military decisions were to be left to the soldier.

Montrose was not far away. He had arrived in the Border area, but had been disappointed not to have been joined by more recruits on the way. The Border Earls of Home, Roxburgh and Traquair who had promised support to the King were nowhere to be seen (Royalists claimed that they were secretly in concert with the Covenanters, and had been leading Montrose on in order to deliver him to the enemy). On 12 September the Royalists camped at Philiphaugh, beside Selkirk, on the banks of the River Ettrick (now the town's rugby ground). It was a secure enough position and Montrose thought they had no need to worry, for his intelligence was that Leslie was still a long way off. But the day before, Leslie, who had got as far as Gladsmuir in East Lothian, had received information (possibly from Traquair, playing a double game) as to Montrose's whereabouts and strength. Unlike his predecessors as Covenanting generals, he was to show no hesitation in taking the initiative. He marched his men hard through the hills to the south, and the next night found himself within three miles of his quarry, who was still oblivious as to his presence.

Montrose spent the night of the 12th in a room in the West Port of Selkirk, staying up late writing letters to the King. Charles had written to him three days before from Ragland Castle, the Marquis of Worcester's seat, assuring Montrose of the importance of his victories. 'How much I esteem those real, generous, indeed useful obligations (and without which, in all probability, before this time, I had not been capable to have acknowledged any) you have put upon me.'[4] According to local tradition Montrose's Selkirk landlady – clearly not a political sympathiser – boiled a sheep's head, stating that if it had been her guest's she would have made sure that she held the lid down!

It was a misty morning on the 13th, and the Royalist army of around 1,000 cavalry and 500 infantry were at their breakfast when they realised that they were under attack. It was a Captain

Blackadder who brought the shocking news to Montrose in his lodgings, and by the time he made it back to Philiphaugh to rejoin his army, the King's Captain-General found battle already well underway, and his own forces in a state of confusion. The Royalists had a strong position partly protected by the River Ettrick on one side, but they were facing overwhelming odds and an enemy that not only had the advantage of surprise, but which was led by a more resolute captain than any they had encountered thus far. Montrose personally led a desperate mounted counter-attack, but with the disparity in numbers had no chance of success. O'Cahan's Irish fought like demons, but were driven back to make a final stand at Philiphaugh Farm, where, with barely 100 left alive, they eventually surrendered when Colonel Stewart, the Adjutant General, was promised quarter.

If the Irish soldiery who had wreaked havoc throughout Scotland for the last year, committing hideous atrocities against innocent civilians, had expected that they would be shown greater leniency than they themselves had demonstrated, then they were soon to be disappointed. Leslie, encouraged by the Covenanting clergy supporting his army, interpreted the offer of quarter for which Stewart's surrender was exchanged as applying only to the officers. Stewart, Laghtnan and O'Cahan were therefore spared, the first later escaping while the other two were afterwards taken to Edinburgh and hanged. For the rank and file there was not to be even a temporary reprieve. They were taken to Newark Castle and to the last man shot without ceremony. Worst of all, 300 of the Irish women and children camp followers were also killed. In order not to waste expensive ammunition, Leslie's troops drowned them in the river, like unwanted kittens in a bathtub, by holding their heads at the points of pikes under the water. They were, after all, Irish Papists, and in the eyes of the Covenanters barely human.

Gordon of Ruthven lamented 'such savage and inhumane crueltie, as nether Turke nor Scithean was ever hard to have done the lyke'.[5] But there was, sadly, nothing novel in this atrocity. The Royalist camp followers had been treated in similar fashion after the battle of Naseby by Cromwell's troops, and the Royalists themselves had of course committed terrible barbarities at Aberdeen exactly a year to the day before. Argyll was a spectator to all of this. Whether he approved personally can only be a matter of speculation, but he would no doubt have recalled the sacking of Inveraray and the harrying of his Campbell territories.

Despite his valiant efforts on the battlefield, Montrose had had no chance against overwhelming odds. Typically, he had been determined to fight to the last: 'he thought of nothing else than to sell his life as dear as he could: and having rallied about thirty of the scattered horse, resolves to fight to the last, rather than fall alive into the hands of the enemy.' His colleagues, among them the Marquis of Douglas and Sir John Dalziel, pleaded with him to save himself, 'seeing that in him alone, under God, all their hopes were centred'. At last Montrose was persuaded, and 'cut his way through the midst of the enemy, who were now more intent in plundering the baggage than pursuit,'[6] making his escape with around 30 others west into the hills. His army was annihilated and there was little prospect in the near future of him raising another. In just a few hours all his great victories had been cancelled out. As he headed for the safety of the Perthshire hills, he may have hoped that the King's cause in Scotland would still have a future, but his chances of ever winning back the realm for Charles must have seemed further away than ever. It was to be a brutally disappointing end to a glorious campaign.

After his string of successes the Royalist Captain-General had been guilty of hubristic over-confidence. Montrose had a strong self-belief and an equally powerful sense of destiny. But he made the fatal error of underestimating his opponent, assuming that

Leslie was no better than the other generals he had faced. Worse, he had failed to learn the lesson from Fyvie and Dundee that he needed information on the enemy's whereabouts. Once again his intelligence had failed, and this time the fates were not so forgiving. Perhaps he was not so great a soldier as he believed himself to be.

In total at least 10,000 were killed directly during Montrose's war, and many more died of disease or starvation as a result of the economic disruption caused. Scotland paid a high price for a vainglorious adventure which ultimately would achieve nothing for the King in whose name it had been made. Indeed it could well be argued that, far from having strengthened the King's position, all Montrose succeeded in doing was substantially weakening it. Montrose's objective had always been to create a diversion in Scotland which would be sufficient to disengage the Scots from their involvement with the Parliamentarians in the English Civil War, or even to secure Scotland for Charles and use it as a base to invade England on his behalf. But by the autumn of 1645 it was arguably already too late for either of these aims to make a difference even if they were to be achieved, such was the strength of the Parliamentary forces.

Worse than that, Montrose's campaign may actually have been counter-productive. Until the point where he raised his standard, Scottish influence with the English Parliamentarians had been substantial. The Covenanters were moderates compared to many of the Parliamentarians; the Scots were monarchists, supporting the retention of a King whose powers would be constrained by Parliament. The Covenanters' main allies within Parliament were the 'Peace Party' (dominated by English Presbyterians) while there was a growing mood amongst the rival and more hard-line 'War Party' (consisting mainly of Independents) that government would be better without a King at all. Amongst the Independents there was little love for their

Scots brethren who were regarded as unwelcome intruders in a conflict which Parliament was now quite capable of winning without their help. The ambitious Cromwell had been quick to claim credit for the earlier victory at Marsden Moor, to the annoyance of the Scots (Baillie observed that it seemed 'that Cromwell alone, with his unspeakably valorous regiments, had done all that service').[7] Such was the hostility towards the Covenanters that it was even claimed that some leaders in the War Party had celebrated Montrose's victory at Kilsyth.

The weakening of the Scots' position brought about as a direct consequence of Montrose's victories simply meant that the Peace Party within the Parliamentarians lost vital allies, and their power was diminished. Had the Scots maintained their strong influence, then even an ultimate Royalist defeat in England might well have led to the establishment of a constitutional monarchy as preferred by the Peace Party. It is one of the great ironies of history that had the great Royalist Montrose never taken up a sword, Charles might still have retained his crown. Far from restoring the King to his throne with all its powers, as he had hoped, Montrose's campaign actually contributed to the removal of his royal head from its shoulders.

Argyll celebrated the victory at Philiphaugh as God's work: 'the Lord hath this day . . . appeared gloriously for his people',[8] he wrote. In the year of defeats that he suffered at Montrose's hands there is no indication that he once lost faith in the rightness of his cause or that he doubted God's purpose for him. But any satisfaction Argyll felt at Montrose's defeat must have been tempered by the knowledge that his rival's adventure had cost him dear. The Royalist army had wreaked devastation on the Campbell lands in the West Highlands, driving their Chief almost to the point of bankruptcy. There was also a political price to pay. Argyll's reputation never recovered from his humiliation at Montrose's hands at Inverlochy and Kilsyth, with the result that even after Philiphaugh he struggled to recover the national leadership role he had once held. Montrose may have turned out a failure, but in failing he helped wreck his rival's career.

With the Royalists defeated, Argyll and his allies now had to restore Scotland's Covenanter government. Edinburgh was still ravaged by the plague, so the Estates met in Glasgow on 20 October. They had to deal with the Royalist prisoners apprehended after the battle, namely Lord Ogilvie, Sir William Rollo and Nathaniel Gordon. The ministers pressed for their execution, and despite reservations on the part of the lay members of the Estates, all were marked for the Maiden. Johnston of Warriston argued that in not dealing severely enough with their enemies in the past the Covenanters had, like the Israelites of old, provoked God's wrath against them. Cutting off the heads of one's enemies was therefore doing the Lord's work, and would ensure future blessings.

Among those condemned to die was Lord Ogilvie, who was being held in St Andrews Castle. On the eve of his execution he made a daring escape, much to Argyll's annoyance. He was visited in his cell by his wife, mother and sister, and he and his sister exchanged clothes. She remained behind while he left in disguise with his mother and wife, got past the guards undetected, and went away free. The rest of the prisoners were not so fortunate. The Maiden was set up at the Cross in St Andrews on 20 January 1646 and went about her grim business with Presbyterian efficiency. Montrose's brave and loyal captain of cavalry, Nathaniel Gordon, was among her victims, dying having repented of his sins, and having been as a consequence readmitted to membership of the Kirk.

In between dealing with the Royalist rebels, the Covenanters were debating amongst themselves their next course of action. Montrose was back in the Highlands trying to raise more men and continuing to try to convince Huntly to join with him.

While his forces were still weak, he nonetheless presented a threat. Despite his crushing defeat at Philiphaugh he had lost little of his self-belief or his enthusiasm for the King's cause, and he was keen to resume his campaign as soon as he could gather a new army. Charles continued to encourage him, writing from Newark on 3 November: 'As it hath been none of my least afflictions, nor misfortunes, that you have had hitherto no assistance from me, so I conjure you to believe that nothing but impossibility hath been the cause of it,' going on to praise Montrose's 'eminent fidelity and generosity you have showed in my service: And be assured that your less prosperous fortune is so far from lessening my estimation of you, that it will rather cause my affection to kythe [show] the cleerlier to you; for, by the grace of God, no hardness of condition shall ever make me shake in my friendship towards you.'[9]

On the other side there was amongst many of the Covenanters a weariness of war, and a growing body of moderate opinion willing to agree terms with the King. This was resisted by Argyll and his more radical colleagues, who thought that too much had been sacrificed already, and wanted no compromise. What they did agree on was that there was a need to both contain Montrose and reinforce the army in England, and a new levy of 10,000 men was ordered.

It was decided to recall the Scots from Ireland to assist, and Argyll himself was sent to bring them back. It is curious that a politician normally so engaged in matters of State would want to absent himself from the vital discussions that were taking place amongst the Estates. Feelers were already being put out towards the King in relation to a possible settlement, and it may be that Argyll welcomed the opportunity to distance himself from these. It was entirely in character for him to want to wait and see how a potentially tricky situation would develop, before he took a firm stance on one side of the argument or the other.

There was another reason for Argyll to be absent, not related to his innate political caution. His own Argyllshire territories were still in a desperate state, under attack from the MacDonalds and Irish, and he needed the Scots troops across the water to assist him. En route to Ireland, Argyll met near Stirling about 1,200 of his own Campbell clansmen who had been forced from his territories by Sir Alasdair MacDonald and had tried to survive by looting Royalist territory in West Perthshire. They had suffered a serious defeat at Callander and were now in a destitute state. Without any resources himself to help – with Argyll's own lands paying no rents, and huge costs having been incurred in campaigning, he was heavily in debt – all he could do was take them to Renfrewshire to try to find new Royalist territories to plunder.

Argyll had not long arrived in Ireland when he was urgently recalled by the news from Scotland. King Charles had left Oxford on 27 April, and on 5 May had arrived at Newark, where the Scots army under David Leslie was besieging the Royalist garrison. The King surrendered himself to Leslie, and ordered the defence of the town at an end. The Scots withdrew with Charles to Newcastle. The Civil War in England was over, and once more the world had changed.

It had been apparent to Charles for some time that winning the war against the Parliamentary forces facing him was now impossible. He had had high hopes for Montrose's campaign and was in despair when he heard of the defeat at Philiphaugh. He could not stay in Oxford with Parliament's New Model Army pressing him hard. Behind the scenes the French diplomat Jean de Montereul had been acting as a go-between with various Scottish nobles, and Charles had good reason to believe that he could get the Scots on his side if he was prepared to make a number of concessions, including the establishment of Presbyterian government in England. Meantime relations between the Scots and the English Parliamentarians continued to deteriorate, with the War Party in Parliament, dominated by Independents who had no love for Presbyterianism, increasingly gaining the upper hand (Fairfax's Parliamentary troops were reported to have shouted the slogan 'No king, no Scot, no Presbyteriall government!').[10]

There were real fears that the Parliamentarians would refuse to stick by the terms of the Solemn League and Covenant. If the Scots still wanted to protect Presbyterianism by establishing it in England as well as Scotland, then it seemed that it was the King, not Parliament, who was now the better vehicle for trying to achieve this. Charles' objective, meanwhile, was no longer military victory but to negotiate a settlement with Parliament on the best terms that could be achieved, and having the Scots as his allies in this concern would be a major advantage.

Charles kept his most loyal Scottish follower abreast of his intentions. He wrote to Montrose on 18 April, encouraging him to join forces with his enemies, if he could be sure that they would now be on the King's side: 'desiring you, if you shall find by . . . de Montereul that my Scots army have really declared for me, and that you be satisfied by him that there is by them an amnestia of all that hath been done by you and those who have adhered to me . . . then you will take them by the hand, and use all possible diligence to unite your forces with theirs for the advancement of my service, as if I were there in person, and I doubt not but you, being joined, will be able to relieve me here.'[11] Writing to the Queen four days later, Charles complained about the Covenanters' 'base, unworthy dealing', and stated his intention to flee England if he could not reach accommodation with 'the rebells; if not, then I resolve to go by sea to Scotland, in case I shall understand that Montrouse be in condition fit to receive me, otherwise I mean to make for Ireland, France or Denmark, but to which of these I am not yet resolved.'[12]

A key issue in Charles' negotiations with the Scots was the future of Montrose. The King may have been weak and indecisive, but he did not lack loyalty to his followers, and he was not about to sacrifice his greatest champion ('From henceforth,' he had told Montereul, 'I place Montrose amongst my children, and mean to live with him as a friend, and not as a king').[13] When the Earl of Lothian put to Charles that 'James Graham' – Montrose had of course been stripped of his titles – would require to lay down his arms, the sharp response was: 'He that made thee an Earl made James Graham a Marquis.'[14] The King would have preferred for Montrose to have been allowed to ally with his former foes, but even for the more moderate Covenanters this was asking too much. In the end they agreed that Montrose would be allowed to go into exile on the Continent; in itself a major concession towards someone who still had a substantial price on his head, dead or alive.

On 19 May Charles wrote from Newcastle to Montrose, 'You must disband your forces and go into France where you shall receive my further directions. This at first may justly startle you; but I assure you that, if for the present I should offer to do more for you, I could not do so much.'[15] Similar instructions were issued to both Huntly and Sir Alasdair MacDonald. Montrose was dismayed, but he had no alternative but to obey his Sovereign. He replied, 'As far as my own leaving this kingdom, I shall in all humility and obedience endeavour to perform for Your Majesty's command,'[16] but he had doubts as to whether the King's instructions were genuine or had been issued under duress. So Montrose wrote privately to Charles asking if his surrender was voluntary or if he had been compelled, and if the latter then Montrose would maintain his men in arms. On 15 June Charles wrote back repeating his earlier commands, giving assurances of protection for other prominent Royalists, and holding out the hope that the exile would be temporary:

'For there is no man, who ever heard me speak of you, that is ignorant of the reason that makes me at this time send you out of the country is that you may return home with the greater glory.'[17] The Royal command to Montrose was quite clear. In any event his Royalist army was again dispersing, with many of the Highlanders leaving to join up with the Earl of Antrim who had recently launched another invasion of Argyllshire.

At the end of July Montrose met the Covenanting General John (later 1st Earl of) Middleton at the River Isla to discuss a settlement. Much to the subsequent annoyance of the Committee of Estates, Middleton proposed more generous terms than Montrose could have hoped for. A free pardon was given to all the Royalists except Montrose himself, the Earl of Crawford and Sir John Hurry (despite commanding the Covenanters at Auldearn Hurry had since thrown his lot in with the King again). These three would be free to leave for the Continent no later than 1 September in a boat to be provided by the Estates. All forfeited lands of Scottish Royalists were to be restored, apart from those of the three being sent into exile.

It was a better deal than Montrose had expected, and he was in no position to negotiate. It was now time for him to go. He gathered what remained of his army at Rattray in Perthshire on 30 July for a sorrowful farewell. It must have been a wrench to leave those who had served so faithfully with him, but he had to obey the King's command. Charles wrote privately to Montrose on 21 August asking him to delay his departure as long as he could without breaking his word. It was not until 31 August that the promised ship appeared at Montrose harbour, but its captain decided it needed time in port for caulking and repair of the rigging, which left Montrose vulnerable and in breach of the agreed terms. Fortunately there was an alternative on hand in the shape of a Norwegian sloop which took most of the party of exiles aboard at Stonehaven on 3 September, but not Montrose himself. There they faced the wrath of the local people, mostly staunch Covenanters, who according to Wishart 'cut the cable while the ship was at anchor, and put them in danger of splitting upon the rocks'. The sloop sailed down the coast to the port of Montrose, where it was met by a small boat containing a minister, Reverend James Wood, and his servant, who turned out to be the Marquis of the town, travelling incognito because of the risk to his life. Montrose was taken aboard the Norwegian ship, and a course set for Bergen.

After two years of virtually continuous campaigning, the King's most loyal Scottish subject was exiting the scene. Still just 33, he had conducted the most spectacular military campaign in Scottish history, he had witnessed horrific scenes, seen loved ones and close friends die, but had failed to achieve any of the objectives he had set himself. His beloved King Charles was in the hands of his enemies, foremost among them the Marquis of Argyll, a man weakened but still powerful and dangerous. As he stood on the ship's deck watching the grey cliffs of his dear land slowly merge into the horizon, the sea salt splashing onto his lips, James Graham must have asked himself what it had all been for. The gambler had rolled the dice, and lost all. The North Sea breeze caught the sail, the ropes strained and the timbers groaned, all carrying him away from the place where he needed to be, his one consolation that he knew he still had the King's favour, and that it must only be a matter of time before he was once again called to serve his Sovereign on his native soil.

'Nothing but Jews'

1646-49

Newcastle, 29 May 1646. The King is technically a prisoner of
the Scots army, but no-one visiting the Royal court would know
it. Business carries on as it has always done, the dandified courtiers dancing around His Majesty's presence like bees at the hive,
the ambassadors, diplomats and messengers coming and going,
the world still revolving around Charles' every utterance. Today
there are more visitors from Scotland; foremost amongst them
Archibald Campbell, Marquis of Argyll, freshly returned from
Ireland, and with him the Earls of Morton and Crawford-Lindsay, all so recently enemies of the King, but here to talk peace.
The courtiers bring the guests in, Argyll in front. It has been
four and a half years since he last saw Charles; Argyll thinks he is
looking older, more care-worn, as well he might, for a man who
has nearly lost his crown. The Marquis advances, bows; Charles
smiles, and offers his hand; Argyll takes it and kisses it. Despite
everything, he is still a King's man. The others come forward,
the performance is repeated, and they sit down in conference,
for there is much to discuss. The meeting is cordial, friendly
even, Charles remembers he once favoured this man. He is well
aware of Argyll's abilities and reputation, and hopes that he can
be useful. Later Charles writes: 'Argyll is very civil and cunning,
but his journey to London will shew whether he be altered or
not (if he be, it must be for the better), being gone with much
professions of doing much for my service.'[1] Argyll has made a
good impression, but he still needs to prove himself.

With Montrose neutralised and heading for exile, the way had seemed clear for Argyll to reassert his authority. Although still suspicious of Charles, and with reservations about the accommodation that the Scots had reached with him, Argyll knew that he had to make up with his Sovereign. To do otherwise would have been to cut himself adrift from the mainstream Covenanters, and Archibald Campbell was always flexible enough to abandon previously held positions where these stood in way of political advancement. And so he had agreed to meet the King at Newcastle, and to start to act in his interests.

Charles reported on 10 June: 'Argyll went yesterday to London with great profession of doing me service there: his errand (as is pretended) is only to chasten down and moderate the demands that are coming to me from thence.'[2] The very fact that Argyll was given this task, and agreed to undertake it, is proof of his new, positive relationship with Charles. What the King was hinting at was the secret mission he had entrusted to Argyll and the Earl of Loudon to meet the staunch Royalists the Duke of Richmond and the Marquis of Hertford in London, in order to determine their views on the consequences of the Scottish army declaring for him. As it happened, the response was that such an alliance would be unhelpful, and might well lead to war between Scotland and England, in which even the English Royalists would feel obliged to take up arms against their Sovereign.

Charles thought that he had the measure of his new Scots allies. Writing to the Queen Henrietta Maria from Newcastle on 17 June, he set out in some detail the four factions that existed: 'Montroses, the neutrals, the Hamiltons, and the Campbells.' The Earl of Callander was the supposed leader of the neutrals. 'The three first seem to correspond, the two last are avowed enemies, the second keeps fair quarter with them all, and none of them trusts one another. At the committees in Scotland the Hamiltons are the strongest, but here the Campbells. Most of the nobility are for the Hamiltons . . . but most of the ministers, gentry and towns are for the Campbells.' It was all ripe for a policy of divide and rule, and a shrewder politician than Charles might have made the most of the opportunity. The King could only conclude disdainfully: 'assuredly no honest man can prosper in these people's company'.[3]

The English Parliament now put forward nineteen Propositions to the King, which included a requirement that he accept the Covenant and agree to the end of episcopacy, the passing of control to Parliament of the armed forces for at least twenty years, and the removal of any requirement for Royal Assent to laws which Parliament should pass. The Propositions represented a dramatic stripping of the King's authority. They were debated at Westminster at the end of June, and it was here that Argyll made the most significant speech of his career, setting out his view of the terms on which peace in both Kingdoms could be achieved.

In his remarks Argyll gave the lie to those who would try to characterise him as a strict doctrinaire, making it clear that he took a moderate approach to the issue of church government, and was prepared to allow a variation of Presbyterianism in England which would permit religious liberty and freedom of operation within a broad framework. He argued: 'upon one part we should take heed not to settle lawless liberty in religion, whereby, instead of uniformity, we should set up a thousand heresies and schisms, which is directly contrary and destructive to our Covenant. Upon the other part; we are to look that we persecute not piety and peaceable men, who cannot, through scruple of conscience, come up in all things to the common rule.'

Argyll went on to suggest a Union of the two Kingdoms, presaging a move which would not in fact occur for another sixty years: 'Therefore let us hold fast that union which is so happily established betwixt us; and let nothing make us again two, who are so many ways one – all of one language, in one island, all under one king, in one religion, yea one in covenant; so that in effect we differ in nothing but the name (as brethren do) which I wish were also removed, that we might be one if the two kingdoms think fit; for I dare say, not the greatest kingdom in the Earth can prejudice both as much as one of them may do the other.'[4] Here was a Scots noble in the role of a British statesman, one of the most pre-eminent of the age. Argyll reassured Westminster of the Scottish people's regard for their King and their continued belief in monarchy, and finished by declaring the support of the Scottish Commissioners to Parliament for the Propositions. He might have made up with Charles, but he still wanted the King's powers reduced to those of a constitutional monarch.

Argyll's next business was to attend the meeting of the Assembly of Divines at Westminster in place of Lord Balmerino. This Assembly had been established in July 1643 to agree a system of church government to apply across both Scotland and England (it was to draw up the Westminster Confession of Faith which remains to this day the principal rule book for the Church of Scotland). Argyll was warmly welcomed with the words 'to crown all the rest is the joy of our hearts to find a person of so great and famous renown and honour, in which the greatest safety of the kingdom of Scotland is reposed. We look upon your lordship as one of the greatest instruments under God.'[5] But while feted in London, Argyll still had his difficulties at home; Baillie reporting: 'The Lord help him out of his trouble; his enemies are many, and friends for any purpose bot few; yet God is not dead.'[6]

All hopes for a lasting peace still depended on Charles accepting the Propositions. They were presented to him at Newcastle on 30 July, and he asked for time to consider. He had no intention of agreeing. Charles' view was that his acceptance of these terms would leave him with the Crown in title only, and with an unacceptable imposition of Presbyterianism on the church in England. The Scots piled pressure on him to bend. The Commissioners begged him, with tears, to accept. He was entreated by nobles, harangued by ministers, and warned by Loudon: 'If your Majesty lose England by your wilfulness, you will not be permitted to come and reign in Scotland.'[7] But Charles, who still harboured hopes of assistance from overseas, was once more playing for time. He asked the English Commissioners for permission to go to London to discuss the issue further, but in a clear signal that he was not for bending stated that he would not 'consent to anything destructive to that just power by which the laws of God and the land he had been born unto.'[8]

The English Parliamentarians were having none of this. They had worked out that Charles was simply stringing them along. It was time to force a resolution one way or another. That meant getting rid of the Scots army from English soil and having Charles handed over to them. Exasperated with Charles' intransigence, the Scots were themselves keen to return home, and anxious to be rid of their obstinate King. The stumbling block was money. The Scots army was due vast sums in arrears by the English Parliament, and without payment it was going nowhere. Quite understandably the rank-and-file, some of whom had been campaigning on English soil for years, had no interest in returning home with empty pockets. Inevitably there were disputes about the amount of money due, but eventually it was agreed that the Scots army would be paid £400,000 sterling, half in advance. Even then it would take Parliament months to raise necessary funds, and it would not be until January of the following year that the Scots would eventually withdraw, and Charles be handed over to Parliament.

At the time and for long after, the Scots suffered abuse for their treatment of their King, denounced as 'traitor Scot sold his king for a groat', but this is a quite unfair interpretation of what actually occurred. The Scots were due the arrears of pay that they demanded, and the delay in paying these was causing real hardship. Moreover they were now thoroughly fed up with Charles and his continual attempts to buy time. Robert Baillie wrote, 'The King's answer has broken our heart; we see nothing but a sea of new more horrible confusions.'9 Charles had offered to go to London and they were simply trying to accommodate him. The army could not stay in Newcastle forever, and bringing Charles back to Scotland with it would simply have been a recipe for more plotting and dissension, and possibly even provoke an English invasion.

While the King and the Scots' army sat in Newcastle waiting for the English Parliament to collect the £200,000 due, divisions within the Covenanters' ranks started to widen. Two broad factions were established. One was centred around Argyll and was for keeping to the agreement with the English Parliament, and delivering the King to them as soon as was practical. The other more moderate faction found its champion in the Duke of Hamilton (now free again), who wanted to protect the King, and argued for retaining the Scots army in England until peace was finally settled. But while he professed loyalty to Charles, Hamilton was not trusted by the Scottish Royalists. It was even rumoured that he had an eye on assuming the throne himself, and it was reported that of the leaders of the two main parties in Scotland, one, Argyll, wished to do without the monarchy, while the other, Hamilton, wished the throne for himself. This was a distortion, at least as far as Argyll was concerned: he was no republican but rather a convinced advocate of constitutional monarchy. That, after all, had been the de facto system of government in Scotland since 1639, and from Argyll's point of view the country had been none the worse for it. In contrast, more and more English Parliamentarians seemed to be aiming for the extinction of monarchy altogether.

As the time came near for Charles to be handed over to the English, he stepped up his efforts to win the Scots army over to his cause, even offering Leslie the Dukedom of Orkney. It was not enough. Eventually, on 16 January 1647, the Scots Parliament resolved to deliver Charles to their English counterparts. It was in line with Argyll's wishes, but vehemently opposed by Hamilton and Lanark. Charles was to go to Holmby House in Northamptonshire, and it was requested that the English Parliament should make no peace with him without the Scots' consent. On 30 January, with the first £100,000 due having already been paid and the second on its way, the Scots marched out of Newcastle heading for the Border. They went with the jeers of the local citizens in their ears, being damned as 'nothing but Jews, people who had sold their King and their honour'.[10]

Argyll and his colleagues had achieved their objectives of getting the army back from England intact, of getting the back pay due, and of ridding themselves of an unbending King who had now become an inconvenience. But they had left a bad feeling in both Kingdoms. Although mostly undeserved, public sympathy for Charles was to grow as a consequence of the way in which he had been treated. With the Covenanters now split into two competing groups it was Hamilton's pro-Charles party which was to benefit, while Argyll would find himself diminished. The removal from the scene of his rival Montrose had simply made space for a potentially more dangerous adversary. Argyll complained to the Earl of Lothian about the attitude he faced from some: 'many being so weak, others so full of by ways and malice to men who have served their countrie, so far as God inabled them, with faithfulness.'[11] The master politician was perhaps getting a taste of his own medicine.

The remaining Royalist rebels in Scotland still had to be dealt with, and with the army now returned from England there was the ability to take action. There was no need for the large force previously required, so Argyll proposed, and it was agreed, that the army be reduced to 1,200 cavalry and 6,000 foot. Operational command was again given to David Leslie, who set about extinguishing the residual fires of rebellion, starting with Huntly in the north. Leslie's men met little resistance. Those Irish troops who surrendered were executed forthwith, just as they had been after Philiphaugh. Huntly himself fled into the hills of Badenoch, vainly trying to get permission to follow Montrose into exile.

The most serious issue to be addressed was in Argyllshire, where Sir Alasdair MacDonald and his army of Irishmen had been wreaking havoc. This was personal business for Argyll, who was determined to have his revenge. When it was put to him that MacDonald and his men should be allowed to leave Scotland, Argyll replied that the only discussion over the Royalist captain's fate was whether they would make him 'shorter or longer than he was'[12] – in other words, whether he should be beheaded or hanged.

Leslie's force, with Argyll as second-in-command, caught up with the rebels in Kintyre on 24th May 1647. MacDonald himself, with his father and the bulk of his 1,300 troops, managed to escape on ship to Islay. The remaining 300 of his men retreated to Dunaverty Castle, where they found themselves trapped by the Covenanters. Within the castle walls, the sea on one side and their enemies hemming them in on the other, hopelessly outnumbered, and without the provisions required to withstand the siege, the defenders surrendered unconditionally. Given the history of the civil war in Scotland they could hardly have expected leniency, but perhaps calculated that whatever end would befall them would be a less painful one than a slow death from starvation. Leslie initially tended towards leniency, but a minister with his army, John Nevoy, encouraged him in the slaughter of the prisoners by reminding him of the punishment of King Saul of ancient Israel for sparing the Amalekites. In the event all but one of the prisoners were killed. According to local tradition, Leslie did not want to waste precious bullets and so ordered his men to dispatch the captives by throwing them from the cliff-top onto the rocks and into the sea below. One eyewitness, Sir James Turner, stated that Argyll encouraged this course of action. Certainly his own Campbell kin had suffered terribly at the hands of these invaders – it was even alleged that they had burned alive a barn full of men, women and children at Lagganmore in Glen Euchar. Archibald Campbell might be a British statesman, but back in the Highlands he was *MacCailein Mor*, and he had the blood of his clan to avenge.

Leslie and Argyll proceeded to Islay in pursuit of the remainder of MacDonald's army. MacDonald himself and many of his Irish troops had by now fled back to their home country, but the Covenanters found MacDonald's father, old Colkitto, together with nearly 200 men, at the castle of Dunyvaig. Colkitto himself was captured and eventually hanged (by tradition from the mast of his own galley) but the remainder of the garrison surrendered in exchange for a promise that their lives would be spared, and in this case the promise was kept. Leslie continued to Mull to stamp out the last of the rebellion there. Meantime Middleton was in the north of Scotland still in pursuit of Huntly, who was eventually captured and taken to Edinburgh to await his fate. Lord Reay in the far north abandoned the Royalist cause and went into exile, and, with that, the war in Scotland was at last over.

Peace may have been restored, but there remained much work for the Scottish Parliament to do. The plague was still rife and had spread both to the north of the country and into Argyllshire. Despite the payment of army arrears by the English Parliament, many of the nobility were still burdened with huge debts. It would take a long time to get the country back into its pre-war condition. And while Scotland now desperately needed a government with a unity of purpose, the rivalry between Argyll and Hamilton was intensifying. Argyll still had the majority faction for the time being, but undoubtedly his popularity was on the wane as a consequence of the manner in which the King had been treated. In the new Committee of Estates, formed in March 1647, Hamilton had the more support, although Argyll continued to have the greater following amongst the lairds and burgesses.

In reality the dividing line between Argyll and Hamilton in policy terms was not so great. Both wished to see the King restored to his throne, and both wished to see him sign the Covenant. While Argyll would insist on the establishment of Presbyterianism in England, Hamilton was less prescriptive. What united both parties was a desire to protect the King's person and position against the more militant elements – the Independent Party – in the English Parliament, who were increasingly coming to the view that there was no need for a king at all, and particularly not one so unwilling to compromise.

The English Presbyterians still had a majority in the Westminster Parliament and were quietly working with the King to try and form a new settlement which was not as extreme as the Propositions of Newcastle. This was not popular with the Independents, nor with the New Model Army which they dominated. Fearing that an agreement would be reached without their consent, the Independents captured Charles and took him to Newmarket on 4 June. This outraged the Scots and led them to make greater common cause with the English Presbyterians, and the Queen in France was urged to send the Prince of Wales to Scotland to lead an army south to support her husband. Argyll wrote to Charles at Newmarket offering to send an army into England to restore him to the throne, but on the condition that he sign the Covenant. Argyll's stance had remained remarkably consistent – he was still keen to see Charles reinstated, but only if he championed Presbyterianism in England. Suspicious of the loyalties of Leslie's army, which he felt was much too close to his rival, Hamilton did not support this offer. Inevitably, Charles declined. Had he known what lay in store he might have been more compliant.

On 17 August the Committee of Estates met with Argyll and Hamilton both present, and agreed on new instructions to the Commissioners in London, to invite the King to the capital to put the Newcastle Propositions to him once more. Hamilton was anxious for Leslie's army to be disbanded; understandably, this was resisted by Argyll. Eventually Argyll was to win, but only by a single vote in the Estates, and only after the army had agreed to accept a pay reduction. The complicated chess game between the two noblemen continued, with neither gaining the clear advantage.

The three Scottish Commissioners met the King on 22 October, and promised him that if he met their demands about the establishment of the Presbyterian religion he would have the Scots' support. They urged him to escape and come to Scotland. Instead Charles suggested going to Berwick, where he could not be accused of deserting England. In the end he did flee, on 11 November, but in the opposite direction, to the Isle of Wight. There he was made a prisoner in Carisbrooke Castle, where he signed up to a new agreement – 'The Engagement'. The terms of this required the establishment of a Presbyterian form of church government in England for three years, after which time there would be further consultation before final settlement would be reached. The Covenant would be signed by all except conscientious objectors, and the King could keep his own preferred style of worship at home. Charles would also pursue a complete union of the two Kingdoms, or at the least establish a free trade area between them. In exchange the Scots would support the

King's return to London by negotiating peace terms with Parliament, and if this could not be achieved would send an army to support him.

It was an agreement in which the King had made remarkably few concessions, and represented a substantial climb-down from the position the Scots had so recently held. All Charles had signed up to was, in effect, a 'trial run' of Presbyterianism with no long-term commitment. The Covenanters' original vision of a permanently Presbyterian England had been betrayed.

Unsurprisingly, the Engagement was not universally popular back home. Hamilton's faction which favoured the Engagement (the 'Engagers' – those opposed became known as 'Anti-Engagers') had a majority in the Estates as a result of careful manoeuvering by their leader, who stuffed meetings with supportive backwoodsmen. Baillie writes that there were, 'Never so many noblemen present in any of our Parliaments; near fyftie Earls and Lords,' all 'ran in a string after Duke Hamilton's vote. That partie, besides the advantage of the number of two at least to one, had likewise the most of the ablest speakers.'[13] For once Argyll found himself outplayed in the game of politics. But popular opinion was considerably more sceptical of the new direction. Many of the clergy who had previously pushed for war in support of the King when they thought that it would be Argyll in charge, now changed their tune, and urged peace. The army were still loyal to Argyll personally, David Leslie being a strong ally (Montereul observed in a letter to Cardinal Mazarin in Paris that 'Argyle has a quite special interest in retaining an army of which all the officers are but his tools'),[14] and there were rumours of a military coup, although nothing came of these.

Relations between former allies, who had fought together against the King, were becoming fraught. Argyll even found himself in a duel with the Earl of Crawford-Lindsay (also Hamilton's brother-in-law) whom the Marquis heard had claimed that he was a better man than he (Argyll) was. Baillie records this 'unhappie incident, that was ready to kindle a fire amongst us all, had not the Lord prevented it'. The background to this was that 'Argyle's enemies had of long tyme burdened him, among many slanders, with that of cowardice and cullionrie [base conduct]'. On hearing the report of Crawford-Lindsay's words, Argyll was furious at this latest slur. He called the Earl to account and the duel date was set for 7 o'clock in the morning of Monday 13 March 1648 at Musselburgh Links, where the two parties would seek satisfaction with the sword. The two noblemen, accompanied by their seconds, rode to that lonely spot far from town, ready to draw blood at the appointed hour. Fortunately word of the encounter had got out, and they were met on the Links by various colleagues, who intervened and ensured that they did not come to blows, with Crawford-Lindsay apparently apologising. According to Baillie, 'by God's Providence, before they began their pley, some fell on them, and made them part without a stroke. The counsel that night, with much adoe, got them to a professed coldryfe friendship.'[15] Argyll's honour was restored, but he was clearly a man sensitive to the jibes of his critics.

The struggle between Hamilton and Argyll at the level of the Estates was mirrored in a division of the country between two factions, the Engagers and the Anti-Engagers. The Engagers might have the majority in the Estates, but the bulk of the clergy were with the Anti-Engagers. Notwithstanding the popular opposition to their policy, the Engagers were determined to press on and take the country to war if necessary.

On 28 April Berwick was seized by English Royalists who had made their way to Scotland to join with the Engagers, and the following day Carlisle was also taken. On 4 May the Estates authorised the raising of a huge army of more than 27,000 foot and nearly 3,000 horse under the command of Hamilton. Argyll deemed it prudent to absent himself to avoid having to sign the bond for the maintenance of the army, and left Edinburgh for Inveraray. But he continued to do all he could to oppose the notion of war.

The Kirk denounced the raising of the army, and in the most strongly Covenanting parts of the country, such as Fife, Ayrshire and Galloway, there was active obstruction of the levy of troops. 2,000 Covenanters gathered at Mauchline in Ayrshire in open opposition. There they were met by Middleton and his cavalry who managed to disperse them, causing perhaps as many as 80 casualties. It was a demonstration by the Engagers that they were not prepared to put up with internal opposition, and had the desired effect in preventing a more general uprising, of which Argyll would doubtless have approved.

In the end Hamilton collected an army of only 10,000 with which to launch his invasion, still a large force but far short of what had originally been hoped for. He had no great track record as a general, but the Covenanters' two greatest commanders, Leven and David Leslie, had refused to serve for political reasons; Leven opposing the Engagement, and Leslie, a key ally of Argyll's, being unwilling to act without the Kirk's endorsement. Hamilton had no choice but to take personal command. The levies who made up the ranks were inexperienced and poorly equipped. The infantry in particular were of dismal quality, with barely one man in five able to handle a pike. This poor shower were about to face in Parliament's New Model Army, the most disciplined and effective fighting force in Europe.

On 8 July 1648, Hamilton's army crossed the border from Annan and headed south through Lancashire, hoping to meet up with English Royalists. It was pursued by Cromwell's Parliamentary forces who attacked the Scots at Preston and again at Winwick, near Warrington, on both occasions inflicting terrible losses. Without finding the substantial English reinforcements he had hoped for, Hamilton eventually had no option but to surrender at Uttoxeter on 25 August. It had been a desperate, humiliating failure.

Argyll was delighted at the news. With Hamilton now off the scene as a prisoner in England, the way was clear for Argyll's faction to regain power. The fightback started in unexpected fashion with an armed rising in the South-west led by the Earls of Loudon, Eglinton, Leven, Cassillis and David Leslie, intended to overthrow the Engagers' regime and put power back in the hands of the radicals. This became known as the 'Whiggamore Raid' (a whiggamore was a cattle-driver, the supposed profession of many of the raiders) and is the origin of the term 'Whig', which for centuries after identified the political party which championed the rights of Parliament against the Crown. Argyll played no direct role in the rising (he was canny enough to keep his distance, at least publicly) but with his kinsman and close ally Loudon a leading figure, there can be little doubt about his prior knowledge and support, and it certainly suited his purposes.

The 6,000 raiders made it to Edinburgh where they were warmly welcomed by the people. Ahead of their arrival the Engagers in the Committee of Estates escaped to Stirling, where by coincidence their enemy Argyll had stopped to break his journey in the opposite direction. Interrupted during his dinner with the Earl of·Mar, Argyll narrowly escaped capture by riding to North Queensferry and from there taking a boat across the Forth to Edinburgh, thus avoiding being a useful hostage for the Engagers. The failure of Hamilton's invasion had undoubtedly lost them popular support, and with the capital now in the hands of Argyll and his allies, the Engagers' position was increasingly weak. And there was another threat on the horizon – Cromwell was on his way northwards, determined to remove any future threat from Scotland.

Oliver Cromwell believed he could make common cause with the Anti-Engagers. He wrote to Loudon, as Chancellor, rejoicing 'to see the power of the Kingdome of Scotland in a hopefull way to be invested in those, who, wee trust, are taught of God to seek his honor, and the comfort of his people,' going on to hope for an alliance: 'so wee hope and pray, that the late glorious dispensation in giving soe happie success against your and our enemyes in our victoryes, may be the foundation of union of the people of God in love and amitye.'[16] Cromwell received a warm response, Loudon welcoming his defeat of Hamilton and assuring him, 'wee doe prefer these to all other interest whatsomevir'.[17]

As de facto leader of the Anti-Engagers, Argyll was best placed to treat with Cromwell. He went to meet him on 21 September just north of the Tweed at Mordington, and agreed the surrender of Berwick and Carlisle (although Berwick refused to co-operate). Both Engagers and Anti-Engagers were desperate to prevent the English army from coming in force into Scotland – the Engagers because of the real threat presented, and the Anti-Engagers because they did not want it to appear that they were gaining political power on the back of an English invasion. The Engagers tried desperately to regroup, but they were outnumbered and had been outmanoeuvred. Eventually, on 27 September, they agreed to relinquish all claims to power. As a military coup the Whiggamore Raid had proved an outstanding success, and civil government in Scotland was back in the hands of Argyll and his hardline followers, the Marquis in his preferred position one step back from the front line, but pulling all the strings.

The new regime set about consolidating its position. On 4 October the Anti-Engagers called a meeting of the Committee of Estates in Edinburgh, with all Engagers excluded from it. With the new 'Kirk Party' (as Argyll's backers became known) in control, Cromwell was increasingly to be viewed as an ally. On the same day that the Estates met, the English general arrived in Edinburgh, dining on the first night with both Argyll and Johnston of Warriston. Relations between Cromwell and Argyll were friendly enough, the former having written of his earlier encounter, 'I must be bold and testify for that noble Lord the Marquis, the Lord Elcho, and the other gentleman with him, that I found nothing in them other than what becomes Christians and men of honour.'[18] The two had plenty in common; a strong religious devotion, a belief in Parliamentary supremacy, an ambition for a closer union between their two kingdoms, and an unswerving confidence in the rightness of their cause. But not everyone was impressed with Cromwell. As an Independent his religious views were still offensive to the Kirk. He was interviewed at Moray House in the Canongate by the three leading ministers, David Dickson, James Guthrie and Robert Blair, and Blair's damning assessment afterwards was: 'If you knew him as well as I do, you would not believe one word he says. He is an egregious dissembler and a great liar. Away with him, he is a greeting devil.'[19]

The purpose of Cromwell's visit was to ensure that the Scots would not again intervene in English affairs on behalf of the King. With the Engagers legally excluded from office, and assurances having been given, Cromwell was able to depart for the south. He left behind at the request of the Estates, and for their protection, two cavalry regiments and two troops of dragoons under Major-General Lambert.

For both Cromwell and Argyll the outcome was highly satisfactory. Cromwell had removed the threat from Scotland to the English Parliamentarians' opportunity to deal with the King as they wished, and he now had in charge north of the Border someone with whom he could do business. On Argyll's part, he had secured his leadership position, and the threat of another English army invading Scotland had been removed. But the prospect of Presbyterianism being established in England, long the Covenanters' main objective, must have appeared further away than ever.

While Argyll and Hamilton were doing battle for power in Scotland, Montrose was far away in exile watching events and biding his time. He had travelled between Hamburg, Paris and Vienna, always looking to rally support for the King. While he received many warm welcomes, offers of practical help were few and far between. Even Queen Henrietta Maria, whom he met at court in Paris and petitioned to raise an army, was unenthusiastic.

Montrose's greatest asset was his reputation. His chaplain George Wishart had published in the Netherlands at the end of 1647 a heroic and highly partisan account of the Marquis' campaign in Scotland. Written in Latin, then the international language, it was an immediate publishing sensation. Throughout the capitals of Europe Montrose was viewed as the epitome of the romantic hero. In Paris Cardinal Mazarin, the effective ruler of France during Louis XIV's minority, offered him a series of positions up to the Captaincy of the French King's Guard and the rank of Marshall of France. In Prague the Holy Roman Emperor Ferdinand IV presented him with the crimson baton of Marshall of the Empire, empowering him to raise troops in any part of his dominions.

Montrose made his way to Flanders in the hope of gathering an army from amongst Ferdinand's followers, but found the imperial troops in disarray. When the news of Hamilton's defeat reached him he turned his attention away from the Queen to the Princes – the Prince of Wales, the Duke of York and Prince Rupert – hoping to convince them to assist him in raising a force to take to Scotland. Rupert had at his disposal the small Royalist navy which Montrose was keen to make use of, but the Prince was reluctant. Eventually the Prince of Wales, now in the Hague, agreed to meet Montrose, but only secretly, for fear of antagonising the Engagers. But before the meeting could take place, terrible, shocking news arrived from London. The English had cut off their King's head.

The Covenanted King

1649-1650

A bitterly cold afternoon in Whitehall; every window crowded with faces. In the street below, a mass of people press up against the lines of halberd-wielding soldiers, six-deep in front of the black-draped scaffold newly erected outside Banqueting House. Most of the common folk have been there, crammed together, since early morning, unwilling or unable to leave their prime vantage spots, and the young Parliamentary officer in command wrinkles his nose at the stench of sweat and piss. The crowd's babble hushes at a sign of movement on the wooden platform above their heads. A first floor window swings open, and out comes the anticipated party: officers, priests, the black-clad and hooded executioners, the King's attendants, and then Charles himself, as elegant and regal as ever, wrapped in a velvet cloak bearing the Garter star. It is two o'clock on the afternoon of Tuesday, 30 January 1649, a date which all present will remember for the rest of their lives: the day they saw the King die.

Charles has the right to make a last speech, but the people are too far away to hear. He speaks instead to those around him, justifying all his actions that have brought him here. Finally he says: 'I die a Christian according to the Profession of the Church of England, I have a good cause and a gracious God.' He takes off his cloak; beneath he has worn two shirts, so even on such a cold day he is not seen to shiver and his subjects think that he is in fear. He lies down, places his head on the block, prays for a moment, then puts out his hands as a signal to the executioner. The axe swings, in a single clean blow severing head from body. To his most loyal followers, Charles completes the transformation from suffering Christian saint to Christ-like martyr, sacrificed for the Anglican faith and his belief in the Divine Right. A great groan rises from the crowd; some rush forward to dip handkerchiefs in the Royal blood dripping on to the street, believing it to possess magical powers. England has killed its King.

*

What brought matters to this tragic pass? The Duke of Hamilton's ham-fisted actions in support of Charles turned out to have had the opposite effect to that intended. The Engagement, and the subsequent Scots' invasion of England, had led to a hardening of attitudes within the English Parliamentarians. If the military exploits of one of the King's Scottish champions, Montrose, had unintentionally weakened his position, then it was those of the other great Royal supporter, Hamilton, which sealed his fate. Those Parliamentarians who had supported the continuation of negotiations with the King in good faith increasingly felt that he was simply not to be trusted. The pressure had grown for Charles to be put on trial for crimes against his people.

The Scots were alarmed at this turn of events. Their objective remained the restoration of Charles to the throne, providing always that he would agree to introduce Presbyterianism to the English church. But increasingly the interests of the Scots and those of the English Parliament had drifted apart. More and more the Independent Party had the upper hand, and the House of Commons was purged of those most sympathetic to the King. Ironically this was an initiative which the Independents had learned from the Scots' purging of the Engagers, the effectiveness of which Cromwell had seen for himself. The Rump Parliament (as it became known) was determined to bring the

King to trial. The horrified Scots protested loudly. Apart from anything else, Charles was still their King, and it was not for the English Parliament alone to decide what might become of him. It was to no avail.

On 20 January 1649 the trial of the King began. Charles' opponents barely made an effort to try to provide legal justification for the unprecedented proceedings – a Sovereign on trial. It was enough that they had concluded, probably with justification, that there could be no peace in England while the King still lived. The country was sick of war, and a Kingly sacrifice was called for to prevent further bloodshed.

Charles conducted himself before his accusers with great dignity, refusing to defend himself as he did not recognise the legality of the Court. He would not even remove his hat as a measure of respect to the judges. The outcome was inevitable. The chief judge, John Bradshaw, read out the verdict that 'He, the said Charles Stewart, as tyrant, traitor, murderer and public enemy to the good of this nation, shall be put to death by severing of his head from his body.' It was only when judgement was declared that Charles started to try to commence his defence, but by then it was too late.

News of Charles' death was met with universal horror by the Scots. For the devoted Montrose, it was the worst outcome imaginable: 'When news of this monstrous parricide was confirmed, and there remained no more room for hope, his grief became passion, his anger was heightened to fury, and his noble spirit was so overwhelmed that his limbs stiffened and he fainted in the midst of his attendants, falling down like one dead.' On waking from his faint, he lamented: 'We must die, die with our gracious king. May the God of life and death be my witness, that henceforth life on earth will be bitterness and mourning,'[1] and with that closeted himself away for two days. It was a monstrous act against God to kill His anointed King, and without a stable government to replace him, a recipe for anarchy and chaos. Such views were not restricted to Royalists; even staunch Covenanters were appalled at this action by their English allies. In Edinburgh the Estates had been meeting to complete the purging of the Engagers with the passing of the Act of Classes, removing from public life those who had supported the Engagement or held dangerous or 'Malignant' opinions (speaking in support of the Act, Argyll described it as 'the breaking of Malignants' teeth'). When the dreadful news from London arrived the Estates adjourned for two days to take stock.

Immediately on their reconvening, the 18-year-old Prince of Wales was proclaimed Charles the Second, King of Great Britain, France and Ireland, but it was made clear that before he would be granted the powers of the throne he would have to meet the same conditions that had so long been resisted by his father. It was a move that reflected popular opinion in Scotland, outraged at the killing of their King. Even amongst the dominant Kirk Party, which with the Act of Classes had strengthened its grip on power, there were very few who opposed the new monarch. One consequence of this proclamation was that it brought to an end the short-lived alliance between Argyll and Cromwell.

The conditions that Charles II had to meet before the Estates would support him were that he had to sign both Covenants and create a Presbyterian government in all his Kingdoms, that he consent that all civil acts be settled and approved by Parliament, that all religious acts and church matters have the same approval by the General Assembly, and that he remove evil counsellors such as Montrose. It was essentially the same list as had so often been put to Charles I and which he had been so reluctant to accept. Four Commissioners, the Earl of Cassillis, Alexander Brodie, George Winrame of Libberton and Alexander Jaffray, were sent to the Netherlands to negotiate with the new King.

Argyll and his allies were unsettled by continual rumours that the Royalists were planning a landing in Scotland, where if they could link up with the remaining Engagers they would prove a real threat to the new regime of the Kirk Party. On 22 February, 700 Royalist horsemen, mainly drawn from Clan McKenzie and led by Sir Thomas McKenzie of Pluscardine, occupied Inverness. The Estates ordered the raising of a new army, again with David Leslie in command. It was intended both to put down internal risings, and provide for defence against invasion either by the English or by the Royalists. Pluscardine found little local support, and as Leslie's forces came closer to the town he left Inverness without a fight. In Atholl there was another rising under Lord Ogilvy and Middleton, and the garrison of Stirling Castle mutinied. Leslie moved quickly to offer clemency to the rebels if they surrendered, and having sorted out the trouble in Inverness he headed back south to pacify Atholl.

Although the putative rising had been quickly put down, the Estates wanted to send a message that such behaviour would not be tolerated. The Gordons had played their part in the insurrection, and there remained in the hands of the Covenanters their Chief, and Scotland's most determined Royalist, George Gordon, Marquis of Huntly, who had been imprisoned for the last two years. He was already condemned to death and it was now decided that the sentence should be carried out *pour encourager les autres*. So devoted had Huntly been to Charles I, and so devastated had he been at the news of the King's death, that he professed himself content to die: 'he was so overcome with melancholie, griefe, and discontentment, that there was no possibilitie of giving him comfort'. The decision to execute was taken in the absence of 'the first and greatest ranks of the nobilitie that satt in parliament',[2] the aristocracy deliberately excluding themselves, fearful of the precedent being set that a nobleman following his king's orders should suffer such a punishment. Huntly was of course Argyll's brother-in-law, and while Argyll did make representations on Huntly's behalf, either he was not forceful enough, or even he was not able to sway the diehards in the Kirk Party. On 22 March Huntly died bravely on the Maiden in Edinburgh, going to his end 'with as cheerful a countenance as if he had gone to a wedding',[3] but lamenting (as well he might) that while he had the chance he had not done enough to assist the late King. His estates were forfeited and transferred to his principal creditor, who happened to be Argyll. This was not such a prize as it might first seem, for like almost all Scottish nobles Huntly was heavily in debt, and his estates extensively mortgaged.

Huntly was not the only prominent Scotsman to die that month. James, 1st Duke of Hamilton, had been held in prison by the English Parliament following his capture by Cromwell. As he held an English title (Earl of Cambridge) as well as a Scottish dukedom, he could be tried in London. Found guilty of treason, he followed his late sovereign in being beheaded by the axeman. His title was inherited by his brother, the Earl of Lanark, who became the 2nd Duke.

Charles II was in the Hague, where three different groups competed for his interest. Firstly there was Montrose and the other staunch Royalists from both north and south of the Border, some of whom wanted Charles to invade Scotland and some who thought his better bet was Ireland, where he could link up with the Catholic Irish. Secondly there were the Engagers, led by the new Duke of Hamilton and the Earl of Lauderdale, who wanted him to ally with the Kirk Party, possibly in the hope that once he was in Scotland his influence would be enough to remove Argyll and have a more moderate administration put in place. Thirdly there was the Kirk Party itself, represented by the Scots Commissioners, which would back Charles if he met their previously stated conditions.

Charles II

The Commissioners got off to a bad start. Charles met them on 27 March in his bedchamber, intending that, by not according them proper respect, he would avoid accepting the legality of their appointment. Their first demand, a precondition of further discussions, was that Charles break with Montrose, 'a man most justly, if ever, cast out of the Church of God . . . upon whose head lies more innocent blood, then for many yeers hath done on the head of any one, the most bloody murtherer in our Nation.'[4] Argyll was determined that his rival would be frozen out of any possible political comeback. The King refused to make any response to this until the Commissioners set out their other demands, which they declined to do. There was much delay, and it was only nine days later, on 5 April, that they revealed their additional conditions. Charles wanted to know that what had been put to him thus far was the full extent of everything that he would be expected to sign up to. The Commissioners knew that the Estates wanted to keep open the option of bringing in further demands at a later date once the King was installed in Scotland, and were evasive. Neither party appeared to be dealing in good faith, and the prospects of reaching agreement seemed remote.

Notwithstanding the Commissioners' demands, Montrose continued to be close to Charles and pressing for military action. James Graham still had plenty of admirers, Charles' Secretary of State, Sir Edward Nicholas, writing, 'it is the opinion and wishes of all men, that his Majesty would imploy him, as the man of the clearest honour, courage, and affection, to his service.'[5] In defiance of Argyll and his allies, Charles agreed, and Montrose was appointed, as he had been by Charles' father, Captain-General of Scotland and Admiral of the Scottish Seas, and was authorised to appeal to foreign nations for their military assistance.

On 19 May Charles eventually gave his response to the Scots Commissioners. He would agree with much of what they demanded if they undertook to help him avenge his father and recover the English throne. But he could not impose the Solemn League and Covenant on England and Ireland without the consent of their Parliaments. Inevitably this was not enough for the Commissioners, who returned home with nothing to show for their efforts, but with a positive report of Charles as a person: 'one of the most gentle, innocent, well-inclined princes'.[6]

Montrose set off around Europe as Charles' ambassador, looking to raise troops for an invasion. He went to Hamburg to see the Duke of Courland, then to Schleswig to meet Frederick, King of Denmark, but nowhere was there much on offer other than good wishes. At least there seemed no prospect of Charles going to Scotland to join with the Covenanters, which was always Montrose's greatest concern. Back in the Hague, Montrose took up with Elizabeth, the widowed Winter Queen of Bohemia (and sister of the late King Charles), renowned for her charm and beauty. The two became close friends, the romantic cavalier hero and the elegant former Queen making a handsome couple, although whether there was anything more than friendship in his relationship with Elizabeth is something that can only be speculated about. Although poor Magdalen Carnegie had only recently died, leaving Montrose a widower, his marriage had effectively ended many years before after his long absences from home. There were also hints at the time of a romantic attachment between Montrose and Elizabeth's daughter Princess Louise, but whatever the truth of the matter Louise would end her days unmarried in a nunnery.

Back in Scotland, Argyll must have been wondering where to go next. His ambition remained to see Presbyterianism established in England and a constitutional monarchy in both Kingdoms. There was no prospect of either objective being achieved while Cromwell was in power. That left only Charles as a possible vehicle for delivering what both Argyll and the Kirk Party desired, and the young King had made it clear that there were other options that he would rather pursue. In the meantime the Kirk Party regime remained vulnerable to potential aggression from both Cromwell and the Royalists, and substantial opposition at home from the purged Engagers.

The Estates, still dominated by the Kirk Party, met again in August and agreed to take forward the only course which was realistically open to it, which was to reopen negotiations with Charles. George Winrame of Libberton was appointed as emissary to the King. Although there was opposition from the Kirk, Argyll was supportive of this new approach. Ever careful, cautious and calculating, he had come to the conclusion that Charles was the key to success. He applied all the pressure he could upon the young King to have him sign the Covenants, even writing to the Prince of Orange requesting his assistance. 'Your Highness cannot doe his Majesty a better service nor in persuading him to concur in the league and covenant, and perfecting what was wanting in his father's answers for satisfaction of his good subjects, especialie in religion . . . so I howpe your Highnes will not leave off to pres it.'[7] But even within the Kirk Party there were many who did not fully trust Argyll, and considered him to be acting in his own self-interest.

By the time Libberton made it to the Hague in October he found that Charles had moved to Jersey, from where he had intended to go to Ireland as Montrose had originally suggested. But there events had moved on, and Cromwell's highly effective and brutal campaign against the Irish had closed that particular door. This proved to be to Libberton's advantage, because with the Irish option now off the table, an agreement with the Scots now looked the best, if not the only, route available for Charles if he wanted to retrieve his Kingdoms.

Charles still had Montrose's unbending loyalty, and the Marquis was energetically making plans for an invasion of Scotland via the Orkneys. Montrose believed that the local population both there, and in the northern part of the mainland, would be sympathetic to the cause. On 19 September Charles wrote to him, 'I entreat you to go on vigorously, and with your wonted courage and care, in the preservation of those trusts I have committed to you, and not be startled with any reports you may hear, as if I were otherwise inclined to the Presbyterians than when I left you. I assure you I am upon the same principles I was, and depend as much as ever upon your undertakings and endeavours for your service, being fully resolved to assist and support you therein to the uttermost of my power.'[8]

Despite the assurances, Charles was, like many of his Stewart forebears, quite capable of playing a double game. He needed to continue talking to the Covenanters, and he needed the threat of Montrose as a bargaining chip in his negotiations. And if Montrose were in the end to prove successful in putting him back on the throne by force of arms, then what would there be to complain about?

At least Montrose was shrewd enough to know that the prospects of his venture depended on the Royalists within Scotland coming to his aid following any invasion, and that they would be reluctant to do so if they thought Charles was about to deal with the Covenanters. He needed a clear statement of intent to reassure waverers. So he issued a declaration from Sweden with the news that he was returning to Scotland, and calling on the rebels to lay down their arms or they would receive no mercy. Johnston of Warriston delivered an uncompromising reply on behalf of the Estates, ordering that the declaration be burned by the public hangman and decrying Montrose as 'that viperous brood of Satan, who the Estates of Parliament have long since declared traitor, the Church hath delivered into the hands of the Devil, and the Nation doth generally abhor.'[9]

By January 1650, Charles and his advisors had eventually concluded that they had no alternative but to try to reach an agreement with the Covenanters. He wrote to the Estates, to Argyll, and to the Commission of the Kirk, asking to meet at Breda in the Netherlands to agree terms. Argyll was strongly in favour, and in this was backed by most of the nobility. But many of the Kirk Party were nervous, still suspicious of Argyll and believing that he sought to advance himself by assuming the position of kingmaker. They warned that there could be no treaty with Charles unless he accepted all of their conditions. After a 'great and hott dispute', the Estates agreed to proceed with negotiations, the nobles voting thirteen to one in favour (only Cassillis was against). Even the production of a letter from Charles to Montrose, urging him to go ahead with his invasion plan as this would force the Estates into a weaker negotiating position, was not enough to affect the decision. It was agreed that the Commissioners would be sent to Breda, but only to offer the terms previously proposed, and that Parliament would have the final say in any agreement.

When Parliament did meet on 7 March, before the Commissioners departed, a number of new conditions were added, including the requirement that Charles cancel any commission he had given to the hated Montrose. Before any power should be granted to him he would have to sign the Covenants, preferably before he left Breda, but in any event as soon as he landed in Scotland. But Charles continued with his double dealing. Montrose set sail from Bergen to Orkney accompanied by several hundred men (mostly Dutch and German mercenaries) with the aim of joining up with a small force which the Earl of Kinnoull had taken there the previous September. Although Kinnoull himself had died, as had his uncle the Earl of Morton, Orkney's feudal superior (and Argyll's father-in-law), their troops were still there.

Three and a half years after leaving Scotland, Montrose was at last on the way home. For too long he had been on the sidelines, in the unfamiliar world of courts and staterooms, surrounded by those who played with words and argument. Now he was free to do what he did best; take a sword in his hand, and lead men in a fight to avenge the dead King and put his son in his rightful place on the throne. It was his chance to save Charles from the oppressive demands of Argyll and his fanatic brethren. As the winds drove his ship into sight of the flat lands of the Orkneys, James Graham's spirits surged: this was his time.

Montrose was in Orkney on 23 March when a package arrived from Charles. With it came the George and blue ribbon of the Garter, and two letters – one private and one to be made public. In the public letter the King advised of his forthcoming discussions with the Covenanters, but assured Montrose that any treaty would not 'do any contrary to that power and authority which we have given you by our commission, nor consent to anything that may bring the least degree of diminution to it; and if the said treaty should produce an agreement, we will, with our uttermost care, so provide for the honour and interest of yourself and of all that shall engage with you, as shall let the whole world see the high esteem we have for you.' It went on to ask Montrose to 'proceed vigorously and effectively in your undertaking', as this would encourage the Covenanters to reach more reasonable terms. The second letter provided further assurances of the King's loyalty and told Montrose 'not to take alarm at any reports, or messages from others, but to depend on my kindness, and to proceed in your business with your usual courage and alacrity', concluding 'I wish you all good success in it, and shall ever remain your affectionate friend.'[10] At least Charles was being open in his strategy of using Montrose as a pawn in the game, although he was reassuring his loyal captain that he viewed him as anything but expendable.

By now negotiations in Breda between Charles and the Scots Commissioners were well underway. Charles was charm personified, keen to give every appearance of good faith: 'the King strokes them till he can get into the saddle, and then he will make them feel his spurs,'[11] one observer wrote. He was still reluctant to sign up to the Covenants and to another condition disowning his treaty with the Catholics in Ireland, and these remained obstacles to a final agreement. Eventually Charles hinted at a compromise, whereby he would sign a declaration attached to the Covenants rather than the documents them-selves, and that he would disown the Irish treaty if he was still required to do so once he reached Scotland. It was just enough for the Scots Commissioners, who were desperate to see agree-ment reached. On 29 April they at last issued an invitation to Charles to come to Scotland. This he accepted two days later, although there were still serious differences between the parties.

For Argyll and the Covenanters, securing Charles' agreement – something which they had never achieved with his father – was, on the face of it, a cause for celebration. They had at last their Covenanted King, while Charles now had the crown of at least one of his Kingdoms, and key allies to help him secure the other two. But, deep down, both parties must have known that they were simply using each other. Charles, with his love of mistresses and fine living (all he wanted was 'a shoulder of mutton and a whore', sneered Cromwell) was the unlikeliest pin-up boy for the devout Scots looking for the equivalent of an Old Testament King of Israel. The Covenanters were deluding themselves if they thought that this was the Christian prince of their dreams, and what is worse they probably knew it. One of the Commission-ers, Alexander Jaffray, noted in his diary: 'We did both sinfully entangle and engage the nation ourselves and that poor, young Prince to whom we were sent, making him sign and swear a Covenant which we knew from clear and demonstrable reasons that he hated in his heart.'[12] As for Charles, he was no better. He was making promises to his new subjects that he had no real intention of keeping. He would put up with this bunch of religious fanatics for so long as they were useful to him, but once he was on his throne he would be doing things his own way. Both parties were being deeply dishonest and acting in bad faith, both deliberately ignoring the pitfalls in the accommodation that had been reached, so anxious were they to secure their objectives. It was no more than a marriage of convenience, and like most such marriages it was all bound to end in bitterness and tears.

Charles was very conscious of the weakness of his position and keen to lessen the grip that the Covenanters had on him. Key to this was Montrose, planning his invasion of the mainland. Alas for the Captain-General, his mission depended on the Royalists within Scotland flocking to his banner, and there was now no chance of that happening. As soon as it became known that the King was close to an agreement with the Covenanters, the ground was cut from underneath James Graham's feet. The terms of Charles' letter to Montrose, setting out in plain English that the purpose behind the Royalist invasion was primarily to improve Charles' negotiating position, were well known throughout Scotland. Few would risk their lives in a political game. Any hopes that Montrose might have had of a widespread Royalist rising were destroyed. Charles had effectively signed his brave Captain's death warrant.

12

The Cavalier's Last Hurrah

1650-51

On a treeless Kirkwall heath, the chill March wind biting at their faces, the Marquis of Montrose drilled his 1,200 men: Danes, Germans and local levies. It was a little army with which to win back a kingdom. What he would have given to have Alasdair MacDonald back at his side, or Magnus O'Cahan, or Lord Ogilvie or Nathaniel Gordon, but they were all long gone, now just ghosts of distant memory. He had to make the best of it, this last throw of the dice. His mission had been rendered even more perilous by the King's actions, but he did not much care. Again leading an army on Scottish soil, Montrose was where he felt he was meant to be. His preference was always for the field of battle rather than the world of politics, and in his chosen arena he had an unmatched track record. And, like his nemesis Argyll, he had an unshakeable belief in the rightness of his cause.

It would have been easy for Montrose simply to have remained in exile as a fêted romantic hero. Since the publication of George Wishart's memoirs, he had found himself celebrated in Continental society, and would have had no difficulty in making a profitable career commanding the armies of any one of a number of the crowned heads of Europe. To return to Scotland, where he was still under sentence of death and with a large reward attached to his capture, dead or alive, was to put himself unnecessarily in a situation of great personal risk. He had already done his bit for the Royalist cause, and could not have been criticised had he now decided to leave the fight to others. But Montrose was still deeply personally committed to supporting the Stewart monarchy, and seeing it restored to its powers in Scotland in place of what he viewed as the extremist and fanatical regime of the Covenanters. He also had scores to settle with those who had opposed Charles I, chief among them Argyll. And, ever the gambler, he relished the challenge and the adventure, as one who had penned the famous lines:

> He either fears his fates too much,
> Or his deserts are small,
> Who dares not put it to the touch,
> To win, or lose it all!

It is tempting to view Montrose as a doomed warrior-hero who, like Achilles, had made a conscious choice of a short spectacular life, and wanted to go out in a blaze of glory. His letters speak of his death: he wrote to Charles from Kirkwall on 26 March, pledging 'with the more alacrity and bensell [vigour] abandon still my lyfe to search my death for the interests of yr Ma[jestsy's] honor and service.'[1] On the same date he wrote to the Earl of Seaforth, promising 'I will serve you with my life, all the days it shall please God to lend me to it . . . I shall tender your friends, and interests, as my own life; and shall live, or die, my Lord, your cousin and faithful friend and servant.'[2] Yet notwithstanding the odds being stacked against him, he still had reason to be optimistic. He already had the core of an army, and high hopes of being joined by the Royalist northern clans once he crossed from Orkney to the mainland. David Leslie was a formidable commander of the Covenanting forces against him, but led little more than 5,000 men in total. The two had only previously met in battle at Philiphaugh, where Leslie had benefited not only from much superior numbers but also the element of surprise, and Montrose must have rated his chances in a more equal fight. He was never one to underestimate his own abilities.

On 9 April Montrose sent Sir John Hurry, now his Major-General despite having changed sides no fewer than three times in the civil war (and whom Montrose had bested at Auldearn), with 500 men over to Caithness as an advance party. The Royalists had hoped that both the Mackays and Mackenzies would come out in force to support them, but they were mostly disappointed. Knowledge of the game that the King was playing was hardly likely to encourage recruits to flock to his banner.

Montrose himself crossed the Pentland Firth to the mainland on 12 April with the rest of his men and headed south. When news of this reached the Estates there was great concern; Loudon and Argyll were summoned to Edinburgh 'to consult the publique safety'.[3] Leslie was ordered to take his army north to meet the threat. An advance party of five troops of horse, numbering about 230 men and commanded by Archibald Strachan, a devout Covenanter, made for Ross-shire. By now Montrose was at Carbisdale on the southern side of the Kyle of Sutherland, still waiting in vain for the much hoped-for reinforcements. On 27 April Strachan caught up with him.

The Royalists were camped in a strong defensive position and had already dug themselves in. The bold Strachan knew it would be difficult to use his cavalry to launch an effective attack on the enemy where they were, and decided to try and draw them out. He concealed the bulk of his forces, sending forward one troop only. The information which Montrose's scouts passed back to him was that there was just a small force ahead. Not for the first time the intelligence was defective. Anxious for a quick victory to improve morale, Montrose gave the order to advance, his men leaving their defensive position and moving on to low ground where they would be vulnerable to cavalry attack. Immediately

Strachan attacked with the full weight of his forces, catching them by surprise.

Had Montrose had at his disposal even a proportion of the brave Irish troops who had once made up his army, then he might have saved the day, but the inexperienced Orkney levies had no stomach for a fight with the Covenanters' well-ordered dragoons, and the Royalist troops broke and ran. Only the 400 or so Danes and Germans put up any sort of resistance before they, too, were overwhelmed. Of Montrose's 1,200 men, there were between 400 and 500 slaughtered, with perhaps 200 being drowned in the River Shin as they tried to make their escape. More than 400 were captured, among them Hurry (who would be taken to Edinburgh and become another victim of the Maiden). Montrose himself lost his horse, shot from underneath him, and it was all he could do to save himself. He had lost his last battle.

With just two companions, Montrose made his way into the trackless hills, trying to make it to the far North-west to find safety in the territory of sympathetic Royalists. He had thrown away his sword belt and coat with the badge of the Garter on it to help avoid detection. It was desperately cold with snow on the ground, and with little in the way of supplies it was a terrible, gruelling journey through wild country. Starving, frozen and exhausted, he dragged himself as far as Assynt, where he sought refuge with the local laird, Neil MacLeod. Montrose was unsure of MacLeod's loyalties, but he had run out of options. He was taken into the laird's castle of Ardvreck, on the shores of Loch Assynt, hoping that the traditions of Highland hospitality would be enough to protect him from the Covenanters who were in hot pursuit. But the temptation of the large reward being offered was too great for MacLeod, and despite Montrose offering money for his freedom and transport to Orkney, on 4 May the Marquis was handed over to his enemies. The game was finally over.

The Covenanters were exultant at the capture of their villain. For the last six years Montrose had been a demon figure, and now the Lord had delivered him into their hands. They were determined to humiliate their prisoner and had him taken to Edinburgh on an unsaddled pony, his feet tied together under its belly. For at least part of the journey there went ahead of him a herald announcing him as a traitor. Montrose's route south took him through Angus, and on 15 May he stopped at the Earl of Southesk's castle of Kinnaird, where he was reunited with Robert and Jean, his two younger children.

Montrose's captors had hoped that the population would turn out to abuse the prisoner, and there were certainly instances of victims of the conflict doing just that. But the dignified manner in which he conducted himself aroused public sympathy. It was now five or six years since he had been considered a real threat to the peace, and with the Kirk Party's regime in Edinburgh becoming less and less popular, Montrose was not the same hate figure to the public as he still was to the leading Covenanters.

On 18 May the prisoner reached Edinburgh, and was taken up the Canongate tied to the hangman's cart, bare-headed, with his arms pinned behind his back so he could not protect himself from missiles thrown by the mob. The common folk lined the street to see this monster, whose name they had used to frighten their children, now humbled before them. But rather than hurl stones and abuse they were silenced by Montrose's noble bearing, some even cheering. The cart passed Moray House, where were assembled many of the leading Covenanters, waiting to see their great enemy at last brought low. On the balcony overlooking the street stood Argyll's heir Lord Lorne, but Argyll himself kept out of view, watching from behind a half-open shutter. Even in his moment of triumph, he did not want to be seen gloating at the humiliation of his rival. Archibald Campbell had himself lived enough of his life on the knife's edge not to feel a measure of sympathy for one who had gambled it all, and lost so dramatically. The moment is captured in typically partisan fashion in W. E. Aytoun's Royalist ballad 'The Execution of Montrose':

> Then, as the Graeme looked upwards,
> He met the ugly smile
> Of him who sold his King for gold –
> The master-fiend Argyle!
> The Marquis gazed a moment
> And nothing did he say,
> But the cheek of Argyle grew ghastly pale,
> And he turned his eyes away.

The previous day it had been decided how Montrose would be dealt with. There was of course no need for a trial, the prisoner having previously been convicted of treason *in absentia* and sentenced to death. Montrose was ordered to be hanged as a common criminal rather than beheaded as a nobleman. The sentence narrates that he was to be: 'taken to the market cross of Edinburgh and there . . . hanged upon a gibbet, where he is to hang for certain hours, and after cutting down his body, his head publicly to be struck off and his two arms and legs separated from his body, which are to be affixed and disposed upon in manner following, namely: his head upon the west gable of the new prison house of Edinburgh, one of his arms upon the top of the tolbooth of Perth and the other upon the tolbooth of Aberdeen, and one of his legs upon the top of the tolbooth of Stirling and the other upon the tolbooth of Glasgow, where they are to be affixed and remain.'[4]

By the time Montrose arrived at Edinburgh, he was aware that Charles had signed the Treaty of Breda with his enemies. The King had written to Montrose advising him of the agreement and ordering him to lay down arms and leave Scotland.

This letter was to be taken by Sir William Fleming, who was also told that if the Scots Parliament did not ratify the Treaty then the instructions were to be withdrawn. A subsequent instruction by the King to Fleming, on 12 May, sought to put distance between him and Montrose. As it happened, neither mattered – Fleming did not arrive in Edinburgh until after Montrose's execution. Charles certainly had had it within his power to protect Montrose, and could have at least tried to make it a condition of his dealings with the Covenanters that his life would be spared. But he chose not to do so, valuing his negotiating position with his new allies more highly than his brave Captain's life. Argyll reported to the Estates that he 'had a letter from the Secretary, the Earle of Lothian, wich shew him that his Majestie wes no ways sorey that James Grahame was defait, in respecte (as he said) he hade made that invasion without and contrarey to his command.'⁵ Protecting Montrose would have used up valuable political capital with the Covenanters, and as a Royalist asset he was simply past his sell-by date. It was a poor reward for the Marquis' unswerving loyalty to both Charles and his father.

Montrose was to be executed on 21 May, just three days after his arrival in Edinburgh. While there was no trial to be held, the prisoner was interviewed at length by many of the leading Covenanters and ministers, and taken before Parliament to hear his sentence. Despite the hopelessness of his situation, Montrose stoutly defended his actions, maintaining his loyalty to the National Covenant and continued opposition to the Solemn League. He had remained a faithful subject of the King, and his last military action had been at his Majesty's just commands. He told his interrogators: 'As for my coming in at this time it was by his Majesty's commands, in order to the accelerating of the treaty betwixt him and you; his Majesty knowing, that whenever he had ended with you, I was ready to retire upon his call: I may justly say, that never subject acted upon more honourable grounds, nor by so lawful a power, as I did in this service.'[6] It was all true, but it made not a whit of a difference.

Montrose spent his last night in the Tolbooth under the watch of the infamous Major Weir, outwardly a prominent and devout Covenanter, but later exposed as a notorious warlock and burnt at the stake for his self-confessed crimes (which supposedly included incest with his sister). Despite being pestered by his captors the prisoner found time to write more poetry appropriate to his situation:

> Let them bestow on every airth a limb,
> Then open all my veins, that I may swim
> To Thee, my Maker, in that crimson lake;
> Then place my parbroiled head upon a stake,
> Scatter my ashes, strew them in the air –
> Lord! Since Thou knowest where all these atoms are,
> I'm hopeful Thou'lt recover once my dust,
> And confident Thou'lt raise me with the just.

On the afternoon of Tuesday the 21st, Montrose was taken out to die on gallows 30 feet high, specially erected for the occasion. Resplendent in a fine black suit, with a scarlet cloak, carnation pink stockings, white gloves, shoes with ribbons, and a black beaver hat with a silver band, he awed the crowd gathered for a last glimpse of this great offender. One observer noted that he looked more like a bridegroom than a criminal, while another wrote: 'I never saw a more sweeter carriage in a man in all my life.'[7] The condemned man delivered a final speech of self-justification, forgiving his enemies, and reiterating his devotion to the King. Copies of Wishart's book and Montrose's final Declaration delivered from Sweden – deemed between them sufficient evidence of his crimes – were hung round his neck. He prayed a little, and legend has it that a ray of sunlight broke through the stormy sky as if heaven was greeting him. His last words were 'God have mercy on this afflicted land', and with that he was hanged. He was 37 years old.

Montrose's body was left suspended for three hours, after which, as ordered, the head was cut off and placed on a spike on the Tolbooth, where the black Edinburgh corbies soon made their foul dinner of his noble features. The limbs were removed and distributed to Stirling, Glasgow, Perth and Aberdeen. What remained was buried beside the public gallows in the Burghmuir, outside the city wall, for as an excommunicate the Marquis was not entitled to burial in the consecrated ground of Greyfriars' kirkyard.

Argyll took no part in the actions against Montrose (the favour was to be repaid eleven years later when Montrose's young heir, the 2nd Marquis, refused any part in Parliament's condemnation of Argyll). James Graham had long since ceased to present any serious threat to his ambitions, and there was no point in being personally vindictive. Argyll was in any event preoccupied with the birth of a baby daughter on the same day as Montrose's execution. 'I confes I am wearie,' he wrote to Lothian the next day, 'for all last night my wyf was crying, who, blissed be God, is saiflie brocht to bed of a dochter, whois birth day is remarkabll in the tragik end of James Grahame at this Cros.' He displayed no pleasure at his rival's demise, but noted dismissively 'he got sum resolution after he cam her, how to goe out of this world, but nothing at all how to enter into aneother, not so muche as once humblling himself to pray at all on the scaffold.'[8] For the devout Christian, Argyll, Montrose had died too concerned about his reputation on Earth, and not sufficiently focused on the afterlife.

Both of Argyll's principal rivals, Montrose, champion of the Royalists, and Hamilton as leader of the Engagers, were now gone, and this should have left him in an all-powerful position.

But their departure from the stage seemed to coincide with the decline of his own influence, as if he had depended on their challenge and threat for his authority. Argyll was becoming more distant from the governing Kirk Party, whose members feared that he was putting self-interest before the greater cause. Increasingly he saw Charles as the coming man, and it was to the Royal star that he wanted to hitch his fortunes. On 24 June the King reached Scotland, landing at Garmouth in Moray, where he was received by Argyll 'with all the outward respect imaginable'.[9] The previous day Charles had finally, and somewhat reluctantly, signed the Covenants. If he wanted the Scots on side he really had no alternative. Charles made his way south by way of Aberdeen, where his late champion's freshly severed arm was now on public display, but if he felt any sense of shame he did not disclose it. Everywhere there was public delight at the new King's arrival, with bonfires and dancing in the streets of Edinburgh. Nicoll's *Diary* records: 'The pure kaill wyfes at the Trone sacrificed thair mandis and creillis, and the verie stooles thai sat upone to the fyre.'[10]

Charles was installed in Falkland Palace in Fife, and quickly brought under the supervision of his new political and religious masters. Presbyterian ministers took it in turns to instruct the young King in his new faith, reprimanding him for frivolous activities such as dancing or playing cards. On one Sunday he had to endure no fewer than six sermons 'without intermission'.[11] Although for a 20 year old it must have been a great ordeal, it was a price worth paying. If Henry of Navarre could renounce the Protestant faith and become a Roman Catholic in order to gain the Crown of France (reputedly with the words 'Paris is well worth a mass'), then Charles could be a good Presbyterian for the sake of three Kingdoms.

Charles recognised that the key politician he needed as an ally was Argyll, and when he approached the Marquis looking for assistance he found a willing recruit. The Duke of Buckingham, who had accompanied Charles as one of his advisors, counselled him to put his trust entirely in Argyll, and the Marquis was more than happy to take charge of Royal interests. 'There was never a better courtier than Argyle,' wrote Clarendon, 'who used all possible address to make himself gracious to the King, entertained him with very pleasant discourses, with such insinuations, that the King did not only very well like his conversation, but often believed that he had a mind to please and gratify him.' But Argyll still kept his trademark cautious approach, deploying his favoured tactic of absenting himself from difficult situations: 'but then, when his Majesty made any attempt to get some of his servants about him, to reconcile the two factions, that the kingdom might be united, he [Argyll] gathered up his countenance, and retired from him, without ever yielding to any one proposition that was made to him by his Majesty.'[12]

The Kirk Party wanted to expel some of the Malignants who had come with Charles to Scotland, among them the new Duke of Hamilton and the Earl of Lauderdale. Following the King's wishes, Argyll proposed in Parliament that their removal should be delayed, but much to his annoyance he was outvoted. At least Parliament unanimously agreed to ratify the Treaty of Breda, on 4 July. The King was immediately granted his Royal power and the coronation date of 15 August was set. But it was not to be. The English Parliament was never going to put up with this threat to its power. On 22 July Oliver Cromwell, fresh from his successful campaign in Ireland where he had with great brutality crushed Parliament's opponents, and now Parliamentary Captain-General, crossed the Border with an invasion force of 16,000 men. The Scots Parliament had already agreed a levy of troops, and with David Leslie once more in command, an army of 15,000 was assembled. Many were inexperienced and ill-equipped and unlikely to provide much of a match for Cromwell's hardened troops, but they were defending home territory and a cause in which they believed, and their ministers assured them that they had God on their side. Cromwell was equally convinced of divine support for his cause. He wrote to the Scots, 'I beseech you in the bowels of Christ think it possible you may be mistaken.'[13] But the Covenanters had no doubts.

Now the Estates made a serious and possibly fatal error. Concerned about the presence of Malignants in the army, it was decided that there would be a purge of those in the ranks who were not pure in their views. Despite opposition from both Argyll and Leslie, thousands of officers and men were expelled, a loss that the Scots army could well do without. Meantime Cromwell had his own problems. He had made it as far as Musselburgh, but had struggled to make more progress, and with supplies running low, and sickness in the camp, he had retired to Dunbar. Leslie pursued him eastwards and drew up his forces on Doune Hill in a commanding position, blocking Cromwell's line of retreat to the south. By this stage Leslie had nearly double the forces of the English, and with adequate supplies, time was on his side. He was initially happy to wait until hunger forced Cromwell's hand. Unfortunately the politicians and clergy intervened and urged him to take action. Having taken the advice of senior officers, and following their unanimous decision, Leslie moved his men onto lower ground, and it was here, early in the morning of 3 September, that battle was joined.

Cromwell could not believe his luck when he saw that the Scots had changed position. He launched a bold surprise attack on Leslie's troops, who were simply outclassed by the experienced English soldiers. The result was an overwhelming victory for the invaders, with as many as 4,000 Scots killed, and an incredible 10,000 taken prisoner, most of whom would die in captivity or be transported as slaves to the colonies. There was many a young minister's son, recruited to the purged Scots army more for his godliness than for any skill he had in battle, who had waved farewell to his parents at the manse door on a summer's morning, never thinking that it was the last he would ever see of them, and that he would end his days in servitude thousands of miles away under the hot sun of the Americas. If God had been on anyone's side that day, He had been with Cromwell. It was a disaster for the Covenanters and for Scotland.

Not everyone, though, was as dismayed at the news as might be expected. When Charles heard of what had happened he fell on his knees and gave thanks to God, 'that he was so fairly rid of his enemies',[14] realising that this might be enough to free him of the tyranny of the extreme Covenanters under whose strictures he had been living. He was right; the greatest political losers from the defeat at Dunbar were the Kirk Party, who understandably were blamed for the ruinous decision to purge the army. There was a growing view that their rule, in many ways socially oppressive (and the closest Scotland ever came to a theocracy), had been disastrous. Robert Baillie had previously observed: 'I am more and more in the mind, that it were for the good of the world, that Churchmen did meddle with Ecclesiastical affairs only.'[15] It was proof positive that religion and politics make a bad mixture.

Argyll had put enough distance between himself and the Kirk Party to ensure his own survival in the event of the latter's decline, but many of his friends and political allies, such as Johnston of Warriston, were prominent amongst the extremists. If the Party was going down, Charles had to make sure that someone as valuable to him as Argyll did not go with it, and that the King retained his loyalty. Charles wrote to him from Perth on 24 September promising to create him a Duke and Knight of the Garter and (perhaps more usefully, given his financial situation) to ensure payment of £40,000 sterling owed to him, once he was properly on the throne. If Charles needed Argyll, then equally Argyll needed Charles. He had burnt his boats with the Kirk Party, he was distrusted by the Engagers, and hated by the Royalists. The relationship between King and Covenanter was one made of necessity, and despite the warm words there was a deep distrust between the two men.

The true nature of the concord between Charles and Argyll was illustrated in the episode which became known as 'the Start' – an attempted coup by Engagers and Royalists from the North in support of the King. Details of this were provided in advance by Buckingham to Argyll, and in the event the whole thing was badly planned and even more poorly executed, and came to nothing. But the Royal fingerprints were all over it, and it would simply have confirmed Argyll's belief that Charles was only allying with him as a matter of expediency until a better option presented itself.

Cromwell, meanwhile, had occupied Edinburgh. Although he had come close to engaging the Scots army which was now at Stirling, he had failed to advance further north to challenge Charles, who was ensconced at Perth, Scotland's ancient capital. The English general was putting out feelers towards the more extreme Covenanters, whom he knew were increasingly suspicious of the true motives of their new King. Partly as a result of the Start, Covenanters from the South-west sent a Remonstrance to the Estates with a complaint against the King that he was not sincere in accepting the Covenants. They called on Charles to be excluded from power until he could demonstrate that he was genuine in supporting the Covenanting cause.

The Remonstrance had no support amongst the nobility, but amongst the middle classes – the lairds and burgesses – in the west, it had a substantial number of subscribers. It was taken seriously enough to be debated by the Estates in November, with Johnston of Warriston speaking in support and Argyll and others opposing. In his diary for Tuesday 19 November, Johnston records: 'Argyll challenged it [the Remonstrance] of sedition and treason, and challenged ministers as taking too much on them, and he pressed ay the declining of the King's authority.' It demonstrated a divide within the Kirk Party, the more moderate members of which wanted to hold faith with Charles as a Covenanted King, and the more extreme thinking (with justification) that this approach was simply naive.

Majority opinion within the country continued to be strongly in support of the King, and preparations were well in hand for his coronation at Scone, ancient crowning-place of the Kings of Scots, on 1 January 1651. In advance of the great occasion there was called a national day of humiliation for sins, and the King himself was required to fast for a day in penance for not just his own sins but those of his father and grandfather. Charles complied – with a crown at stake it was no time for quibbles – but was unimpressed, remarking afterwards: 'I think that I must repent too that ever I was born.'[16]

The coronation, conducted under the rites of the Presbyterian Kirk, took place in the parish church of Scone with all due ceremony. It was New Year's Day, and the kirk was packed with leading nobles, splendid in their finest clothes, for what would be a historic day: the last ever coronation of a monarch on Scottish soil. All the traditional formalities were observed with the exception of the anointing with oil, which was deemed to reek too much of Popish superstition. Robert Douglas, Moderator of the General Assembly, could not have found a more appropriate text for his sermon (which lasted two hours) than the passage from 2nd Kings 11, on the coronation of the young King Joash of ancient Judah, and the priest Jehoaida's covenant between God and the King and the people. Charles, in whom all hopes rested, sat patiently throughout the whole ludicrous charade, appearing 'very seriously and devoutly, so that none doubted of his ingenuity and sincerity'. At last the crown was placed on the King's head by none other than Argyll himself, as the one who had done more than any man alive to ensure that this day happened. One by one the nobility came forward to touch the crown and swear allegiance to their long-awaited Covenanted King. Charles then spoke to the ministers present, assuring them of his good faith, and requesting 'that if in any time coming they did hear or see him breaking the Covenant they would tell him of it, and put him in mind of his oath'.[17] He was playing his part to perfection.

Argyll was certainly seeking to make the most of his position while he could. Charles had already promised that his title would be elevated to a Dukedom. Now Argyll suggested that his eldest daughter Anne, 'a gentlewoman of rare parts and education',[18] be taken by Charles as a wife. The King treated this suggestion courteously enough, writing to seek his mother's advice. Queen Henrietta Maria replied to this in diplomatic fashion, warmly praising Argyll as an individual but stating that the times were too troubled for any such decision to be made at this juncture. Whether Charles had any personal interest in this match is not known, but Lady Anne herself was seriously disappointed, and ended up by dying unmarried; 'she lossed her spirit and turned absolutely distracted', wrote Kirkton, 'so unfortunately do the back wheels of private designes work in the puppet playes of the publick revolutions in the world.'[19]

While Argyll's role in the coronation made him appear as the kingmaker, in reality his power and influence were dwindling. None of the three main political factions in the country trusted him, and he was almost entirely reliant on the King's patronage for his position. The Malignants were being allowed back into both the Estates and the army, and the Act of Classes was rescinded on 2 June. With both Engagers and Royalists now readmitted to public life, Argyll's power base had gone. 'The statesman who had given over Scotland to the rule of the middle class, and had taught her that her safety lay in associating herself with England while preserving her own national independence, fell unaided and unregretted because a base intrigue for the maintenance of his own influence had taken the place of a manful championship of his nations' cause',[20] is Gardiner's assessment. Nor was there much public sympathy for him, a newspaper of the time reporting that 'Argyll is gone down the winde; nobody takes any notice of him; as he rides along, private troopers jostle him sometimes almost off his horse.'[21] A little more than a year after the execution of his great rival Montrose, Argyll now found his own political career effectively at an end.

While Charles was extending his influence over the Estates and army in Scotland, Cromwell continued with his military conquest. On 1 August he seized Perth. The Scots army under Leslie was still at Stirling but lacking both arms and supplies. They had just two options: either stay where they were and await Cromwell's attack, or instead invade England in the hope of rousing the Royalists there. The second option might have seemed a desperate one, but it was the less bad of the two. Argyll was opposed, but in a minority of one, and so retired to Inveraray. As it happened his wife was dangerously ill, and Charles gave him permission to leave the army. They never saw each other again.

*

Charles took his army south to Carlisle, and then on through Lancashire towards the Midlands. The hoped-for English recruits to the cause simply did not materialise; indeed the Scots were looked on as an invading force. Cromwell marched south in pursuit, catching up with Charles at Worcester. There, on 3 September 1651, precisely one year to the day after his famous victory at Dunbar, he smashed the Royalists to pieces. 2,000

Scots were killed, and nearly 10,000 captured, most to be sold as slaves for the Americas. Charles himself escaped, eventually making it to France, where he stated that he would rather be hanged than ever return to Scotland (he never did). He had had his fill of the Scots and their wretched Covenants.

Cromwell had left General Monck in Scotland with between 5,000 and 6,000 men. The Committee of Estates tried to rally Scots resistance to the army of occupation, but without success. The Estates met at Kirriemuir in Angus on 24 August, but without a quorum, and then again on the 28th in the small town of Alyth in East Perthshire. Here they were surprised by Monck and nearly every member captured. And with that the independent government of Scotland, with its experiment in the empowerment of the middle-class, was extinguished, and shortly thereafter the whole country came under Cromwellian control. Thirteen years after the Scottish Revolution, power was back in the hands of an unsympathetic London ruler, only this time he did not wear a crown.

13

A Better Crown

1651–1661

Archibald Campbell, Marquis of Argyll, had always had two principal objectives in his political career: the creation of a constitutional monarchy and a system of civil government where Parliament was supreme, and the establishment of Presbyterianism as the state religion in England, as a necessary bulwark to protect the freedom of the Kirk in Scotland. With the King in exile, and Cromwell, who had no religious sympathies with Presbyterians, effectively established as a dictator, these two aims now seemed further away than ever. However, there was still work to be done in protecting both the Kirk and the Scottish national interest against the worst excesses of Cromwellian rule, and Argyll was adaptable and pragmatic enough to want to try to reach an accommodation with the new regime.

Argyll already found himself sidelined from a leadership role in what remained of the Scottish political class. This was taken up by his relative John Campbell, Earl of Loudon, as Chancellor. Loudon attempted to call a meeting of the Scots Parliament for November 1651 for those members who had not been captured by General Monck, to be held at the Campbell stronghold of Finlarig at the west end of Loch Tay in Perthshire, hopefully far out of reach of Cromwell's troops. In advance of this Argyll wrote to Monck asking for a meeting. 'I beleeve all Christians in every business do propose a good end (or at least ought to do) so should they resolve upon just and righteous wayes to attain it (I judge no man) yet I desire to know from you, as one having chiefe trust in this Kingdome, if it were not fit that some men who have deserved Trust in both Kingdomes may not meet to good purpose on some convenient place, as a meanes to stop the shedding of more Christian blood?'[1]

Monck replied that he could not enter into an agreement without Parliamentary authority – as far as he and his superiors were concerned they were in command of Scotland now, and they did not recognise any separate Scottish government with whom they had to deal. Monck wrote on 31 October, 'Argyle hath summoned a Parliament; for what end tis not yet known; the people generally are desirous of a settlement.' He also noted 'there is no news of the young Lad [Charles II] being here in Scotland.'[2] In the event it was agreed that a meeting would be useful, and Argyll was given permission to travel to Perth to meet Monck's representatives, but only on condition that he used his utmost endeavours to prevent the meeting of Parliament previously called. Argyll made it neither to the arranged meeting in Perth nor to the session of Parliament, which turned out to be a non-event, as only three of its members turned up.

In December the English Parliament appointed commissioners in order to run affairs in Scotland and create a political union with England. These commissioners were anxious to meet Argyll to obtain a guarantee that he would not seek to frustrate their actions. Argyll was understandably reluctant to submit to the invaders, and exceedingly concerned about his future under the new regime. He played for time, blaming gallstones for preventing him from acting more quickly. He wrote again and again to the commissioners seeking assurances as to his position, with increasing persistence.

Cromwell still had the Highlands to bring to heel, and he sent out an expeditionary force under Major-General Deane to suppress any latent Royalists, and to start the process that would lead to the creation of English garrisons at strategic points. Before these troops reached Inveraray, to which they had doubtless been sent to try and force his hand, Argyll eventually surrendered, accepting both the authority of English Parliamentary rule and the terms of a Union between the two countries. Facing a military threat he had little alternative. His new allies were well aware of his dilemma; writing from Tarbert on 18 July 1652, one Cromwellian officer observed: 'The Marquesse of Argyle doth entertaine Col. Overton, Col. Read, and Col. Blackmore in much state: and makes many pretences of love and affection, but who knows not that it is but constrained? The Marquesse is no stranger in the art of Politicks; but we shal make use of him accordingly.'[3]

On 19 August Argyll signed Articles of Agreement with Major-General Deane, promising to do nothing either directly or indirectly to the prejudice of the Parliament of the Commonwealth of England or other authority in Scotland, and to use his utmost endeavours to secure that his family, vassals and tenants should do the same. He was obliged to inform on any who were inclined to breach these terms. Should notice be given to that effect by the English Parliament, either Argyll or Lord Lorne would have to travel to England as hostages until such time as Parliament would deem it fit to see them released. In return for accepting these terms, Argyll's person, property, and rank would be respected, there would be (except in exceptional circumstances) no military garrisons in his main properties at Inveraray and Carrick, but five garrisons were to be established within Argyllshire at Dunstaffnage, Dunolly, Lough, Kincairn and Tarbert. Additionally, Argyll would not be prevented from pursuing 'his good endeavours for the establishing religion according to his conscience'.[4] Despite these concessions it seemed like a deal with the Devil.

Argyll had another reason to want to reach an agreement with the English Parliament. Years of war and campaigning had left him with terrible debts which he had no hope of repaying unless the very substantial sums owed to him by the Scottish Government were forthcoming. Until he made his peace with the new regime, there was no prospect of any of these payments being made and he faced financial ruin. His signing of the Articles of Agreement meant that the debts due to him would be repaid, but even then his financial position continued to be precarious.

Meantime, the Marquis' treatment at the hands of the English soldiers had raised the ire of his loyal Campbell clansmen. Under the pretext that they believed Argyll had been taken prisoner, they gathered in substantial numbers to threaten the Cromwellian troops, capturing three out of the five Argyllshire garrisons. Anxious to keep the peace, Argyll had the prisoners released. The episode demonstrated not only the continued loyalty of his clansmen to their chief, but also the military power that he still held. The outcome was that the English decided to abandon the three affected garrisons, leaving them with only a presence at Dunstaffnage and Dunolly.

Charles, in the Hague, was kept abreast of his former favourite's activities. In April 1653, Sir Robert Moray reported to the King: 'All I shall say of My Lord Argyle, that with how great disadvantage soever he may be represented to your Majesty, and whatever grounds of jealousy there may possibly be against him, the course he takes is merely for self-preservation.'[5] According to Moray, whatever the King might be hearing to the contrary, Argyll's true loyalties were still with him. Charles himself wrote some months later to the Marquis, in the warmest terms, assuring him of the King's friendship and desire to reward him for his past loyalty. Charles needed to keep the Royalist flame alive in Scotland, and the last thing he wanted was as powerful a man as Argyll making deals with the enemy.

Charles still harboured hopes for military victory against Cromwell, and appointed the Earl of Glencairn as his Commander-in-Chief to start a new rising. Glencairn raised the

Royal Standard at Killin on 27 July 1653, gathering to him volunteers from across Scotland. Having so recently signed his peace with Cromwell, Argyll could hardly himself commit to this venture, but the young Lord Lorne was an enthusiast for the Royalist cause and his father could not prevent him, nor his younger brother, from joining the rising. It might have appeared that the Campbell family were simply hedging their bets by having different members of the household on opposite sides, as many great Scottish houses were to do in the Jacobite risings of the following century, but Argyll seems to have made strenuous efforts to prevent his sons joining with Glencairn (or at least he wanted to give the appearance of having done so). He wrote in forceful terms to Lord Lorne, copying it to the English Colonel Lilburne: 'If there be in you either feare of God, or respect to His law in your obedience to your Parents, or any feare of the curse pronounced in God's Word against the setters lightly of either father or mother, or if you desire not their curse to follow you in all your waies, These are requiring you as you will answere for it one day before the Throne of God, and as you desire to be free of all the guiltinesse and prejudice which will follow such waies, and as you desire to enjoy anything that is mine, or would eschue to deserve my curse, that you will harken to my counsell to forbeare such courses.'[6] Lorne paid no attention.

Having secured Argyll as a political ally, Cromwell's forces sought military assistance from him. These requests were resisted by the Marquis for whom this was a step too far. He told the English that due to the popularity of Lorne with his clansmen, he could not rely on them to take up arms against the Royalists. But Argyll did intervene on the English side to support a Colonel Cobbett who landed in Mull. Argyll himself travelled to the island and persuaded the local population to accept English rule, an action which won the gratitude of the Cromwellians. Monck reported to Cromwell: 'the Marquesse of Argyll is resolved to engage in blood with us on our side with a partie'.[7] Even this minor intervention raised the ire of the Royalists, with Glencairn's instructions to a Major Strachan highlighting: 'First, and above all, the warrant under the King's hand declaring Argyle traytor ... for his being in open hostility against his Majesty's forces at Dowart [Duart], for assisting the English with ... and for causing all the Country people lift up their hands and swear to obey the Common wealth of England.'[8]

Glencairn's rising continued rather ineffectually for the next year, providing more of an irritation to the authorities than a real threat. One consequence was a continued deterioration in the relations between Argyll and his eldest son. Argyll travelled to Dalkeith in November 1654 to denounce Lorne to Monck as part of his continued efforts to demonstrate good faith with the English occupiers. It was not until August of the following year that Lorne would eventually surrender, and thereafter move back to Inveraray and start to rebuild the relationship with his father.

Argyll had other problems. His financial position had continued to deteriorate to the extent that he was now unable to leave his Argyllshire territories without facing action at the hands of his many creditors. When he visited Monck, the Marquis suffered the humiliation of having his horse, harness, and 'all other household stuff' poinded in Dalkeith and at Newbattle, and brought to Edinburgh and forcibly sold at the Mercat Cross to repay debts. His straitened circumstances won him no sympathy from the population, Baillie noting that 'The people's great hatred lyes on him above any other, and whatever befalls him, few does pittie it.'[9] Matters became even worse when, in November 1655, Argyll made the journey to London to kiss Cromwell's hand (by now the English leader had been appointed 'Lord Protector of the Commonwealth of England, Scotland and Ireland') and to ratify the agreement which he had made with Deane. The principal purpose of the trip was to ensure that Cromwell's regime paid to Argyll the huge sums owed by the Scottish Government. But while in Westminster he was arrested on the action of one creditor, Elizabeth Maxwell, the Earl of Dirleton's widow, for a debt of £1,000 sterling for supplies to the Scottish army in England during the civil war campaign. Argyll found himself imprisoned, and was not released until February 1656 when the Dowager Countess was eventually repaid from sums he was able to recover from the Government. For Scotland's once most powerful man to have found himself languishing in an English jail must have been both embarrassing and frustrating, but imprisonment for debt amongst the nobility was more common than one might think, and conditions in jail were in keeping with the prisoners' status.

On his release from prison Argyll remained for some time in London, not returning to Scotland until 1657. John Evelyn notes in his diary that Argyll visited him twice, making him laugh with his ignorance of birdlife: 'he tooke the Turtle-Doves for Owles'.[10] Argyll played little active part in political affairs, declining to participate in sittings of Parliament, although following the death of Oliver Cromwell in September 1658 he did sit briefly in Richard Cromwell's Parliament as a member for Aberdeenshire. He had to all intents and purposes retired from public life.

The Protectorate which had been created for Oliver Cromwell ended with the resignation of his son in May 1659. General Monck restored the rule of Parliament and arrangements were made for the recall of Charles II from exile as a restored monarch in 1660. There was jubilation in Scotland; the Covenanted King was coming back to his throne. Now surely, at last, all the Covenanters' ambitions would be fulfilled. But of course it was not to be, and wiser heads in Scotland viewed the restoration of Charles with foreboding. Ministers in Edinburgh told their congregations to be afraid of Charles' return rather than celebrate it, talking about bishops being reinstated, the reintroduction of liturgies and the destruction of the Covenants. The more radical amongst the Covenanters knew that Charles had little love for them, and feared that once back on the throne he would be looking to settle old scores.

On one level, Argyll surely had no reason to be personally concerned. While those who had played a part in the trial and execution of Charles I would now be nervous, in no sense could Argyll be placed among their number. He had always been loyal to the current King, to the extent of even placing the crown on his head. While he had co-operated with the Cromwellian regime, he had done so only under duress, and had held out longer than many of his contemporaries. But strange omens were suggesting black consequences for the Marquis. His sister, the Countess of Kenmure, had foreseen through the art of physiognomy (the ability to tell a person's fate from their facial features) that he would 'die in blood'. On the night of Charles II's return to British soil, all the dogs at Argyll's house at Roseneath 'did take a strange yowling and glowering up to my Lord's chamber windows for some houres together'.[11] While at a game of bowls with Argyll and some colleagues, a friend of his fell pale, and said to those about him, "Blesse me! What is that I see? My Lord with his head off, and all his shoulder full of blood".'[12]

However concerning the portents were, sooner or later Argyll would have to face the restored King. With Charles established at Court in London, a succession of Scottish nobles made the journey to present themselves to him and were warmly received. These included Lord Lorne, and the friendly reception he obtained seemed to have been enough to convince Argyll to make the trip himself, against the advice of some of his friends who felt it would have been better for him to stay in the safety of Argyllshire and await developments. Baille records: 'Argyle, by his son Lorne's letter, being advertised that the King took kind-lie with all men, ventured to goe to London.'[13] He had already purchased (for £80) a 12-ton pleasure boat on the Thames, the *St Lawrence of Dorft*, not so much for social purposes but more to provide a means of escape to the Continent should matters take a wrong turn. The Marquis knew from past experience on at least three occasions of the value of a convenient ship when his life or liberty were in danger.

Argyll arrived in London on 8 July 1660 and sought out the Lord Chancellor, the Earl of Clarendon, at his home to ask for his assistance in arranging a meeting with the King. Clarendon refused to see him. Undeterred, the Marquis simply waited out-side and doorstepped him as he left his lodgings to make the journey to Court, but the Lord Chancellor declined to stop and speak. Clarendon was travelling by carriage while Argyll had the advantage of his boat on the Thames, so the latter was able to get to Whitehall first. He tried to catch Clarendon again in the Royal antechamber, but once more the Chancellor refused to speak, whispering to his son 'that is a fatal [i.e. doomed] man'.[14] Undeterred, Argyll waited in the room while sending Lorne into the King's inner chamber to advise of his father's presence, as he wished to present himself and kiss the royal hands. Charles made no reply, but summoned his secretary, and quietly asked him to instruct Sir Edward Walter, the Garter King-at-Arms, to arrest Argyll on the charge of treason. Still standing in the outer room, 'extremely crowded and gazed upon',[15] with the English courtiers wondering what to make of this visitor from Scotland, a man once so vital in the nation's affairs, Argyll was seized by the King's officers. The Marquis was taken from Court to the Tower of London, begging to be allowed to see the King, but his requests falling on deaf ears. His fall from grace was complete.

Notwithstanding Argyll's caution in advance of his trip to London, his arrest for treason must have come as a brutal shock.

He had believed himself loyal to Charles, and they had always enjoyed good personal relations; this was the man, after all, who might have been his son-in-law. Despite the risks, he hoped that being able to present his case face-to-face would be enough to win the King over. But it was not to be. Charles had already made up his mind.

When the news reached her of her husband's arrest, Argyll's wife Margaret went to London to try and get him an audience with the King, without success. He lay in the Tower for some five months until December 1660 when he was transported by sea to Edinburgh to await trial. Unlike Hamilton, Argyll had no English title and therefore could only be tried by his peers in Scotland. The sea journey, in rough weather, took two weeks, and on arrival at Leith Argyll was conveyed to Edinburgh Castle for imprisonment. As he made his way through the streets, thousands turned out to stare at this noble prisoner making what was to be his final journey, just as they had watched Montrose a decade before.

Argyll's trial for treason before the Scottish Parliament began on 13 February 1661. It would last for weeks; 'many hearings had he on his long lybell; his defences were very pregnant'.[16] The setting was Parliament Hall, ironically the scene of so many of his political triumphs. His defence was led by the advocate Sir John Gilmore, assisted by the brilliant young lawyer George Mackenzie, later to be elevated to the position of Lord Advocate and to earn himself the nickname 'Bluidy Mackenzie' for his callous treatment of the next generation of Covenanters. Prosecuting the case was the then Lord Advocate, Sir John Fletcher, an unpleasant character subsequently forced to resign office for receiving bribes, who was 'some tymes uncivilie tart'[17] to the accused. Presiding over the trial was the Earl of Middleton, the Lord High Commissioner, and an old enemy of the prisoner.

The charges against Argyll were in three groups. The first related to his actions during the civil war, including his part in the 1644 invasion of England and the delivery of Charles I to the English, and also his role in the executions of Huntly and Montrose. The second related to cruel and barbarous murders and other mistreatment of the enemy by officers acting under his command. And the third related to his collaboration with both Oliver and Richard Cromwell and his opposition to the Glencairn Rising. In addition there was a further charge of complicity in the death of Charles I. The fact that there were many other Scottish nobles who could easily have faced the same list of charges was immaterial to the proceedings.

Argyll's attempt to build a defence was hampered by restrictions put on him and his legal team, which limited their ability to prepare answers to the charges. Realising that the cards were stacked against him, the Marquis asked for permission to throw himself upon the Royal mercy, but this was immediately refused; the authorities were anxious that the trial should proceed so the full extent of the prisoner's wickedness could be exposed. Nonetheless, and notwithstanding the magnitude of the case against him, Argyll was defiant. He believed that he had sound defences to most of the charges that had been brought. For his conduct during the civil war he had merely acted as instructed by the Estates of Parliament, and in any event Acts of Indemnity passed in both 1641 and 1651 prevented proceedings being taken against him for actions prior to these dates. In relation to the charges of cruelty, he vehemently denied these, stating 'I never took any man's life, or what was done in conflict, or by order of law, for notorious crimes, according to standing Acts of Parliament.'[18] While there had been some terrible cruelties during the time of civil war, these had occurred on both sides, and if perpetrated by those under his command, were the consequence of anger caused by the savageries they themselves had suffered.

The accused had a strong case, and he presented it with elegance and eloquence. Bishop Burnet writes that Argyll spoke 'with so good a grace and so skilfully, that his character was as much raised as his family suffered by the prosecution'.[19]

On Saturday 11 May, with the trial still ongoing, the nobility of Scotland turned their attention elsewhere. Charles had ordered that it was his 'express pleasure that the bodies, bones and head of that late marquis of Montrose . . . should be gathered and honourably buried at his majesty's expense'.[20] Parliament agreed unanimously, even those who had treated Montrose as an enemy and who had happily condemned him to death now wanting to be seen to do the King's bidding. The citizens of Edinburgh, who eleven years before had turned out to witness James Graham having the life choked out of him at the end of a rope, now crowded the streets for his funeral. In 1650 Montrose may well have been an excommunicate traitor to the nation, but today he was a hero, and to be buried with all national honour, 'with a greater solemnitie than any of our Kings ever had at their burial in Scotland'.[21]

✳

Montrose's heir, the 2nd Marquis, had ingathered as much as he could of his father's remains, which were wrapped in linen and placed in the coffin which had then lain in state for four months in the Abbey Kirk of Holyrood. Now a great procession wound from the Palace of Holyroodhouse between high Edinburgh tenements up the hill to St Giles, the coffin carried by no fewer than fourteen Earls, followed by twelve Viscounts or Barons with the pall. Nearly every major Scottish peer took part in the parade, with one obvious absentee. The sounds of musket volleys and cannon fire which greeted the procession reached high above the masses to the cell in Edinburgh Castle occupied by the Marquis of Argyll. He cannot but have reflected on how easily fortunes changed.

Lord Lorne still retained the King's affection and had been busy making representations on his father's behalf. He managed to get Charles to write to Middleton to instruct him that the Lord Advocate was to drop all charges which related to the period before 1651, when the second Act of Indemnity was passed. This was only fair, and ignoring that Act would have put in danger many others beyond Argyll. Lorne's intervention also resulted in a direction from Charles that on conclusion of the trial no sentence was to be pronounced until the King had the opportunity to see the whole record of it. This second instruction was vehemently opposed by Middleton as seeking to undermine the independence of the Parliament as a court, and Charles backed down and reversed it.

With the first two sets of charges now dropped, the case hinged on the issue of Argyll's collaboration with Cromwell and his part in the regicide of Charles I. The Marquis' camp were optimistic about their prospects. His second son, Lord Neil Campbell, saw Lorne in London and talked openly about the likelihood of their father's acquittal. They had reason to be upbeat. No evidence could be produced in support of the charges of involvement in Charles I's trial and execution, and Argyll was able to point to his numerous public denunciations of the King's treatment at English hands. By a substantial vote in Parliament the prisoner was acquitted of this charge. That left only the allegations of complicity with Cromwell, but Argyll could demonstrate that he had been one of the last in Scotland to surrender, and that only at the point of a sword. He jousted in court with the Lord Advocate, wryly pointing out that there were many others who similarly had reached terms with Cromwell's regime, including more than a few who were present and sitting in judgment on him (including the Lord Advocate himself). If Argyll was guilty then so were they, and none would wish to find themselves facing similar charges. This enraged Fletcher, who called Argyll 'an impudent villain'. The prisoner gravely replied, that 'he had learned in his affliction to bear reproaches, but if the parliament saw no cause to condemn him, he was less concerned at the king's advocate's railing'.[22]

The accused may have thought at this stage that his ordeal would soon be over. But he had underestimated his enemies. When the point was made that if Argyll was guilty then so were they all, Middleton responded, 'we are all of us, or most, guilty, and the King may pitch on any he pleases to make examples'.[23] Any sense of a fair trial was fast disappearing. If the King could decide who was guilty or who was not, what need was there for Parliament or courts?

✳

Just as proceedings were drawing to a close, with every expectation on Argyll's part that he would be walking out a free man, the fates intervened. Monck (now elevated by a grateful King to the Dukedom of Albemarle), had a long-standing enmity towards the Marquis: 'In his heart,' he had written in 1659, 'there is no man in the three nations does more disaffect the English interest than he.'[24] Now, on hearing that Argyll might be acquitted, Monck 'by an inexcusable baseness searched among his letters, and found some that were written by Argyle to himself, that were hearty and zealous on their side.'[25] The business at Parliament Hall was interrupted by the arrival of a messenger from London, who 'knockt most rudely at the Parliament door',[26] and presented a packet of letters to Middleton. The nobles present were curious: what could this be, at this late stage? Triumphantly, barely able to conceal his delight, Middleton had read to the court this private correspondence from Argyll to Lilburne and Monck, written in 1653 and 1654. Argyll's heart sank as his fellow Parliamentarians took in the implications of what they heard.

The contents of Monck's letters were damning. They disclosed that Argyll at the time of the Glencairn Rising had been providing detailed information to the English occupiers about the movements of the Scottish Royalists, and had been acting always in Cromwell's interests. The production of these letters at this stage in the trial broke every rule of legal procedure, as the time for production of new evidence had passed, but the contents were so explosive that no legal niceties would stand in the way of their deciding the trial: 'the reading of them silenced all farther debate'.[27] Argyll had no alternative but to accept his authorship of the letters, and the matter was sealed. When it came to the vote Argyll was convicted unanimously and condemned to death. Only the young 2nd Marquis of Montrose refused to participate, honourably arguing that his family's personal enmity against Argyll meant that he could not act as an unbiased judge on the issue (and thus reflecting Argyll's abstention in the proceedings against his own late father).

Inevitably there was a proposal made to hang Argyll, as Montrose had been, but this was not agreed. On the next day, Saturday 25 May, the sentence was declared against the prisoner: 'that he was found guilty of high treason, and had judged to be executed to the death as a traitor, his head to be severed from his body at the Cross of Edinburgh, upon Monday, the 27th instant; and affixed in the same place where the Marquis of Montrose's head was formerly, and his arms torn before the Parliament and at the Cross.'[28] Only fourteen days before, Montrose's funeral had taken place with great pomp and circumstance, and the spike atop the Tolbooth on which his head had been displayed now lay empty, and awaiting its next adornment.

When Argyll was brought to the bar of Parliament to hear the sentence he reminded the gathering that the Roman Emperor Theodosius had ruled sentence of death should not be executed until thirty days after it had been passed. He asked that the sentence be delayed for ten days to allow the King time to be told of it, and if necessary act. This request was refused. He was then ordered to kneel down to receive the sentence, pronounced by the Earl of Crawford-Lindsay as President of the Parliament. Despite having once come close to fighting him in a duel he was still an old friend of the Marquis, and he read out the words of condemnation with tears pouring down his face. On hearing the sentence Argyll replied, 'I had the honour to set the crown on the King's head, and now he hastens me to a better crown than his own,' then adding, 'you have the indemnity of an earthly King among your hands, and you have denied me a share in that, but you cannot hinder me from the indemnity of the King of Kings, and shortly you must be before His tribunal. I pray He mete not out such measures to you as you have done to me, when you are called to account for all your doings, and this among the rest.'[29] George MacKenzie records: 'The Parliament seem'd much affected with this great revolution of fortune, and his own carriage, which drew tears from his very enemies.'[30] And with that he was taken to the Tolbooth, the commoners' prison, to await the sentence being carried out.

The next evening, on the eve of the day appointed for execution, the Marchioness of Argyll sought out Middleton at Holyrood, hoping to win a reprieve for her husband for at least long enough to allow an intervention by the King. She found him drunk, but he was still able to tell her that he had received three instructions from the King: 'to rescind the Covenants, to take the Marquis of Argyll's head, and to sheath every man's sword in his brother's breast'.[31] There was no hope for a stay of execution. Argyll had too many enemies to be allowed another chance to live.

The prisoner spent his last Sunday attended by some of his friends amongst the Presbyterian clergy, including Robert Douglas, George Hutcheson, and David Dickson. His fellow prisoner was another minister, James Guthrie, also under sentence of death. Far from being melancholy at what awaited them, Argyll was in good spirits, entirely at peace and confident in his faith that a heavenly crown awaited him.

On the morning of his execution, Monday 27 May, he spent time settling his accounts and business. He wrote to the King protesting his innocence and asking that his family as faithful subjects should not be held responsible for any of his faults. He dined with his friends at noon, displaying no hint of nervousness and happily consuming a partridge. Then, in a detail from history which demonstrates an astonishing calmness of mind in the circumstances, we are told that he lay down for his customary afternoon nap. At two o'clock he received the summons to go to the scaffold, and drank a glass of wine, saying his farewells to those who were not going to accompany him. Mindful of Montrose's 'tragik end', he remarked to his advocate George Mackenzie that he 'would not die as a Roman braving death, but as a Christian without being affrighted'.[32] He walked with his supporters, among them the Earls of Caithness, Lothian and Loudon, the short distance down the High Street to the place of execution at the east end of St Giles, watched in respectful silence by the crowds.

✳

It was customary for the condemned man to deliver a speech to the assembled masses. Argyll spoke for half an hour, justifying all of his actions, encouraging his listeners to be strong in their Christian faith, and forgiving those who had condemned him:

> I desire not that the Lord should judge any man, nor do I judge any but myself: I wish, and as the Lord hath pardoned me, so may He pardon them for this and other things, and that what they have done to me may never meet them in

their accounts. I have no more to say, but beg the Lord that since I go away, He may bless them that stay behind.[33]

With that he prayed once more and approached the Maiden. The minister George Hutcheson told him, 'My Lord, hold thou your grip sicker [sure]' to which he replied, 'Mr Hutcheson, you know what I said to you in the chamber. I am not afraid to be surprised with fear.'[34] Perhaps he had expected to lose his nerve at the end, but it was not to be. He had been observed fiddling with the buttons on his waistcoat when addressing the crowd, but his doctor took his pulse and found it entirely steady. His last words to those around were, 'I desire you gentlemen, and all that hear me, again to take notice, and remember, that now when I am entering on eternity, and am to appear before my judge, and as I desire salvation and expect eternal happiness from Him, I am free from any accession, by knowledge, contriving, counsel, or any other way to his late Majesty's death; and I pray God to preserve the present King his majesty, and to pour his best blessings on his person and government, and the Lord give him good and faithful counsellors.'[35] With that Argyll put his head on the block, and after a moment's prayer lifted his hand as a signal. The Maiden did her work, and Archibald Campbell entered the presence of a King more constant, and more forgiving, than any he had served on Earth.

14

Post Mortem

1661–

As had been instructed in his sentence of death, Argyll's severed head was put up on the very spike on the west end of the
Tolbooth where Montrose's had been displayed for so long. His
other remains did not suffer the ignominy of dismembering
which had befallen his rival. The body was taken to St Magdalen's Chapel on the Cowgate and from there to Newbattle
Abbey, the Earl of Lothian's residence. When the stomach was
examined it was found that the partridge which the Marquis
had consumed for his last lunch had been entirely digested,
which was taken as another sign that he had been quite free
from nerves in his final hours. A month later, the body was
taken in a grand procession, borne in a carriage drawn by six
horses, across the country to the Campbell family mausoleum
on the Holy Loch in Argyllshire. Three years later, on the King's
orders, the head was removed from public display and reunited
and buried with the body.

The day after Argyll's death, the Scottish Parliament passed
the Act Rescissory which abolished every Act of Parliament
since 1633. 27 years of history were wiped out, and all the
reforms instituted as a result of the Scottish Revolution of 1637
extinguished. One of the consequences of this Act was that the
government of the Kirk reverted to what had existed prior to the
National Covenant, and so episcopacy was reintroduced. At a
stroke, all that Argyll and his colleagues had fought so long and
hard for was overturned.

The retribution against leading Covenanters did not stop with the death of Argyll. There were three others marked for death. Firstly there was Reverend James Guthrie, who had been imprisoned in the Tolbooth with Argyll, and was executed two days later. Secondly there was the eminent preacher and writer, Samuel Rutherford, whose extraordinary polemic against the unfettered power of monarchs, *Lex Rex*, was deemed offensive and inflammatory. Rutherford cheated the hangman by dying of disease before he could be brought to trial. And lastly there was Johnston of Warriston, who of all the Scots had been closest to Cromwell. Having been warned in advance of the warrant for his arrest, he escaped with his family in the nick of time on a boat from Leith, finding sanctuary on the Continent. Two years later the authorities caught up with him at Rouen in France, from where he was taken to London and eventually back to Edinburgh, where he was hanged in the Grassmarket in July 1663.

Charles II trusted the government of Scotland to the Earl of Lauderdale in place of Middleton, who was pensioned off eventually to become Governor of Tangier. A new system of administration was put in place whereby the King would choose Lords of the Articles to propose legislation to Parliament, thus effectively ensuring that real power was vested in the Crown, and Parliament neutered. All the post-revolution reforms which had brought an element of democracy to Scottish government were swept away. New bishops were appointed in the Kirk and the system of Presbyterian church government reduced. Throughout Scotland, ministers who refused to recognise the new regime were put out of their pulpits and manses. In areas like the South-west where Covenanting sentiments had been the strongest, those who were evicted were in the majority. Many continued to carry on preaching and ministering to their flocks in defiance of the authorities, holding open-air services which became known as 'conventicles'. Increasingly Lauderdale tried to stamp out such activities, using the military to enforce the law. All this did was harden attitudes further.

There were armed risings in 1666 and 1679, the Covenanters rebelling against the civil authorities and taking up arms in defence of their right to worship God as they saw fit. Another member of the Graham family, John Graham of Claverhouse, later ennobled as Viscount Dundee, led the Government forces in suppressing the rebels, acting with great brutality (Royalists called him 'Bonnie Dundee', but to his opponents he was 'Bluidy Clavers'). But the more the Covenanters were suppressed, and the more atrocities were carried out against both men and women who refused to declare allegiance to the King, the more the resistance grew.

Charles II died in 1685. He left at least twelve children by seven assorted mistresses, but no legitimate issue. The Crown passed to his younger brother James, Duke of York, who was crowned James II of England and Ireland and VII of Scotland. James was a Roman Catholic and therefore immediately a controversial monarch, even in England. In Scotland the oppression of the Covenanter rebels (or 'Whigs' as they were increasingly known) was stepped up.

Charles II's bastard son, James, 1st Duke of Monmouth and 1st Duke of Buccleuch, led an invasion from the Netherlands seeking to capitalise on anti-Catholic sentiment and have himself put on the throne as a Protestant monarch. His forces landed at Lyme Regis in Dorset in June 1685. A parallel invasion led by the 9th Earl of Argyll, the late Marquis' eldest son, came ashore at Campbeltown in Kintyre, but failed to gain enough support to make any real impact. Argyll was captured on 19 June and taken to Edinburgh, where eleven days later he was beheaded by the same Maiden which had dispatched his father 24 years before. Less than a week after, Monmouth was defeated at Sedgemoor, and from there taken to London and beheaded in the Tower. He died horribly, the bungling axeman Jack Ketch taking at least five blows to sever his head. Monmouth cannot have been the only English nobleman to wish that his uncivilised countrymen had embraced the more humane Scots Maiden.

But time was running out for King James. The tipping point came when the Queen gave birth to a son who would be brought up as a Roman Catholic. Faced with the prospect of a Catholic monarchy in perpetuity, the English rebelled. The invitation was made to the King's eldest daughter, Mary, who was married to Prince William of Orange in the Netherlands, to come and take the throne jointly with her husband as Protestant monarchs. It was a virtually bloodless coup. James and his family fled into exile, and Protestant monarchy was re-established. Regime change had come again.

'The Glorious Revolution' ensured that absolute monarchy would never again play a part in the British constitution. A form of constitutional monarchy, with a strong Parliament, was secured. William and Mary's Act of Settlement for Scotland abolished the Lords of the Articles. Crucially it also abolished episcopacy in the Scottish Kirk for good. The Church of Scotland and the General Assembly were established as Presbyterian, with the Westminster Confession of Faith as the rule book. Half a century after the signing of the National Covenant in Greyfriars, the Covenanters had finally won.

Archibald Campbell, Marquis of Argyll, did not live to see the fulfilment of his life's work. His principal objectives had always been the establishment of constitutional monarchy and the protection of Presbyterianism in the Kirk. In the end the Church of England did not become Presbyterian, but that did not matter; no British monarch after 1688 would have the ambition of either of the Charleses to try to unify religion throughout their Kingdoms. The threat of bishops in the Scottish church was removed forever.

Argyll's view on the need for limited Royal power was drawn from his personal background as head of one of the country's great noble families, and entirely in tune with established Scottish political thinking. There had never been a traditional view of the Scottish monarch as an absolute ruler; rather the king ruled through, and with the consent of, the nobility. The Declaration of Arbroath of 1320 makes this approach clear – the king amongst the Scottish earls was *primus inter pares* rather than a supreme overlord. This just reflected the reality of government on the ground. With a large landmass and a small population, and travel challenging at the best of times (and often impossible in winter), a king in Edinburgh relied on the nobles to administer justice, maintain order and collect taxes in their own fiefdoms. Folk living in Argyllshire, far distant from the capital, would never have seen their king, but would know and recognise their earl (and clan chief) as the one to whom they owed their loyalty.

The sixteenth-century Scottish theorist George Buchanan, whose writings inspired many of the Covenanters, developed this basic notion into a concept of contractual monarchy. As kings were at first chosen by the people, the powers that they had were those that the people allowed them to exercise. As the people themselves were incapable of directly holding the king to account and preventing him acting in tyrannical fashion, it fell to the nobility to keep his power in check. Argyll approved of this theory, writing: 'Princes begin to lose their estates when they begin to break the ancient laws, manners and customs under which their subjects have long lived; for princes must have as much regard for the safety of their subjects (which consists in the protection of the laws) as of their lives.'[1] It goes without saying that as a powerful noble himself, such an approach was manifestly in his own interest.

The logical end-point of this was that if the king broke his faith with the people (or at least the nobility as the protectors of their interests) then he could be deposed and replaced with another (there was no Republican sympathy here, as the nation required a strong leader and figurehead – this essential point was the key dividing line between the Covenanters and the Cromwellians). In view of this, the opinions that the unfortunate Stewart of Ladywell claimed that he heard Argyll express at the Fords of Lyon – that the King could be replaced – do not seem incredible. Whether Argyll genuinely had designs on the crown for himself can only be a matter of speculation, but such an ambition would not be inconsistent with his general political approach.

In order to strengthen the position of the nobility against a centralising monarch, Argyll proposed and delivered the empowerment of the middle classes – the barons and burgesses. But this was essentially a tactical move rather than one founded in ideology. With its weighting towards the great nobles, the pre-1639 Scots Parliament was too sympathetic toward Charles I. Diluting their power meant bringing in those much more radical in outlook and more committed to a stronger Parliament and a weakened King. Argyll got the result he wanted, but he would have been horrified had this meant a permanent power-shift away from great men like himself.

Great historic reforms may not be seen as such at the time of implementation, and the motivations of their instigators are invariably more complex than first appears. Argyll's move towards a more democratic Parliament was driven not by any high-minded desire to broaden the political base in Scotland, but rather to gain him a short-term advantage over more conservative opponents. And the fundamental purpose of the Covenanters' reforms was nothing to do with civil government at all, but entirely about restricting the King's opportunity to meddle in religious matters. It is only with hindsight that such changes can be seen as being of great historical significance, fitting in to a centuries-long transition from centralised Royal power to a modern democracy; it would have been far from apparent at the time.

Argyll understood the inevitability of closer political links between Scotland and England. There is no evidence that he favoured the incorporating Union that was to happen less than half a century after his death (as his biographer Allan Macinnes points out, he opposed Charles I's attempts to establish administrative, social, economic and religious uniformity throughout the British Isles). Rather, Argyll was interested in a confederate arrangement, with separate parliaments in both London and Edinburgh with clearly defined powers, working together if necessary to prevent the extension of the Crown's executive powers. There would be free trade between the countries, respect for the rights of each other's citizens, and military co-operation.

In all this it is impossible to overestimate the importance of religion as a driver for political change. What motivated the Covenanters was their fundamental belief in the Reformed faith, with the Presbyterian Kirk as its safeguard. It was (just) within living memory that Scots Protestants had been burned at the stake for their beliefs, and the threat of counter-Reformation, while diminished, still hung in the air. The greater danger lay in a creeping undermining of Reformed principles through changes such as the reintroduction of bishops and Anglican liturgies, pursued by monarchs who were suspected of being privately sympathetic to Catholicism. The legacy of John Knox was one which had to be jealously guarded if the future well-being of the country was to be secured.

Today religion is regarded (at best) as a private matter, and any public figure who professes more than the most nominal faith is regarded with suspicion. The situation could not have been more different in seventeenth-century Scotland. Piety was not simply a personal concern but something of the utmost concern for the nation as a whole. Just like the ancient Israelites, the Scots would only enjoy God's favour if they were collectively faithful to his Word, and divine punishment would automatically follow apostasy and sin. Thus the defeat at Dunbar was taken by the Kirk Party as a sign of God's displeasure that the purging of the army had not gone far enough – an entirely sensible conclusion to draw for anyone using the Old Testament as their guide. And the nation's leaders had therefore to be godly men who could demonstrate in their lives their adherence to true religion.

So the maintenance of the Reformed Kirk was about more than religion, it was in the collective national self-interest. The political reforms implemented by Argyll and his allies were all introduced with a single aim in mind – not the extension of democracy, not the curtailing of Royal authority *per se* (although both were to be consequences) – but the removal of the King's power to interfere in the Kirk. Had Charles Stewart not tried to unify the form of Christian worship throughout his Kingdoms then there would have been no National Covenant, no Scottish Revolution and (almost certainly) no English Civil War.

And what of Montrose? He championed Charles, even though the Stewarts' belief in the Divine Right of Kings was out of step with mainstream Scottish political thought.

Montrose supported monarchy as a bastion against anarchy, which he believed would inevitably lead to dictatorship. He believed in 'Sovereign Power' which needed to be strong and unquestioned, although limited by the laws of God and nature, the laws of nations, and the fundamental laws of the country. It was not a necessity that the Sovereign Power should be a king – in the ancient Roman republic it was representatives of the people – but that was the system of government which Britain and Ireland were accustomed to. Montrose's approach might be summed up in the famous lines of poetry he penned:

My dear and only love, I pray,
That little world of thee,
Be governed by no other sway,
Than purest monarchy;
As Alexander I will reign,
And I will reign alone;
My thoughts did evermore disdain
A rival on my throne.

These views on politics drew heavily on those of Lord Napier, the principal theorist amongst the Scottish Royalists (and Montrose's brother-in-law). Indeed, it may well be the case that the writing on Sovereign Power which is usually claimed as Montrose's is in fact Napier's work. According to the theory, the king had to operate within the law and be accountable to free parliaments. As long as the king did not breach these requirements then he must be left to govern as he chose. In the end it was better for the people to put up with a monarch acting in ways that they disapproved of, than for them to rebel against him, as the alternative would be disorder and the decline of the society. As the people were simply not up to the job of ruling themselves, without a strong king they would fall prey to powerful and ambitious men and the whole country would be worse off as a result.

Strong nobles were very capable of exploiting a situation to strengthen their own positions in relation to the monarchy, but doing so on the pretext of protecting the people. Montrose claimed: 'The perpetual cause of controversies between the Prince and his subjects, is the ambitious designs of rule in great men, veiled under the specious pretext of religion and the subjects' liberties.'[2] The rise of Argyll and the more radical faction within the Covenanters, once Royal power had been broken, would have been sufficient proof for Montrose that his views were right.

This belief in Sovereign Power seems to us today curiously old-fashioned and out of step with any modern view of government. Yet it is worth remembering that similar arguments were used as recently as the early twentieth century to defend Tsarist rule in Russia. Even today, those who would seek to justify the authoritarian regime of Communist China would claim, as Montrose and his colleagues did, that a strong central power was essential to avoid a descent into anarchy and chaos where the ordinary citizens would be the losers.

It seems strange that one holding these views would have been involved in challenging royal power in the first place. Montrose was an early, and energetic, supporter of the National Covenant and the Scottish Revolution. His break with the Covenanters only came when he felt they were overreaching themselves by allying with those in England who sought to bring down the King, the personification of the Sovereign Power, and at the same time promoting those whom he viewed as political and religious extremists and those (undoubtedly including Argyll) he thought were mainly in it for their own interests.

Although Montrose and Argyll had different political perspectives, it is possible that both could have been satisfied with the settlement that was eventually reached after 1688. Scotland still had a Stewart on the throne (although, in this case, Mary Stewart ruled jointly with her husband), and the power of monarchy was limited by a strong parliament. A constitutional monarchy, arguably a modified Sovereign Power, had been achieved. Presbyterianism in the Kirk had been secured in perpetuity, an outcome which would have contented both rivals. Both their families prospered under the new regime. Archibald Campbell, the 10th Earl of Argyll and the Marquis' grandson, was elevated to be made the first Duke of Argyll in 1701. In 1707, as a reward for his support of the Act of Union, James Graham, the 4th Marquis, became the first Duke of Montrose. Both lines continue to this day.

So the end result of all that happened in Scotland over the period occupied by these two great protagonists was an outcome that both might well have been happy to live with. Could that end-point have been arrived at with less strife and bloodshed? For a long time, there was very little between the two rivals in terms of political or religious difference. It could be argued that the split came as much because Argyll emerged as a Covenanting leader ahead of the ambitious Montrose, as it did because of any great ideological divide. But whatever the reason for the division, conflict drove the two further apart.

There are few things in this world more terrible than civil war. It is a cliché to say that such wars set brother against brother, and neighbour against neighbour, but that does not make it any less true. There are many who view civil war as an opportunity to settle old scores, to use the mask of conflict to put down rivals in politics, business or love. Atrocities against civilian populations are commonplace. And reasonable men find themselves shouting to be heard. What happens when a nation divides is that extremism flourishes, moderation is driven out, and the centre vanishes. Room for compromise is lost. Those who were once allies find their differences magnified and exaggerated by their followers, and reconciliation becomes impossible. Even if Montrose and Argyll had had a mind to make peace, their respective supporters would never have allowed it.

The 'camps' which congregated around the rivals were jealous of their champions' reputations, and capable of much greater bitterness towards the opposition than the leaders were themselves. Both factions employed energetic propagandists on their behalf. Even in the era before mass democracy, winning popular support for the cause was important. One way in which this was achieved was the circulating of pamphlets putting a highly partisan gloss on the words, or actions, of the various leading players, and exaggerating victories over opponents while seeking to blacken their reputation (the claim that Lord Elcho flew a banner with the words 'Jesus and No Quarter', which derives from a contemporary Royalist pamphlet, is a very good example of this). The political spin-doctor is not an invention of the late twentieth century.

Reading the historical records it is difficult to discern exactly what was the personal relationship between the rivals. Certainly they must have known each other well – they were not far off in age, and the Scottish nobility was a small enough group that they would have encountered one another regularly from when they were both young. As Argyll assumed a leadership role amongst the Covenanters, Montrose undoubtedly came both to be jealous of his position, and to fear his power and ambition. Perhaps, like Caesar, Montrose could not endure a superior. On Argyll's part, he seems to have viewed his counterpart with more disdain and irritation than personal animus, despite the sufferings of both his clansfolk and political allies (Argyll's comments on Montrose's execution point to this).

Argyll certainly did make efforts to win Montrose over to his side when the Scots were planning to ally themselves with the English Parliamentarians, but was rebuffed. Montrose did not have the influence to prevent Scots intervention in the English Civil War, but perhaps if he had stayed within the Covenanters' camp the weight of his authority would have been enough to have ensured a more moderate approach towards dealing with the King. It is worth remembering that Montrose could not have had an objection *in principle* to war against his Sovereign, given that is exactly what he had done in the Bishops' Wars. Certainly if he had not taken up arms on the King's behalf in Scotland, then the more extreme elements on the English Parliamentary side might have seen their influence reduced, and a peace settlement with Charles achieved which included the establishment at that stage of a constitutional monarchy.

A more considered Marquis of Montrose, a better politician, might have played a longer game instead of rushing to take up the sword on his master's behalf in a counter-productive, albeit spectacular, venture.

Or what if Montrose had, instead of pursuing his own agenda, worked harder to forge alliances with the Marquis of Huntly and the Duke of Hamilton to create a broad-based centre-ground coalition of Royalists and moderate Covenanters? Argyll and his radical faction would have been sidelined. There would have been no Solemn League and Covenant, no Scots military assistance to the Parliamentarians, and probably no regicide, no Commonwealth, and no Cromwellian Protectorate. Charles might well have retained his crown, although whether he would then have kept his promises to the Covenanters must be highly debateable. But such a course of action would have required Montrose to be more inclined to compromise than his nature permitted, and more prepared to work with, and perhaps under, those for whom he had little patience.

There are striking parallels in the lives of the Montrose and Argyll, in their family backgrounds, in their education, in military experience, in political involvement, in the manner in which they were both betrayed by their King, and how they each faced an untimely death. Both had enormous self-belief and an unshakeable conviction in the rightness of their cause. Both were devoted to their Masters – Montrose to his King; Argyll to God and his Kirk – and would see anything done to advance their interests. Both demonstrated courage that was at times breathtaking: Montrose on the battlefield, Argyll on the scaffold. Both died as heroes, and martyrs, to their followers.

Yet they were very different in their characters. Where Argyll was cautious, considered, pragmatic and realistic, Montrose was principled, loyal, unbending and reckless. Argyll would do deals with anyone – Hamilton, both Charles I and Charles II,

Cromwell, Montrose himself – in the wider interest. Montrose had difficulty working even with those who shared his outlook, such as Huntly and Hamilton. Faced with a difficult choice, Argyll, like his great contemporary Oliver Cromwell waiting on the revelation of God's will, would take his time carefully to weigh the options before settling on a course. Montrose was more impulsive, rushing in and acting on instinct. One was a chess-player, the other a gambler.

Montrose's historical contribution to Scotland is undermined by the very dash and verve which make him such an appealing romantic figure. He sparkles on the scene like a firework, catching all eyes for a few moments of brilliance, but then disappearing in an explosion of light. In contrast Argyll's role is less ostentatious but ultimately more important, deftly steering the nation through troubled times. Despite the claims made by his detractors about his being motivated by self-interest, Argyll's part in the affairs of the time was principally focused on securing political and religious stability, and a long-term settlement of the troubled relationship between Scotland and its southern neighbour. From our historical perspective it is he who emerges as the greater figure; a statesman of British significance whose views have better stood the test of time, even though his rewards in the end were debt and death. It is hard to disagree with Baillie's conclusion that he was 'the best and most excellent man our State of a long tyme had enjoyed'.[3]

Despite the bad press he has sometimes suffered from over the centuries, we have to admire Argyll for his skills and success as a politician. But which of us, deep down, would not prefer to be like Montrose? Proud, headstrong, and ultimately a glorious failure, he put his life and his career on the line for an unpopular King to whom he was devoted. He failed, and paid the ultimate price. But history will always judge more kindly those who display courage, even in the wrong cause, rather than calculation.

Montrose may not entirely deserve the level of popularity that his memory still enjoys, but it is hard to begrudge it to him.

Towards the end of his life, Argyll wrote of himself as 'a distracted man, of a distracted subject, in a distracted time wherein I lived'.[4] Montrose might equally have said the same. Scotland may have been spared more than 50 years of wars, strife, persecutions, tortures, brutalities, and executions, had things been different, had they held different beliefs and had different temperaments, had they been allies rather than enemies. They were both products of their age, driven apart by ferociously held views on subjects which seem to us today obscure and unimportant. Whichever we regard as the ultimate winner, both played crucial roles in forging the Scotland that we know today, and both deserve to be remembered and celebrated for their contribution to our nation. Archibald Campbell and James Graham may lie in effigy in St Giles Kirk, but it is the modern country they both helped mould that is the real memorial to these two great men.

Notes

Introduction:
1. Smellie, A., *Men of the Covenant,* p.74.
2. Seymour, D. *Battles in Britain*, p.129.
3. The Open University. http://www.open.edu/openlearn/history-the-arts/history/world-history/archibald-campbell-marquis-argyll-1598-1661

Prologue:
1. Baillie, R. and Laing, D. (ed.), *The Letters and Journals of Robert Baillie 1637–1662*, Vol. II, p. 263.
2. Guthry, H., *Memoirs*, p. 140.
3. Baillie, *Letters*, Vol. II, p. 263.
4. Napier, M., *Life and Times of Montrose*, p. 293.
5. Gordon, P., *Britaine's Distemper,* p. 100.
6. *Ibid.*, p. 101.
7. *Ibid.*, p. 101.
8. *Ibid.*, p. 101.
9. *Ibid.*, p. 102.
10. Guthry, *Memoirs*, p. 140.
11. Napier, M., *Memoirs of the Marquis of Montrose,* Vol. II, p. 175.

Chapter One:
1. *Historical Manuscripts Commission*, Vol. VI, p. 631.
2. *Ibid.*, Vol. IV, p. 482.
3. Campbell, A., *Instructions to a Son*, p. 77.
4. Burnet, G., *History of his own time*, Vol I, p. 30.
5. Gardiner, S. R., *History of England from the Accession of James I to the Outbreak of the Civil War 1603-1642*, Vol. II, p. 183.
6. Gordon, *Britaine's Distemper,* pp. 56-57.
7. Hyde, E., *The History of the Rebellion and Civil Wars in England*, Vol. II, p. 100.
8. Burnet, G., *History,* Vol I, p. 49.
9. Wishart, G., *The memoirs of James, Marquis of Montrose, 1639–1650*, pp. 406-7.
10. Hyde, *History*, Vol. VI, p. 422.

11. Brodie, G., *A History of the British Empire,* Vol. IV, p. 272.
12. Balcanquhall, W., *A large declaration concerning the late tumults in Scotland,* p. 6.

Chapter Two:
1. Gordon, J., *A History of Scots Affairs,* Vol. I, p. 7.
2. *Ibid.*, Vol. I, p. 7.
3. Row, J., *History,* p. 409.
4. Rothes, J. L., *Kirk of Scotland, p.* 199.
5. *Ibid.*, p. 199.
6. Row, *History,* p. 409.
7. Rothes, *Kirk of Scotland,* p. 199.
8. Spalding, J., *Memorialls of the Trubles in Scotland and in England*, Vol. I, p. 79.
9. Gordon, *Scots Affairs,* Vol. I, p. 9.
10. Rothes, *Kirk of Scotland,* p. 200.
11. Baillie, *Letters*, Vol. I, p. 18.
12. *Ibid.*, Vol. I, p. 18.
13. Balfour, J., *The historical works of Sir James Balfour of Denmylne and Kinnaird*, Vol. II, Note 229F.
14. Baillie, *Letters*, Vol. I, p. 23.
15. *Ibid.*, Vol. I, p. 52.
16. Gordon, *Scots Affairs,* Vol. I, p. 33.
17. Johnston, A., Lord Wariston, *Diary* 28 February 1638
18. Yorke, P., *Miscellaneous State Papers*, Vol. II, p. 106.
19. Guthry, H., *Memoirs*, p. 36.
20. Baillie, *Letters*, Vol. I, p. 73.
21. Gordon, *Scots Affairs*, Vol. I, p. 49.
22. *Ibid.*, Vol. I, p. 145.
23. Yorke, *State Papers*, Vol. II, p. 113.
24. Wodrow, R., *Analecta*, Vol. II, p. 116.
25. Yorke, *State Papers*, Vol. II, pp. 115-7.
26. Gordon, *Scots Affairs,* Vol. I, pp. 171-2.
27. *Ibid.*, Vol. I, p. 172.
28. Baillie, *Letters*, Vol. I, p. 145.

Chapter Three:
1. Spalding, *Memorialls*, Vol. I, p. 130.

2. Baillie, *Letters*, Vol. I, p. 111.
3. *Ibid.*, Vol. I, p. 213.
4. Spalding, *Memorialls*, Vol. I, p. 153.
5. *Ibid.*, p. 153.
6. Gordon, *Scots Affairs*, Vol. I, p. 228.
7. *Ibid.*, Vol. I, p. 228.
8. *Ibid.*, Vol. I, p. 230.
9. *Ibid.*, Vol. I, p. 239.
10. Spalding, *Memorialls*, Vol. I, p. 486.
11. Gardiner, *History of England*, Vol. IX, p. 16.
12. Baillie, *Letters*, Vol. I, p. 212.
13. *Ibid.*, Vol. I, p. 111.
14. Rushworth, J., *Historical Collections*, Vol. III, p. 938.
15. Baillie, *Letters*, Vol. I, p. 220.

Chapter Four:
1. Guthry, *Memoirs*, p. 60.
2. Gordon, *Scots Affairs*, Vol. III, p. 132.
3. Spalding, *Memorialls*, Vol. I, p. 264.
4. Napier, *Memoirs of Montrose*, Vol. I, p 253.
5. Baillie, *Letters*, Vol. I, p. 224.
6. Napier, *Life and Times of Montrose*, p. 128.
7. Gordon, J., *A History of Scots Affairs*, Vol. III, p. 182.
8. Napier, *Memoirs of Montrose*, Vol. I, p. 477.
9. Guthry, *Memoirs*, p. 60.
10. Baillie, *Letters*, Vol. II, p. 261.
11. Bruce, J., Douglas Hamilton, W., and Lomas, S.C., *Calendar of state papers, Domestic series, Reign of Charles I. 1640-41*, p. 616.
12. Gordon, *Scots Affairs*, Vol. III, p. 165.
13. Historical Manuscripts Commission, *Sixth Report of the Royal Commission on Historical Manuscripts*, p. 616.
14. Napier, *Life and Times of Montrose*, p. 131.
15. *Ibid.*, pp. 135-136.

Chapter Five:
1. Napier, *Memoirs of Montrose,* Vol. I, p. 359.
2. Cowan, E. J., *Montrose, for King and Covenant,* p. 103.
3. Baillie, *Letters*, Vol. I, pp. 305-6.

4. *Ibid.*, Vol. I, p. 262.
5. Argyll, *Letters to the Argyll Family,* p. 36.
6. Spalding, *Memorialls*, Vol. I, pp. 47-8.
7. *Ibid.*, p. 48.
8. Guthry, *Memoirs*, p. 93.
9. *Ibid.*, p. 93.
10. Spalding, *Memorialls*, Vol. I, p. 48.
11. Balfour, *History*, Vol. III, pp. 40-42.
12. Napier, *Memoirs of Montrose*, Vol. II, p. 5.
13. Yorke, *State Papers*, Vol. II, p. 301.
14. *Ibid.*, Vol. II, p. 302.
15. Napier, *Memoirs of Montrose,* Vol. I, pp. 317-8.

Chapter Six:
1. Argyll, *Letters,* p. 37.
2. Baillie, *Letters*, Vol. II, p. 43.
3. *Ibid.*, Vol. II, p. 41.
4. Morrison, W., *Johnston of Warriston*, p. 119.
5. Baillie, *Letters*, Vol. II, p. 51.
6. *Ibid.*, Vol. II, p. 47.
7. *Ibid.*, Vol. II, p. 90.
8. *Ibid.*, Vol. II, p. 156.
9. Napier, *Memoirs of Montrose,* Vol. II, p. 146.
10. Spalding, *Memorialls*, Vol. II, p. 374.

Chapter Seven:
1. Napier, *Memoirs of Montrose,* Vol. II, p. 146.
2. Gordon, *Britaine's Distemper,* p. 70.
3. Napier, *Memoirs of Montrose,* Vol. II, p. 147.
4. Gordon, *Britaine's Distemper,* p. 160.
5. Napier, *Memoirs of Montrose,* Vol. II, p. 149.
6. Terry, C. S., *The Life and Campaigns of Alexander Leslie*, p. 301.
7. Steele, R., *A bibliography of royal proclamations of the Tudor and Stuart sovereigns and of others published under authority,* Vol. II, p. 325.

Chapter Eight:
1. Parliamentary Register, 6th March 1645.
2. Baillie, *Letters*, Vol. II, pp. 416-19.

3. Napier, *Memoirs of Montrose,* Vol. II, p. 175.
4. Guthry, *Memoirs*, p. 141.
5. Baillie, *Letters*, Vol. II, p. 263.
6. Napier, *Memoirs of Montrose,* Vol. II, p. 490.
7. Guthry, *Memoirs*, pp. 180-1.
8. Baillie, *Letters*, Vol. II, p. 263
9. Gordon, *Britaine's Distemper, p.* 123.
10. *Ibid.*, p. 124.
11. Baillie, *Letters*, Vol. II, p. 418.
12. Wishart, *Montrose*, p. 148.
13. *Ibid.*, p. 149.
14. Gordon, *Britaine's Distemper,* p. 129.
15. Wishart, *Montrose,* p. 149.
16. Parliamentary Register, 9th July 1645.
17. Baillie, *Letters*, Vol. II, p. 304.
18. Wishart, *Montrose*, pp. 167-8.

Chapter Nine:
1. Buchan, J., *Montrose*, p. 294.
2. Baillie, *Letters*, Vol. II, p. 305.
3. Howell, T. B., and Howell, T. J., *A Complete Collection of State Trials and Proceedings*, Vol. V, p. 1327.
4. Napier, *Life and Times of Montrose*, p. 376.
5. Gordon, *Britaine's Distemper,* p. 160.
6. Wishart, *Montrose,* pp. 203-4.
7. Baillie, *Letters*, Vol. II, p. 170.
8. Willcock, J., *The Great Marquess*, p. 387.
9. Napier, *Memoirs of Montrose,* Vol. II, pp. 613-4.
10. Gordon, *Britaine's Distemper,* p. 193.
11. Bruce, J., *Charles I in 1646: Letters of Charles I to Queen Henrietta Maria*, p. 101.
12. *Ibid.*, p. 38.
13. Gardiner, *History of England*, Vol. III, p. 23.
14. Turner, J., *Memoirs of His Own Life and Times*, p. 41.
15. Napier, *Memoirs of Montrose,* Vol. II, pp. 277-84.
16. *Ibid.*, pp. 277-84.
17. *Ibid.*, pp. 277-84.

Chapter Ten:
1. Bruce, J., Douglas Hamilton, W., and Lomas, S. C., *Calendar of state papers, Domestic series, Reign of Charles I. 1640–41*, p. 49.
2. *Ibid.*, p. 47.
3. *Ibid.*, pp. 48-9.
4. Journal of the House of Lords, Vol. VIII, p. 392.
5. Gardiner, *History of England*, Vol. II, p. 494.
6. Baillie, *Letters*, Vol. II, p. 398.
7. Rushworth, *Historical Collections*, Vol. IV, pp. 319-20.
8. Gardiner, *History of England*, Vol. II, p. 514.
9. Baillie, *Letters*, Vol. II, p. 386.
10. Montereul, J. De, *The Diplomatic Correspondence of Jean De Montereul and the Brothers De Bellievre*, Vol. I, p. 444.
11. Laing, D., *Ancrum and Lothian Correspondence*, Vol. I, p. 212.
12. Montereul, *Correspondence*, Vol. II, p. 140.
13. Baillie, *Letters*, Vol. II, p. 35.
14. Montereul, *Correspondence,* Vol. II, p. 261.
15. Baillie, *Letters*, Vol. II, pp. 35-36.
16. Thurloe, J., *State Papers*, Vol. I, p. 101.
17. *Ibid.*, p. 102.
18. Carlyle, T., *Oliver Cromwell's Letters and Speeches*, Vol. II, p. 51.
19. Row, W., *The Life of Robert Blair*, p. 210.

Chapter Eleven:
1. Wishart, *Montrose,* pp. 335-336.
2. Gordon, *Britaine's Distemper, p.* 223.
3. *Ibid.*, p. 224.
4. Baillie, *Letters*, Vol. III, p. 512.
5. Carte, T., *Original Letters and Papers*, Vol. I, p. 232.
6. Baillie, *Letters*, Vol. II, p. 88.
7. Gardiner, S.R., *Letters and Papers illustrating the relations between Charles II and Scotland in 1650*, p. 1.
8. Wishart, *Montrose*, pp. 447-8.
9. Steele, *Royal Proclamations*, Vol. II, p. 343.
10. Napier, *Life and Times of Montrose*, p. 465.
11. Gardiner, *Letters and Papers*, p. 49.
12. Jaffray, A., *Diary of Alexander Jaffray, Provost of Aberdeen*, p. 56.

Chapter Twelve:

1. Gardiner, *Letters and Papers*, pp. 42-3.
2. Napier, *Life and Times of Montrose*, p. 755.
3. Gardiner, *Letters and Papers*, p. 68.
4. Parliamentary Register, 17th May 1650.
5. Balfour, *History*, Vol. IV, p. 25.
6. Napier, *Memoirs of Montrose*, Vol. II, pp. 787-8.
7. *Ibid.*, Vol. II, p. 805.
8. Laing, D., *Ancrum and Lothian Correspondence*, Vol. I, p. 262.
9. Hyde, *Civil War*, Vol. III, p. 474.
10. Nicoll, J., *A Diary of public transactions and other occurrences*, p. 17.
11. Burnet, *History*, Vol. I, p. 55.
12. Hyde, *Civil War*, Vol. III, p. 496.
13. Abbott, W.C., *The writings and speeches of Oliver Cromwell*, Vol. II, p. 325.
14. Gardiner, S.R., *A History of the Commonwealth and Protectorate 1649–1656*, Vol. I, p. 331.
15. Baillie, *Letters*, Vol. III, p. 38.
16. Gardiner, *Commonwealth and Protectorate*, Vol. I, p. 385.
17. Ibid, Vol. I, pp. 346-7.
18. Gardiner, *Letters and Papers*, p. 114.
19. Kirkton, J., *The Secret and True History of the Church of Scotland*, p. 50.
20. Gardiner, *Commonwealth and Protectorate*, Vol. I, p. 353.
21. Willcock, *The Great Marquess*, p. 271.

Chapter Thirteen:

1. Firth, C.H., *Scotland and the Commonwealth Letters and Papers 1651–1653*, p. 333.
2. *Ibid.*, p. 337.
3. *Ibid.*, p. 363.
4. *Ibid.*, pp. 48-9.
5. *Ibid.*, p. 134.
6. *Ibid.*, p. 167.
7. *Ibid.*, p. 145.
8. *Ibid.*, pp. 308-9.
9. Baillie, *Letters*, Vol. III, p. 288.
10. Evelyn, J., and Bray, W. (ed.), *Diary and Correspondence of John Evelyn*, Vol. III, p. 175.

11. Baillie, *Letters*, Vol. III, p. 466.
12. Wodrow, *Analecta*, Vol. I, p. 73.
13. Baillie, *Letters*, Vol. III, p. 467.
14. Willcock, *The Great Marquess*, p. 303.
15. MacKenzie, G., *Memoirs of the Affairs of Scotland from the Restoration of King Charles II*, p. 13.
16. Baillie, *Letters*, Vol. III, p. 465.
17. *Ibid.*, p. 465.
18. Howell, T. B., and Howell, T. J., *A Complete Collection of State Trials and Proceedings*, Vol. V, p. 1385.
19. Burnet, *History*, Vol. I, p. 83.
20. Parliamentary Register, 4th January 1661.
21. Baillie, *Letters,* Vol. III, p. 466.
22. Burnet, *History*, p. 134.
23. Willcock, *The Great Marquess*, p. 319.
24. Firth, C.H., *Scotland and the Protectorate. Letters and Papers 1654–1659*, p. ix.
25. Burnet, *History*, p. 84.
26. MacKenzie, *Memoirs*, p. 39.
27. Burnet, *History*, p. 84.
28. Wodrow, R., *Analecta*, Vol. I, p. 73.
29. *Ibid.*, p. 150.
30. MacKenzie, *Memoirs*, p. 40.
31. Wodrow, *Analecta*, Vol. I, p. 68.
32. MacKenzie, *Memoirs*, p. 47.
33. Wodrow, *Analecta*, Vol. I, p. 156.
34. *Ibid.*, Vol. I, p. 157.
35. *Ibid.*, Vol. I, p. 157.

Chapter Fourteen:
1. Campbell, *Instructions to a Son*, p. 95.
2. Napier, *Memoirs of Montrose,* Vol. II, p. 43.
3. Baillie, *Letters*, Vol. III, p. 466.
4. Campbell, *Instructions to a Son*, p. 95.

Bibliography

Abbott, W. C. (ed.), *The writings and speeches of Oliver Cromwell* (1839)

Baillie, R., and Laing, D. (ed.), *The Letters and Journals of Robert Baillie 1637–1662* (3 vols., Edinburgh, 1841)

Balfour, J., *The historical works of Sir James Balfour of Denmylne and Kinnaird, knight and baronet* (4 vols., London, 1825)

Balcanquhall, W., *A large declaration concerning the late tumults in Scotland* (London, 1639)

Birch, T. (ed.), *A collection of the state papers of John Thurloe* (7 vols., London, 1742)

Brodie, A., *The Diary of Alexander Brodie of Brodie MDCLII-MDCLXXX and of his son, James Brodie of Brodie, MDCLXXX-MDCLXXXV consisting of extracts from the existing manuscripts, and a republication of the volume printed at Edinburgh in the year 1740* (Aberdeen, 1863)

Brodie, G., *A History of the British Empire* (Edinburgh, 1822)

Brodie, G., *A Constitutional History of the British Empire from the Accession of Charles I to the Restoration* (3 vols., London, 1866)

Bruce, J., *Charles I in 1646: Letters of Charles I to Queen Henrietta Maria* (London, 1856)

Bruce, J., Douglas Hamilton, W., and Lomas, S. C., *Calendar of state papers, Domestic series, Reign of Charles I. 1640-41* (London, 1882)

Buchan, J., *Montrose* (Edinburgh, 1928)

Burnet, G., *History of his own time: from the restoration of King Charles the second* (2 vols., London, 1850)

Campbell, A., Marquis of Argyll, *Instructions to a Son* (London, 1661)

Carlyle, T., *Oliver Cromwell's Letters and Speeches with elucidation* (2 vols., London, 1845)

Carte, T., *Original Letters and Papers* (2 vols., London, 1739)

Cawdor, J., *The Book of the Thanes of Cawdor* (Edinburgh, 1859)

Cowan, E. J., *Montrose, for King and Covenant* (London, 1977)

Dalrymple, D., *Memorials and Letters relating to the History of Britain in the Reign of Charles I* (Glasgow, 1866)

Evelyn, J., and Bray, W. (ed.), *Diary and Correspondence of John Evelyn* (4 vols., London, 1852)

Firth, C. H., *Scotland and the Commonwealth, Letters and Papers 1651–1653* (Edinburgh, 1895)

Firth, C. H., *Scotland and the Protectorate, Letters and Papers 1654–1659* (Edinburgh, 1899)

Fotheringham, J. G., *Montereul Correspondence* (2 vols., Edinburgh, 1898)

Gardiner, S. R., *A History of the Commonwealth and Protectorate, 1649–1656* (4 vols., London, 1903)

Gardiner, S. R., *History of the Great Civil War, 1642-1649* (London, 1893)

Gardiner, S. R., *History of England from the Accession of James I to the Outbreak of the Civil War 1603–1642* (10 vols., London, 1899)

Gardiner, S. R., *Letter and Papers illustrating the relations between Charles II and Scotland in 1650* (Edinburgh, 1894)

Gordon, J., *A History of Scots Affairs* (3 vols., Aberdeen, 1841)

Gordon, P., *Britaine's Distemper* (4 vols., Aberdeen, 1844)

Guthry, H., *Memoirs, wherein the conspiracies and rebellion against king Charles I. of blessed memory, to the time of the murther of that monarch, are briefly and faithfully related* (London, 1702)

Historical Manuscripts Commission, *Sixth Report of the Royal Commission on Historical Manuscripts* (1877), p. 616

Hope, T., *A diary of the public correspondence of Sir Thomas Hope of Craighall, Bart. 1633–1645* (Edinburgh, 1843)

Howell, T. B., and Howell, T. J., *A Complete Collection of State Trials and Proceedings*, Vol. V (London, 1828)

Hyde, E., *The History of the Rebellion and Civil Wars in England begun in the year 1641* (6 vols., Oxford, 1732)

Jaffray, A., *Diary of Alexander Jaffray, Provost of Aberdeen* (London, 1856)

Johnston, A., Lord Wariston, *Diary* (Scots History Society, Edinburgh, 1911)

Journal of the House of Lords, Volume VIII, 1645–1647 (London)

Kerr. R., and Laing, D. (ed.), *Correspondence of Sir Robert Kerr, First Earl of Ancram and his son, William, Third Earl of Lothian* (2 vols., Edinburgh, 1875)

Kirkton, J., *The Secret and True History of the Church of Scotland* (Edinburgh, 1817)

Laing, D., *Ancrum and Lothian Correspondence*, Vol. I (Edinburgh, 1875)

Macray, W. D. (ed.), *Letters and papers of Patrick Ruthven, Earl of Forth and Brentford, and of his family, A.D. 1615–A.D. 1662. With an appendix of papers relating to Sir John Urry* (London, 1868)

MacBain, A., and Kennedy, J. (eds.), *Reliquae Celticae: texts, papers, and studies in Gaelic literature and philology left by the late Rev. Alexander Cameron* (2 vols., Inverness, 1844)

Macdonald, A. (ed.), *Letters to the Argyll Family from Elizabeth, Queen of England, Mary Queen of Scots, King James VI, King Charles I, King Charles II, and others* (Edinburgh, 1839)

Macinnes, A., *The British Confederate* (Edinburgh, 2011)

MacKenzie, G., *Memoirs of the Affairs of Scotland from the Restoration of King Charles II* (Edinburgh, 1821)

Mackenzie, J., *The History of Scotland* (London, 1867)

Meikle, H. W. (ed.), *Correspondence of the Scots Commissioners in London 1644-1646*, (Edinburgh, 1917)

Montereul, J. De, *The Diplomatic Correspondence of Jean De Montereul and the Brothers De Bellievre* (Edinburgh, 1898)

Morrison, W., *Johnston of Warriston* (Edinburgh, 1901)

Munro, N., *John Splendid* (Edinburgh, 1898)

Napier, M., *Memoirs of the Marquis of Montrose* (2 vols., Edinburgh, 1856)

Napier, M., *Montrose and the Covenanters* (2 vols., Edinburgh, 1838)

Napier, M., *Life and Times of Montrose* (Edinburgh, 1840)

Nicoll, J., *A Diary of public transactions and other occurrences, chiefly in Scotland: from January 1650 to June 1667* (Edinburgh, 1836)

Peterkin, A., *Records of the Kirk of Scotland: containing the acts and proceedings of the General Assemblies, from the year 1638 downwards, as authenticated by the clerks of assembly: with notes and historical illustrations* (Edinburgh, 1838)

Rothes, J. L., *Relation of proceedings concerning the affairs of the Kirk of Scotland: from August 1637 to July 1638* (Edinburgh, 1830)

Row, J., *The History of the Kirk of Scotland from the year 1558 to August 1637* (Edinburgh, 1842)

Row, W., *The Life of Robert Blair* (Edinburgh, 1848)

Royle, T., *Civil War: The War of Three Kingdoms 1638–1660* (London, 2004)

Rushworth, J. (ed.), *Historical Collections* (8 vols., Edinburgh, 1691)

Rutherford, S., and Bonar, A. A., (ed.), *Letters of Samuel Rutherford, with a Sketch of his Life and Biographical Notices of his Correspondents* (Edinburgh, 1891)

Sadler, J., *Scottish Battles* (Edinburgh, 2010)

Scott, W., *A Legend of Montrose* (Edinburgh, 1819)

Seymour, W., (1975) *Battles in Britain,* London

Smellie, A., (1903) *Men of the Covenant,* Edinburgh

Spalding, J., *Memorialls of the Trubles in Scotland and in England, A.D. 1624–A.D. 1645* (2 vols., Aberdeen, 1851)

Sprott, G. W., *Scottish liturgies of the reign of James VI* (Edinburgh, 1871)

Steele, R., *A bibliography of royal proclamations of the Tudor and Stuart sovereigns and of others published under authority, Vol. II 1485–1714 Scotland and Ireland* (Oxford, 1905)

Stevenson, D., *The Scottish Revolution* (Edinburgh, 1973)

Stevenson, D., *Revolution and Counter-Revolution* (Edinburgh, 1977)

Stuart, P. C., *Scottish Coronations* (Paisley, 1912)

Terry, C. S., *The Life and Campaigns of Alexander Leslie* (London, 1899)

Thurloe, J., *State Papers,* Vol. I, 1638-1653 (London, 1742)

Turner, J., *Memoirs of His Own Life and Times* (Edinburgh, 1829)

Whitley, E., *The Two Kingdoms* (Edinburgh, 1977)

Willcock, J., *The Great Marquess* (Edinburgh, 1903)

Wishart, G., *The memoirs of James, Marquis of Montrose, 1639-1650* (Edinburgh, 1819)

Wodrow, R., *Analecta: Or, Materials for a History of Remarkable Providences; Mostly Relating to Scottish Ministers and Christians* (4 vols., Edinburgh, 1842)

Yorke, P., *Miscellaneous State Papers* (2 vols., London, 1778)

Index